D1162740

THE BEST OF McDERMOTT

THE BEST OF

McDERMOTT

THE SELECTED WRITINGS OF

William F. McDermott

FOREWORD BY JOHN MASON BROWN

THE WORLD PUBLISHING COMPANY

CLEVELAND AND NEW YORK

PUBLISHED BY The World Publishing Company
2231 West 110th Street, Cleveland 2, Ohio

Published simultaneously in Canada by
Nelson, Foster & Scott Ltd.

Library of Congress Catalog Card Number: 59-12869

FIRST EDITION

Contents

FOREWORD BY *John Mason Brown*   9

1. THE THEATER

John Galsworthy   13
Bernard Shaw   18
Somerset Maugham   22
Franz Molnár   27
John Barrymore and Hamlet   32
A Russian *Hamlet*   36
A Visit to Reinhardt Castle   40
Brooks Atkinson and Irony   44
Bing Crosby's Radio Rehearsal   47
Katharine Cornell   50
Criticism   52
Judith Anderson in *Medea*   55
Good Will   57
Good Plays   60
Theatergoing   63
Oscar Wilde   65
Shavian Self-Portraits   67
Charm   70

CONTENTS

2. REFLECTIONS ON POLITICS

Oratory: The Radio and Politics 77
Roosevelt: Thinking in Terms of the Nation 79
Democracy 82
Mankind 84
Europe: History Repeats Itself 86
A Paradox 89
Japan: War in the Pacific Is Inevitable 91
The A-Bomb 94
Germany 96
The Air Lift 98
Jealous Nations 101
The President's Power 103
The Declaration of Independence 105
Foreign Aid 107

3. WAR

Slaughter 113
Cassino Pulverized 115
Lava Annihilates a City 118
The Anzio Landing 121
Ghostly Berlin Ruins 124
Normandy 128

4. THE WRITER AT HIS TRADE

A Newspaperman's Prayer 133
The Press: A Man's Love for His Newspaper ... 135
Invective 137
Censorship 140
Writing 142

Charles Dickens   144

5. THE SPORTSMAN AND HIS DOG

Squash: Health or Fun?   149
Tennis: Perverse But Fascinating   152
Horses   155
Hunting   157
Dogs   159
Spring Comes to Gyp   162
Gyp the Blood   165

6. THE FIBER OF SOCIETY

Charity: A Lesson in Sociology for Two Bits   171
Law: Faith in Legislation   173
Schools   176
Lost Duty   178
The Death Penalty   180
Christmas   183
Hospitals   185

7. THE WANDERING JOURNALIST

The Birthplace of Lenin   191
War-Scarred Barcelona   196
Warsaw: City of Squalor and Luxury   199
Budapest's Beauty   202
Hong Kong   205
Memories   209
The Castle at Elsinore   211
An Amusement Park in Copenhagen   214
Swedish Hospitality   217
Bali   220

CONTENTS

A Baby Bull   222
Vienna at a Waltz Tempo   225
The Orient Express   228
The Lido   232

8. THE DAILY ROUND

The Outdoors: Urban Aromas vs. New-Mown Hay   237
Dentistry   239
Moving   241
Quartets and Snobbish Harmonizers   244
Cravats   246
Independence Days Abroad   249
"I Give You—"   251
A Snow Shovel   254
Accents   256
Hats   259
Smoking   262
Canes   265
The Death of a Friend   267
Modern Art   269
Old Books   271
Old Book Marts   274

MEMORIAL BY *Philip W. Porter*
"A Whole Man If There Ever Was One"   279

Foreword

BY JOHN MASON BROWN

FAR ALONG in the following pages is a piece called "I Give You—" in which Bill McDermott has, and provides, fun describing how he used to introduce me year after year when I spoke in Cleveland. Now it is my turn to introduce Bill, though, heaven knows, in lecture parlance "he needs no introduction." Certainly, he does not to the thousands and thousands of people who hung as I did on his daily column in the *Cleveland Plain Dealer*, to any person who has followed dramatic criticism in this country since the twenties, or who has been reviewed by him.

I have always resented the chairman's phrase, "I give you," which reduces the speaker so freely disposed of to an inanimate, though unwrapped, object purchased at a store and not good enough to keep. It is the speaker's and the writer's business to do the giving, meaning to give of himself. That is what Bill did in person and in print, and does again abundantly in these reprinted columns. They are sharply observed and admirably written pieces. They range from interviews with Shaw and Somerset Maugham and warmly re-creative and discerning reviews to humorous personal sketches, vivid battle and travel accounts, and tough-minded, commonsensical political comments. And Bill McDermott is in them all, a wise, kind, penetrating, amused, and lively person, widely read, widely traveled, and widely exploring, learned but always human and never pretentious, whose every piece bears the signature of his giving personality.

Among the most remunerative lecture fees that I have ever known, I count the many evenings I used to have in Cleveland,

9

when the lecture stint was done, with Bill and his wife, Eva, at their baronial house, book-lined and talk-and-laughter filled, on Lake Erie. I don't think I ever saw the lake from their windows or wanted to. It is hard to look away from a blazing fire, and that is what companionship with the McDermotts provided. They were, and gave, the view. Dinner mattered, but what mattered most was the feast of talk which lasted from cocktails on until well past midnight. The real stimulants were Eva's gaiety and realism, and Bill's igniting curiosity and candor plus the flood of his ideas, comments, memories, anecdotes, and deductions.

If I first came to know Bill when he was "giving me away," I came to know him differently and even better during the Second World War in Algiers, Naples, London, and Prestwick when he was serving overseas as a correspondent. Being small and seeming fragile, he appeared miscast in a Richard Harding Davis-Clark Lee role. He was a pale, round-faced, little man, with a skyscraper forehead, small hands, thin fingers, and an unexercised body, who kept puffing cigars as if he were laying down a barrage. But he had a cherub's smile, eyes bright as searchlights, and a giant's courage. Eva has this same courage. Both of them brought it to their living, and to his dying, which was long, painful, and met by the two of them with incredible gallantry.

I know some people have no liking for collected journalism. As an old offender in this field, I have an open and unashamed fondness for it. I like to savor the day that was, in all its first freshness, as well as the day that is. Hence, having read *The Best of McDermott* with pleasure, I shall proudly and happily put it on the shelf in my study next to H. T. Parker's *Eighth Notes,* Heywood Broun's *Pieces of Hate,* Percy Hammond's *This Atom in the Audience,* George Jean Nathan's long serialization of George Jean Nathan, Alexander Woollcott's *Going to Pieces,* Stark Young's *Immortal Shadows,* Brooks Atkinson's *Broadway Scrapbook,* and Wolcott Gibbs's *More in Sorrow,* glad to have Bill in book form at least and delighted to be with him again.

ONE

The Theater

John Galsworthy

JULY 30, 1922

London—I suppose nobody would attempt to make up a list of
the three or four greatest English-writing dramatists without
including the name of John Galsworthy. There are competent
judges, in fact, who would not make up a list of the two greatest
English-writing dramatists without including the name of the
author of *Justice, Strife,* and *The Silver Box.* If you except the
occasional gallant and fugitive essays of the amateur groups,
Mr. Galsworthy is about all that Middle Western America has
lately seen in the way of drama that is of any very serious intent
or consequence.

Barrie's last play, *Mary Rose,* was not in that well-endowed
writer's most felicitous vein. Maeterlinck's pen is lately reluc-
tant. Shaw never gets past New York so far as professional pres-
entations go. Arnold Bennett's last work likewise got no farther
than Broadway and not very far there. Galsworthy's *The Skin
Game* was generally ranked at the top mark of the late road
season and it was surely the only play of real consequence
which reached here from abroad last year.

Mr. Galsworthy has a reputation among the London penmen
for exceptional aloofness. He has persistently and quite sen-
sibly eluded the pestiferous interviewer, allowing his work to
be its own spokesman and reserving his private life for himself.
The world knows that Bernard Shaw lives at No. 10 Adelphi
Terrace in the heart of the city, but you cannot find Mr. Galsworthy's home address either in the London telephone book or
in *Who's Who.*

However, I discovered the truth to be that there is nothing
aloof about Mr. Galsworthy but his place of residence. He lives,
I hazard a guess, at the top of the highest hill on the loftiest

13

eminence in London at the suburban Hampstead Heath in a house that hides coyly up a narrow road and baffles the most anxious searcher. It was a bad afternoon for the taxi driver, who had no heart for literature and complained only of burning tires on stiff, slippery hills.

The fleeting difficulties of the chase and some concern over the fear of being late for an appointment were immediately allayed when I was ushered into the Galsworthy living room, where the table was set for tea. With uncommon thoughtfulness and a profound understanding of conditions in America Mr. Galsworthy asked if I should prefer a cocktail to tea. I, of course, demurred. A little later I was being disabused of another nationally prevalent illusion that the English do not know the secrets of the American mixed drink.

I have never had a more agreeable host, or a more tactful interviewee, or one who gave so definite an impression of speaking candidly and with the utmost desire to give measured and exact expression to his views and to have them clearly understood.

A man of good size, a little gray, wearing glasses, erect and carefully dressed, he looks and talks like the popular idea of the English gentleman. He is free of an eccentricity of manner, laughs easily and pleasantly, talks a little hesitatingly when struggling with difficult ideas, but is more fluent than most writers, and gives the impression of exceptional warmth of personality—the sort of man, in short, that you'd like to play golf with.

After the preliminaries of getting settled in a comfortable and attractive room, a room that is usually described as "charming" in these interviews, we got around to Mr. Galsworthy's ideas of literary America. The subject is in the air over here since Hugh Walpole in the London *Daily Mail* recently expressed the view that America is developing a literature that cuts away sharply from the English tradition and is perhaps more vital and important.

Mr. Galsworthy, who knows more than some American writers about American literature and who is friendly toward much that is American, cannot quite see this viewpoint.

"I don't think," he said, "that since we have a common language there can be any very pronounced or fundamental differences between the two literatures. That which must be different and increasingly so is the life described. But much of what some of your writers and critics have regarded as 'new' is not confined to America, it is only the American expression of a new way of looking at things to be found over here, too.

"Then again, the newness, say of Sinclair Lewis's *Main Street* lies in its being satire. But satire is not new in the world of literature.

"Willa Cather, another of your American novelists of the 'new' group, writes with exceptional simplicity and beauty, but there is nothing particularly new or even distinctively American in her work. Her methods and her point of view as a novelist, in fact, are decidedly traditional.

"Joseph Hergesheimer, another of those mentioned by Hugh Walpole as 'new,' has in his excellent work adopted the word-painting methods used before him by Flaubert, Joseph Conrad, and others, and cannot be said to represent anything new or peculiarly American.

"Sherwood Anderson, perhaps, and Mencken, certainly, have a flavor and vitality that is distinctively American. But on the whole the present difference between American and British fiction lies much more in the forms of slang and the facts and conditions of life described than in the way of describing them, and I suggest these are matters of surface rather than of fundamental difference.

"You must not forget," he continued, "that there are writers here breaking away from tradition, too. There is Joyce, for instance, and there is Katherine Mansfield and D. H. Lawrence."

I suggested that there were a half-dozen of the younger writers in America who, in their hardheaded skepticism and continual questioning of political and social creeds, coupled in some cases with a fervency and gift of phrase, were not matched by any similar British group, Floyd Dell, Scott Fitzgerald, Sinclair Lewis, Ben Hecht, Eugene O'Neill.

"You know more about American writers than I do," he replied, "and if you say there are, I shall take it lying down."

"What about Eugene O'Neill?" I asked.

"Strong. I have not seen *The Hairy Ape*, of course, but I do know *Ile* and *Diff'rent* and they seemed to me to have uncommon flavor and vigor. In O'Neill you have a most unquestionable dramatist."

Mr. Galsworthy is not at all downhearted about the British theater. About as many good plays are being successful now as ever. He cited the record of a single theater, St. Martin's, where *The Skin Game, A Bill of Divorcement*, and now *Loyalties* and *Shall We Join the Ladies?* have had long runs successively. Revivals of first-grade plays are given regularly, such as *Quality Street, The Second Mrs. Tanqueray*, and *Dear Brutus*.

"You have seldom written, have you, without some thoughtful undercurrent," I suggested. "In *Justice* wasn't it the cruelty in an exceptional case of judicial system; in *Strife* the struggle between capital and labor; in *The Silver Box* and *The Eldest Son* the disparity between moral standards for poor and rich; in *The Skin Game* the moral slackening induced by war; in *Loyalties* racial prejudice?"

"Well," he replied, "I shouldn't find it interesting to write without touching on some question of a general nature."

"Your plays, then," I ventured, "take their start in your mind with some abstract idea?"

The answer was surprising.

"No, they do not. It is very difficult to say exactly how plays come into being; but I am sure that mine start with some character or some incident which awakens an idea. But it is quite true that characters or incidents which don't awaken an idea never set me going."

"But," I asked, "aren't you deeply interested in the racial question which you discuss, for example, in *Loyalties?*"

"Not at all," he replied, smilingly. "I have no feeling about it one way or another."

"Yet you give the impression in the play of seeing all of both sides of the question."

"Perhaps the reason for that is that I have no great feeling about the matter. It is the balance of things that interests me in life and that I try to get into plays. I do not know whether I can make myself plain. I am always conscious of that mysterious and unreachable meeting point of union with variability; of the irony and insolubility of life and human relationships. *Loyalties*, for instance, is broader than a racial question. It applies to all prejudice and all loyalties and their seeming irreconcilability."

"It is curious and tragic, isn't it," I said, "that 'loyalty is only the other half of prejudice.'"

"Yes," he replied, "one is the foundation of the other and would be unthinkable without it. It is such matters that interest me in working out a play after I have found the primary incident."

Those who conceive of the work of a finely talented writer as being done in a sort of inspired divine ecstasy will be shocked by Mr. Galsworthy's answer to another question, though I have put the same question to many distinguished authors and have never received but the one answer.

"Do you get any real pleasure out of the actual process of writing?"

"I do not. Getting started in the morning is pretty hard work. The pleasure, such as there is, comes in having done the job. Yet I would not be happy if I weren't writing."

"Do you assign yourself regular union working hours," I asked, "or labor as the spirit moves you?"

"I used to work every morning and every afternoon between tea and dinner, but in later years I have found the morning's work is quite enough for one day."

Mrs. Galsworthy about this time stepped in to borrow some cigars for her husband's American publisher, who had been waiting in another room for an hour and had concluded that the course of literature had been interrupted long enough. I shortly afterward took my leave with the grateful feeling of having come into personal contact with an uncommonly considerate and likable gentleman and a fine, tolerant, and understanding mind.

"Of course you've been too kind about me, but otherwise I much admire the way you've remembered and recorded," writes Mr. Galsworthy to whom a draft of the foregoing was sent, adding: "By the way, you know that I am a novelist, don't you? More of a novelist than a dramatist, I think."

The reprimand is likely deserved, but I here overlook Mr. Galsworthy's excellence as a novelist simply because this article is intended for the dramatic and not the literary section.

Bernard Shaw

JULY 25, 1922

London—Bernard Shaw, as you know, is a shy and modest gentleman who profoundly dislikes publicity and uses every honorable means to keep his name and his opinions out of the public prints. His hatred of the limelight is only equaled by that of the star actor or the circus press agent. It is only unwittingly, of course, that he gets his name into the papers every day or so in reference to every conceivable subject sacred or profane. Try as he may, he cannot escape public attention.

So I was not surprised, after submitting proper credentials and explaining the publicity advantages of his seeing a representative of the *Cleveland Plain Dealer* for the purpose of an interview, to receive from him the following blushing reply:

> Dear McDermott: You forget that I am myself a professional journalist and that I make my views known directly and not by interview. If The Plain Dealer wants an article by me, I am open to a business proposal. I can put the article in the form of an interview if the editor would prefer it that way. The price will be not less than $750 per 1,000 words; but I cannot under-

take to supply it on these or any other terms, as I am heavily
in arrears with other commissions at present.

Faithfully
G. Bernard Shaw

There you have the ultimate height of modesty. Mr. Shaw
so dislikes newspaper attention that he will not submit to it
for less than $750 the thousand words.

Nevertheless, I was eventually successful in seeing this most
remarkable and elusive man of the age. It was at the International Theater Exhibit in the Victoria-Albert Museum, where
he had gone to inspect the designs made for the New York production of *Back to Methuselah,* which he, of course, has not seen.

A tall, bearded, straight, keen-eyed gentleman, he looks precisely like his pictures, only perhaps a little older. He talks
explosively and fluently. You get the idea of an enormous vitality
and energy behind the words. There is an Irish twinkle in his
eyes and he laughs often, putting all his heart into it. Here is
a man, you say, who would lead by the nose any group in which
he happened to be, whether he had ever written a line or not.

Prompted by the designs of play settings hanging before him,
he told amusing tales of his experience in connection with play
production and the theater generally. He was much impressed
with the work of the American designers Norman Bel Geddes
and Robert Edmond Jones, and devoted nearly all of his time in
the galleries to them. He talked—

But I haul up. Mr. Shaw will undoubtedly present a bill if
I repeat what he said, and no talk, not even Mr. Shaw's, is worth
seventy-five cents a word.

Because Mr. Shaw will not talk for publication, however, is
no reason why the *Plain Dealer* readers should be deprived of
hearing him. He who will not talk stands always in danger of
having his views understood by inference and surmise. It might
be equally informative, as it would certainly be much cheaper,
to interview Mr. Shaw theoretically. The following interview,
then, is to be understood as something that conceivably might
have taken place, but which did not take place.

Mr. Shaw lives modestly at No. 10 Adelphi Terrace, off the Strand, in the center of the London business and hotel district. It is not such a place as you would picture the most famous of English dramatists to be living in. The building is unpretentious, resembling one of our older and second-rate office blocks. Below are stores and offices. Mr. Shaw lives on the second floor.

To get to his quarters you have to go through an anteroom leading to an insurance company or something of the sort which is on the ground floor. A visitor unfamiliar with the Shavian haunts is likely to conclude he is in the wrong place, as I did, but a girl in the office below reassured me and directed me to the second floor.

Mounting the steps, I was met at the top with a small iron gate, locked against encroachers and marked "Bernard Shaw," together with an additional counsel to ring the bell. I did so, and it was immediately answered by a gray-haired woman servant who informed me, with what seemed to be a foreign accent, that Mr. Shaw was at home.

Comfortably seated in a Shavian armchair and the preliminaries over, I began:

"How do you account for the fact, Mr. Shaw, that America, the barbarous country which lynches innocent Negroes, as you recently pointed out, is so much friendlier to your plays than England? *Heartbreak House* was more successful in New York than in London, and your last play, *Back to Methuselah*, though presented in New York, has not been seen on the English stage at all."

Without any hint of a twinkle, Mr. Shaw replied:

"When I spoke unflatteringly about your country it was before your countrymen had seen *Back to Methuselah* or *Heartbreak House*. Conditions since then have, of course, changed. A few of my plays, properly produced, would convert the Fiji Islands to Christianity and civilization in three months.

"The exact degree of culture in any country may be determined by their attitude toward my plays. My plays, now as ever, have always been most successful in Germany, the only genuinely cultured nation on the globe today except China, and, unfortunately, the Chinese, who are prevented by lingual and racial difficulties from seeing and comprehending my plays, are only able to overcome that deprivation through the beneficent effect of being civilized some thousands of years before any European nation."

"You think, then, that if your plays were to be produced in China the yellow peril would be more genuinely menacing?"

"Without doubt. I have heard an account of a Chinese student, ambitious to be a writer and political leader in his own country, who read the preface to my volume of plays, *Pleasant and Unpleasant,* and who thereafter was so impressed by its clarity, compactness, and vigor that he despaired of his own ability and promptly killed himself as the only sensible thing to do. You can see what would happen to his race if the New York Theatre Guild were to move to Peking."

"What interests me, Mr. Shaw, is what would have happened to the Chinese student you speak of if he had read the plays as well as the preface?"

"He would probably have killed me" was the Shavian answer.

"What do you think," I asked, trying to edge away from China, "of the present state of the English theater?"

"An absurd question. No new play of mine has been produced in England for years."

"Do you think that that has anything to do with the present unrest and unemployment?"

"Everything. My plays gave the English public something to think about. Now they have nothing to think about, even if they were capable of it. Satan finds more evil for idle minds than for idle hands."

"Mr. Shaw, you are generally regarded as a shrewd and farseeing man, an unerring seer. That being the case, as you will admit, how do you account for the fact that in predicting Carpentier would knock Dempsey out in a round or two, you were so terribly, unconsciously wrong?"

"You really must excuse me," replied the great vegetarian, rising. "I believe the cook is burning the beefsteak."

Some other hardly less noted men offer lesser problems to the interviewer from America. Mr. John Galsworthy, in response to a request, writes a two-page letter, expressing gratitude "at the compliments you pay me," and giving the caller the friendliest reception, including cigars and cocktails. Somerset Maugham replies with an invitation to lunch, also excellent. Henry Arthur Jones proffers several letters and tea. A. A. Milne is out of town, but will be delighted to meet the interviewer on his return later in July. Arnold Bennett, the plutocrat, is away on a yachting trip, but will be glad to be seen on his homecoming, etc.

After all, people do buy books and go to plays in America.

Somerset Maugham

SEPTEMBER 17, 1922

London—Of the many Englishmen who eke out a more or less pampered livelihood by writing plays and novels for America, W. Somerset Maugham perhaps most piques the present curiosity. His new spectacular melodrama, *East of Suez*, just unveiled in London looks like a gorgeous hit. Its apparent success is possibly not displeasing to A. H. Woods who will present the same play in New York next week. The première, with Florence Reed in the company, will be one of those theatrical events commonly known as auspicious. This, therefore, may not be an inopportune time to write of Mr. Maugham as he appeared this summer "in his habit as he lived" to the pilgrim from America.

By an unhappy conspiracy of booking office Cleveland missed seeing Mr. Maugham's *The Circle* last season, though it was presented in several less hospitable neighboring communities. As enacted in New York by John Drew and an otherwise dis-

tinguished cast, the comedy was elected the top mark of the
season by a standing vote of critics and ticket speculators. A
sly, smooth, gayly ironic work, it was of the stuff that only rarely
gets into the native theater and when it does is pretty sure to
fail. *The Circle* not only pleased the gravest of our theatrical
scholars but tickled the ticket dealers almost as much as *The
Music Box Revue.*

The perpetrator of so exceptional a feat can hardly hope to
escape public attention. Mr. Maugham, of course, has not been
hitherto wholly neglected by the trumpeters for he has been
writing plays and novels with varying success for twenty years,
but he has only lately hit his best stride with *The Circle* and
The Moon and Sixpence, a first-class novel and a best-seller
of a season or so ago.

If you can believe a modest man no one was more surprised
at the success of both *The Moon and Sixpence* and *The Circle*
than Mr. Maugham himself.

"*The Moon and Sixpence,*" he told me recently during the
course of a luncheon in his London home, "was written—all of
it—while I was ill with tuberculosis in a sanitarium."

The book, you will remember, is a lusty and sanguine tale
of adventure in Tahiti. Not the sort of thing at all you would
imagine as emanating from a sanitarium.

"I'm entirely cured now of my illness," continued Mr.
Maugham—and his appearance bore him out, for though not
of robust build he has none of the appearance of the consump-
tive. "I've been traveling a good deal since I've been able and
I'm going to keep at it. I'm getting ready now to go to Siam
where I expect to do some exploring in a part of the country
little known to white men."

Prompted, Mr. Maugham returned to *The Circle.*

"I had no faith in it," he said. "You know it's the sort of thing
that doesn't usually take well. It was a trifle bitter and it was
mostly a comedy of talk. Plays of that kind usually fail pretty
quick. I wrote *The Circle* not because I expected to make
money out of it—though that hope is never wholly out of a

sensible author's mind—but because I had to get it out of my system.

"Its success has scared me a little. I'm afraid I may not be able to follow up. You hate not to keep up the pace. So I'm not working on any new play now, though, of course, I'll have to get back to it eventually. *East of Suez*, written some time ago, will be produced in London some time the latter part of August. A. H. Woods will present it in New York in the fall, probably after he sees what happens to the London production.

"*East of Suez* is different from anything that I've done before. It's a spectacular play, requiring a large scenic equipment and full of color."

"That will be something of an experiment for Mr. Woods as well as yourself," I suggested.

Mr. Woods has lately leaned to the very intimate type of bedchamber drama.

"Woods produces a great many different sorts of plays," he replied. "We get along very well together."

Mr. Maugham has never seen *The Circle* and only knows from hearsay how it goes on the stage. He is coming to America in the fall on his way to Siam and expects to have a look at it then. It will be sent on tour again the forthcoming season and should, in the course of time, reach Cleveland, though probably not with all the members of the first cast.

Mr. Maugham, though a veteran at the business of writing plays, lines up with the younger crowd in his literary sympathies. He admires Floyd Dell, Sinclair Lewis, and some of the other newcomers. Hergesheimer he is not ecstatic about, therein differing somewhat from Mr. Galsworthy, who has *Java Head* and other of the Hergesheimer fictions prominently on his bookshelves.

He saw a good deal of Sinclair Lewis on the latter's recent visit to England and liked him, though he has been a bit perturbed by the interview attributed to Mr. Lewis on his homecoming. Lewis's remarks—I gathered secondhand from several

English authors who seem to take it to heart—have been interpreted as embodying a slight to British writers.

Mr. Maugham grinningly found ample excuse for Mr. Lewis's expressions about English penmen.

"But what I can't forgive," he said, "is his libel against English cocktails, because some of the cocktails about which he generalizes unflatteringly were drunk in my house. He seemed to enjoy them at the time."

This, of course, was said with a chuckle which suggested that Mr. Maugham might still grasp Mr. Lewis's hand in friendship despite everything. The two appear to have a pretty solid basis of understanding.

While not one fairly describable as an ardent prohibitionist Mr. Maugham believes that prohibition is helping the theater to a better life.

"The success of comedies as against melodrama or melodramatic farces in America recently—I mean such plays as Milne's *The Dover Road* and my own *The Circle*—indicates that comedy is coming back, and I believe it's a reasonable theory that prohibition has had something to do with it. Comedy—pure comedy —is conversation; if it's a good comedy, interesting conversation. A tippler or a tippling crowd doesn't want to hear conversation however brilliant or amusing it might be. A sober crowd would be more likely to be entertained by conversational comedy. It needs all its wits to enjoy such a play. Where there is drinking there is likely to be a preponderant interest in noisy farces and girl shows."

There are some obvious weaknesses in the theory, but as a theory it is as good as most.

While marking time before writing another play Mr. Maugham is amusing himself by turning out short stories. He can afford an artistic success now and he is going to lay his hand to it when the spirit prompts. Unlike some of our other popular writers Mr. Maugham doesn't believe that a play can be too good for the public.

"Speaking without any thought of my own work, and I've had

some gorgeous failures in my day, I believe the more honestly and sincerely that a dramatist writes and the more he gives of what is genuinely best in him the more likely his plays are to succeed. Writing down to the public is a good deal bunk."

For those avid for the bloody details Mr. Maugham is a slightly built chap, youthful looking, the possessor of a trifling moustache, much too short, Mrs. Maugham believes. Like Booth Tarkington and Frisco, the jazz dancer, Mr. Maugham talks hesitantly and jerkily, and like both of these gentlemen, when he gets it said, it's worth hearing. A man more like an American —he has traveled much—than some others of the English writers. He strikes you as absolutely candid without straining himself to be so and altogether free of anything resembling a pose.

His comment on a revered fellow novelist is illuminating: "Takes himself prettily seriously, doesn't he?"

Mr. Maugham, you are quite sure, doesn't take himself seriously and he has some genuine excuse for it. He is of the sort that some of us in America are wont to call "a regular fellow," a good mixer, a man who likes his fellow men and the social contacts that the ordinary man likes. He has lately taken up dancing, at Mrs. Maugham's behest possibly, and is wearing himself out at it.

They have one child, a pretty girl seven years old.

I suppose that I am violating no family confidence and I submit that it is one of that kind of important facts which are usually and inexcusably missing from these accounts when I tell you that Mrs. Maugham calls her husband "Willie."

That is probably what Anne Hathaway called her husband.

Franz Molnár

AUGUST 5, 1923

Budapest—It was the people of Budapest, you remember, who clamorously insisted on unhitching the horses of Theodore Roosevelt's carriage, when that inimitable American was their guest, a shouting mob taking the place of the exiled horses and dragging the distinguished democrat in royal style over the cobblestone roads. No potentate, however mighty, had ever received a more rousing welcome. A city capable of such things, you would say, ought to have a vigorous if somewhat exuberant drama.

The sun beats hot on the Blue Danube this midsummer, and the theaters now are given over to the lace and ruffles of operetta, but one hears of a winter season as spectacular and lively as the crowd that played horse for an American ex-president. No less than ten Shakespearean productions were made during the last year, the visitor is informed, and a clerk in a music store explains in faltering and laggard English that he guesses Shakespeare is more popular in Hungary than anywhere else except America. It would have been too difficult going to tell him that Avery Hopwood was more popular than Shakespeare in America.

Besides the classics from alien literatures, which are regularly presented, Budapest has her own young crowd of stimulating, talented playwrights whose works, often of literary excellence, are continuously in the theaters. More than in any other capital there seems to be here in Budapest, a genuine, organized artistic life. Writers, painters, and kindred craftsmen are banded in clubs or meet informally at cafés. Their intercourse is close and regular to a degree certainly not approached by the same class of workers in New York.

Such frequency and intimacy of contact probably develops a craft consciousness that is good for the soul of the artist and good for the theater or for whatever else may be his field. Nothing so stimulates a writer, even so humble a one as the youngest reporter, as to be told by the next youngest reporter that that last story of his was pretty good.

I do not mean to say that the Hungarian drama is vigorous and interesting because Mr. Franz Molnár goes about telling his compatriots at the Hungarian Writers' and Artists' Club that they're good, while they respond in kind, but I do mean that the free exchange of ideas and the stimulation of close contact with men of their own trade has strengthened the standards of the Hungarian theater and nursed, encouraged, and emboldened its writers. Fine literatures have usually been the fruit not of isolation, but of sociable, convivial spirits, who argued it out with their own kind and had the most frequent and convenient access to one another—Jonson, Shakespeare, and the Elizabethans of the Mermaid Tavern, Pope, Garrick, Gay of the coffeehouses, and Dr. Johnson, Lamb, and Goldsmith of the same coffeehouses.

The most important of the Hungarian writers in both Hungary and the United States is Franz Molnár, or to give him the name his mother calls him, Ferenc Molnár. Mr. Molnár, as those know who go to the theater, is the author of *Liliom,* a drama that Joseph Schildkraut and Eva Le Gallienne played in Cleveland last season, and a genuine piece of dramatic literature, one of the most imaginative and finely poetical plays of these times. So great was the success of that play—a success, incidentally, that has left most American theatrical men puzzled and gaping —that three other plays of Mr. Molnár's will hopefully see the light of day in New York this fall. Considerations of quality aside, if Mr. Molnár is to have three plays in New York in one season he will become by sheer force of numbers a leading figure in the American theater, to be outshone numerically perhaps only by Shakespeare and Winchell Smith.

At any rate, the one play *Liliom* establishes him as an artful playmaker of fine poetical imagination, one of the greatest now living. He has never visited America and, unlike everybody else in Europe, has no immediate intention of going there. So something about the man as he lives and has his being in Budapest may entertain you.

He doesn't live, I discovered, very much at home. His valet vouches that he is never in the house ten minutes at a time, rushing home to change clothes and then back to his club, where he stays until late at night or early in the morning. When I ultimately reached him he asked me to meet him late in the evening at his club, an organization of Hungarian writers and artists, handsomely housed in French Renaissance style and with many rooms surrounding a large terraced garden, open to the air.

He came down the stairs, a short, very broad-shouldered man, with a fine, full, compelling face, and quick, nervous eyes. There was none of the air of the wistful dreamer about him. He is personally not at all suggestive of the poet who wrote *Liliom*. With a heavy, determined face, a keen glance, and an intense, taut manner, he seems much more the able politician than the spinner of airy webs theatrical. He wears a monocle and he talks quickly, nervously, fluently too, I imagine, though I listened through an interpreter, my knowledge of Hungarian being somewhat less than three useful words.

He talked first of *Liliom,* as perhaps the subject that would most interest American playgoers. The critics were at it heavy and hot in dissecting *Liliom* and attaching strange meanings to it, trying to find in it some deep, hidden theme. Mr. Molnár has his own ideas about what he meant in *Liliom* and he may perhaps be trusted for firsthand information.

"I was, of course, essentially trying only to tell a story in *Liliom*. The story as a story seemed to me to justify itself. There is no conscious and deliberate symbolism in *Liliom* whatever. But when a poet tells a story it is bound to happen that the story will take on some symbolic meaning. Otherwise he would not be a poet. Many different symbolic meanings have been found in *Liliom* by different critics. All of them in one sense are right."

"And all of them, in a stricter sense," I interpolated, "are wrong."

"That," replied Mr. Molnár, "is the critic's prerogative. If *Liliom* has any meaning beyond what it obviously says, it is to symbolize the struggle for self-expression of two inarticulate souls. Both Liliom and the woman in the play are creatures whose words and acts do not, cannot, express their true feeling. Liliom, outwardly a braggart and a bully, is at bottom a fine soul, but so pulled and tortured by exterior forces, so helplessly unable to express his essential nature, that his acts and words are in bizarre incongruity with what he really intends and what he really feels. He is everywhere and always misunderstood. Even God"—here the translator denoted Mr. Molnár's smiling apology —"even God misunderstands him."

I ventured to tell him that Liliom and the scene in heaven seemed sometimes to be grossly misunderstood by others as well as God in America, a few in the audience seeming to take it for a musical comedy libretto.

"That's nothing. When it was first produced here in Budapest fifteen years ago some of the scenes that are essentially tragic were laughed at. The play was not a success at that time and it was not a success for the reason that people laughed at it. It was shown at a theater, the Gaiety, where comedies were usually given and people going there had made up their minds that anything given there must, of course, be funny.

"*Liliom* had its first success in America, as you know, fifteen years after the time it was first written. And it is due to that success that the play has been successfully revived in my own city, Budapest, as well as in other European capitals, Milan and Paris, where it has been very successful."

One does not habitually think of New York and Cleveland as artistic mentors to Budapest and Paris, but that appears to be the case here. Success in America succeeds even in France and Italy. If it were not for the adventuresomeness of the little coterie that guides the New York Theatre Guild, *Liliom* might still be in the dust and the Hungarian, Ferenc Molnár, not nearly so well known or so highly respected a figure as he is today.

Mr. Molnár reminded me of what many of us have been inclined to forget—that he is the author of a piece called *The Devil* which George Arliss produced in America twelve or fifteen years ago and which was an even greater monetary success than *Liliom*.

"It was not comparable as literature to *Liliom*," Mr. Molnár went on, "but it was very popular over there."

"What do you like best of your own pieces," I asked, "*Liliom?*"

"Yes," he answered. "First *Liliom* and after that *An Officer of the Guards*." The translator had difficulty with the latter title for in the Hungarian it is but one word.

"*An Officer of the Guards* was produced in America some years ago by Belasco, but it was not a success. It had been much modified to meet American requirements. I don't believe either a literary or a commercial success can be made that way. I should never write a play particularly for America myself. Plays written for special audiences cannot be good plays. A poet's best work is always done to please himself. If he's a good poet and it pleases him, then it ought to be a good piece of work.

"*An Officer of the Guards* is going to be revived in its original form by the Theatre Guild in New York this fall. Another play of mine, *The Swan*, which ran for about three hundred nights in Budapest will be produced by Gilbert Miller in New York soon."

You get an idea of the standing of Mr. Molnár among his neighbors when you reflect that Budapest is about the size of Cleveland and that three hundred nights would be a considerable run in Cleveland for the most popular play that the native Avery Hopwood ever wrote. It would, in fact, be miraculous.

The third play that Mr. Molnár will have in New York was originally called *Heavenly and Profane Love*. Because Arnold Bennett wrote an undistinguished play two or three years ago of somewhat similar title, a new name will be found for the piece in America. Mr. Molnár says it will likely be known as *The Angel* and that Arthur Hopkins will produce it.

Mr. Molnár's working hours are a bit unusual. He writes from one o'clock in the morning until he is tired. The obvious advantage of this is that it leaves the day and the evening free for the writer's amusement. But Mr. Molnár avers that it has other advantages.

"You are not disturbed by visitors, by telephone calls, by servants, or by noises of any kind. It is the ideal time for work. My years of life as a journalist on a morning newspaper have accustomed me to working when everybody else is asleep. All of *Liliom*, in fact, was written between three and five o'clock in the morning after newspaper working hours."

"Such finely spun things as *Liliom*," I hazarded, "are not very quickly written."

"One can never tell. I'm a very uncertain workman. The last act of *Liliom* was written in two hours. The second act of *The Devil* I was six months in writing."

The last act of *Liliom* is one of the finest specimens of dramatic writing in the modern catalog, suave, exalted, poignant. The second act of *The Devil,* if not the worst of the generation, may be mentioned as a contender for that distinction.

To quote Dulcy, "It's not how long you do it, but how you do it that makes books your best friends."

I write this from a window that overlooks the Blue Danube and beg leave to report in the name of honest journalism that the Blue Danube is yellow. Also I find Irish stew but no Hungarian goulash listed on the hotel menu.

John Barrymore and Hamlet

JANUARY 27, 1924

John Barrymore's *Hamlet* was laid to rest in Cleveland last evening, flushed with success and garlanded with honor. Mr. Barrymore was tired. Frayed with the strains and excitements of his role, he asked for a little peace. It may give you comfort to know that Mr. Barrymore's Prince of Denmark was as popular here as he has been in his travels to other marts; and the Hanna Theatre as early as Wednesday afternoon found itself too small to hold the crowd that gathered to encourage the nobler drama.

Music shows abundantly feminine and foolish have rarely done so well among us. The event is the more noteworthy in that we have seen much of Shakespeare recently and might be expected to be a little weary of him, though neither Mr. Sothern's nor Mr. Mantell's caused many of us to leave home.

Barrymore's *Hamlet*, of course, is only off on a furlough. When its star is rested, the production will be taken to London. If one may make a guess, Mr. Barrymore's *Hamlet* will be intermittently visible as long as Mr. Barrymore lives. It is an exalted and eloquent and persuasive performance he gives, and unless one errs egregiously, it has that quality of greatness which is permanent.

It will live in the records as long as old men are left to write them and very likely the children of today, when age begins to sit on their shoulders, will be telling their wondering and doubtful grandchildren, years hence, that if they think that young jackanapes who plays Hamlet in the radio theater is any good they ought to have seen John Barrymore in his prime. Those were the days!

For the enlightenment of those unborn grandchildren one may be permitted to set down here a fact not, I believe, hitherto printed, that this player of *Hamlet*, the greatest of his time, thinks that *Hamlet* is a rotten play. Mr. Barrymore is chary of interviewers, regarding them as a bore, and it is a pity, for he talks engagingly, picturesquely, and often printably.

I had just been reading an article of the elderly critic, William Winter, when Mr. Barrymore, accompanied by his manager and nevertheless his friend, David Wallace, knocked at my door a little after teatime, about one o'clock in the morning.

"Here's a critical gent," I said to Mr. Barrymore, pouring out the ginger ale, "who has the degree of Hamlet's insanity exactly figured out. He says, if I can remember, that Hamlet was suffering from 'compound-confusional-intermittent-emotional' insanity."

"An elegant ass," responded Barrymore approximately. "That stuff gives me a pain. Hamlet was a normal, healthy, lusty young fellow who simply got into a mess that was too thick for him. I don't see where these fellows get all that stuff. Did you ever read *Hamlet*? He was no more weak in his mind than he was in his body.

"He was a great fencer, an athlete, a man who led an active, healthy life. How can you make a sickly half-wit out of a man like that? Can you imagine how this quick-witted young fencer made love to Ophelia in the Elsinore garden? Polonius was a wise father when he warned Ophelia to watch out for that fellow.

"But *Hamlet* is a rotten play. Terrible. I don't see why some of you birds don't say so once in a while."

"It's pretty good poetry," I suggested.

"Maybe. But look at the rest of it. Shakespeare had a fine chance to make a real and penetrating study of middle-aged love in the affair between the king and the queen and he makes nothing of it. It's blah, nothing real, nothing deep.

"He couldn't or didn't do anything either with the love affair between Hamlet and Ophelia. There is not a spark in it. It's no good, rotten, empty, silly."

From Shakespeare it wasn't far to Shaw. Mr. Barrymore has a no more complete adulation for the one than for the other.

"Shaw," he said, "once came near writing a real play."

"Which," I guessed, "*The Devil's Disciple?*"

"Yes. That's a good play. A great play up until the last act. Then it takes an awful flop.

"I was going to play the part of Dick Dudgeon for the Theatre Guild. I read the play and thought it a great part until I came to the last act. Then Shaw lost the character. Lost him completely. He simply died on his hands.

"I'd like to meet Shaw. My wife knows him. And if I ever meet him I'm going to have nerve enough to ask what in hell he meant by writing that last act of *The Devil's Disciple* in the way he did.

"I'm even going to have the nerve to ask him to rewrite it so that I can play it."

"When do you leave for Paris?" I asked, expressing some nostalgia for the boulevards and the Café de la Paix, still months off for me.

"I don't know why anybody wants to go to Paris," he answered. "I leave February second, but I hate the place. Too much bunk. I've been there too often."

"If you don't like Paris, what in the name of sweetness and light, do you like?"

"I like Hollywood," was Mr. Barrymore's somewhat disturbing response.

"Why? Well, because I like the atmosphere of work about the place. Everybody is up to his neck in his job. The people are amusing. You get both extremes there. Fourflushers so wrapped up in themselves that they're funny, and the other kind, mostly mechanics, cameramen, etc., who are simple, friendly, kindly men.

"It's nice to live in a place, too, where you're a figure with the headwaiters. Makes you more comfortable."

"But you must find headwaiters in New York equally accommodating."

"Yes. But I don't like New York. I hate it. Too many horn-rimmed fellows there who write for the *New Republic*. I like the road. I've had a fine time this trip. The first time I've been out for years. I like Pittsburgh. I like Cleveland, too, though I mistook it for Pittsburgh in one of my curtain speeches the other day."

A merry fellow, this Barrymore, the greatest, I believe, of a great family; a scorner of pose, interested in many things, a reader, a brilliant, rangy, erratic mind; a noncomformist, restless under leash of any kind, strung high, careless of fools, a man destined to live turbulently. Genius sits very close to him.

A Russian *Hamlet*

AUGUST 7, 1932

Moscow—When I wrote a few weeks ago about the agile Hamlet of Monsieur Yonnel at the *Comédie Française* I thought I had done with Denmark's prince for the rest of the summer and we could pass on to matters more contemporary. But I couldn't have anticipated the Moscow *Hamlet* at Vahtangoff's theater. Bear with me while I unfold the tale. It is the first real news of *Hamlet* since the evenings when John Barrymore was pinching Ophelia's ears.

This Bolshevik *Hamlet* is heroic, grandiose, startling. It is Ringling Brothers' circus merged with Morris Gest and a Shriners' parade. It is impudent and ingenious and full of juice.

I liked it so much that I stayed for the full four and one-half hours of it to see how everything came out. It was the first time in ten years that I have seen the last act of *Hamlet*.

Give heed to what happens to *Hamlet* when the new Russians turn loose on Shakespeare. To begin with, Hamlet is the ghost of his own father. He keeps a set of the old man's armor hidden in a cabin near the Elsinore platform and when he wishes to impress the simple court folk with the terror of the supernatural he picks out a dark night, puts on his dead father's armor and walks the platform, making hollow, unearthly noises by speaking through a porcelain vase or pot, which he carries for that purpose.

Only his friend Horatio is in on the secret. Occasionally Horatio gets hold of the pot and draws it from under his cape to put it to his mouth and terrorize the assembled ghost-watchers.

In this unrouted *Hamlet* Queen Gertrude gallops in on a horse, and at the rear of the stage can be seen at another moment a file of fake horses racing along like the last act of *In Old Kentucky*.

The play scene is completely omitted from this production of *Hamlet*. Its place is taken by a scene showing Hamlet rehearsing and coaching the players. But you never see the play itself. You see only the king and his frightened couriers rushing down the stairs at the finale of the play within a play.

The king is a popinjay king, unbearded and faintly diabolic, who likes to have his portrait painted by artists and is shown sitting for a painting while lackeys hold above him his crown and scepter.

In one scene the king is carried in sitting on the arms of several couriers while Hamlet is hauled in over the shoulders of several others from the opposite side of the stage. They meet in the center, glare at one another like unamicable cats, and carry on an apparently bitter colloquy while being held in the air.

Horatio wears horn-rimmed glasses, which would have been news to the Danes of the tenth century, and Guildenstern wears a beard and employs the manner of the old-time Jewish comedian on the American stage. Hamlet himself is a lively, redheaded little fellow, full of zest and *joie de vivre*, and Polonius has an obtrusively long mustache that keeps wiggling comically as he talks.

Now all these details are misleading because they suggest a mere comic-opera sort of freakishness, though I have not enumerated a tenth of the quaintnesses of the interpretation. The truth that you might not suspect from this introduction is that there is a great deal of acute thought in the production, some interesting Shakespearean criticism, and a magnificent skill in the theatrical management of details.

The director who devised this production is no mere show-off but a fellow with an engaging mind and an active imagination.

Take what seems to be the most fantastic innovation, the assumption that Hamlet played the ghost of his father. It is not merely a humorous idea.

Hamlet was shrewd in the ways of the world. The Russian director assumes that he wanted it known that his father had been murdered and that the quickest way of spreading the news about among a timid and superstitious people would be for him to play his father's ghost and then pledge everybody to secrecy, since nothing travels faster than a secret.

I should guess that in reading the play the director noticed Hamlet's insistence on the members of the watch keeping the secret of his father's ghostly prowlings and concluded that a man as shrewd as Hamlet had, by this insistence, intended to scatter the news widely. It is incredible to a modern mind that one who saw so clearly and who understood so deeply as Hamlet could have shared the vulgar belief of his time in ghosts and hobgoblins.

With these premises it is not too farfetched to suggest that Hamlet was the ghost of his own father.

The effect of another extraordinary amendment is magnificent. Hamlet is shown rehearsing the actors for the play that is to catch the conscience of the king, and you are prepared for it. Instead of seeing the play you see the distilled essence of the play. You see what Shakespeare wanted you to see, multiplied and intensified five times over; that is, the devastating and annihilating effect of the play on the king and his court.

A great, wide, palatial staircase runs from the forestage back and up to the depth and height of the spacious stage. You hear music from the upper rooms and you know the play is on and what is happening, for you have seen the play rehearsed and know its purpose.

Suddenly there is a shout and a turmoil and the king comes running in fright down the long staircase, his cape trailing, his arms over his eyes, the very mold of terror, as he negotiates each long step. Tumbling after him comes an immense procession of frightened courtiers, great ladies with tempestuous skirts, swords dangling, faces pale with fear, splendid clothes awry. A kind of regal terror is in the very breath of the scene.

It is one of the most forceful and haunting spectacles I have seen in a theater. Elmer Rice, author of *Street Scene*, who is visiting Moscow, says that Shakespeare would have used the scene himself if he had thought of it. He couldn't have used it because of the scenic poverty in his day, but if you can conceive of Shakespeare as living today he might have thought of it.

I think this Bolshevist *Hamlet* is without question the richest, most spectacular, most interesting production of the play I have ever seen.

Scene follows scene in prodigal succession, novelty piles on novelty, great arches mingle with forlorn battlements, fantastic constructions combine with a laborious realism, wide, smashing effects mix with delicately laced, richly colored costumes.

There is nothing hackneyed in the play. All of it is intensely theatrical, hotly colored, original and audacious, humorous and ironic and splendid. There is more imagination in it, a freer play of the faculties than in ten American spectacles.

It is not *Hamlet,* but it is something infinitely gustier than the *Hamlet* to which we are accustomed.

How strange it was, I thought, that this rich and expensive and vivifying production of a great English classic should be encountered in a summer theater in a remote country supposed to be desperately poor and lacking in appreciation of esthetic values.

There was not a vacant seat in the large theater on the evening I was there. Even the *strapotins,* those backless supplementary seats that buckle onto the aisle chairs, were occupied by men and women in shabby clothes, the men in shirt sleeves.

Immediately next to me, drinking in the color of this *Hamlet,* was an old peasant woman with a shawl over her head and shoes made of bark fastened on with thick pieces of twine. During the entr'acte I saw her munching a caviar sandwich. Only in Russia can these things be.

A Visit to Reinhardt Castle

SEPTEMBER 7, 1924

Salzburg—This drowsy mountain village that comes up for air out of the hills and lakes of the Austrian border, struggling to make itself seen against the overwhelming competition of nature, had a population of 30,000 souls one hundred years ago. It still has a population of 30,000 souls, many of them doubtless being the same souls, for it is hard to imagine anybody dying in this celestial and renovating air or being removed from scenes of such prodigal loveliness much before reaching the age of a hundred.

Leaving out the surrounding mountains, the whole of Salzburg might be assembled, with a little crowding, in the Cleveland Public Auditorium. One would not think of so small and far off a hamlet as a center of the world's theater, the Broadway and Forty-sixth Street of the Alps. But so it has seemed in the last few days.

A quiet walk around the lobby of the leading hotel, a hostelry, incidentally, where one pours his own wash water and the grandeur of nature is permitted to compensate for unimportant defects of plumbing—and you may meet, as I did today, these gentlemen of the theater: Morris Gest, the purple prince of show fellows, archbishop of *The Miracle* and the greatest figure in picturesque and spectacular American theatricals; Edward Knoblock, English author of *Kismet, My Lady's Dress*, collaborator with Arnold Bennett on *Milestones* and other pieces, and manufacturer of many scenarios for the Hollywood mill; Leopold Jacobson, the Viennese author of the operetta *The Chocolate Soldier* and *The Dream Girl*, great successes in America and Europe; Max Reinhardt, the foremost stage director and artist of the contemporary world stage, and Helene Thymig, one of the best of Viennese actresses.

You might also rub elbows with the gentleman who translated Shaw's plays for Central Europe and whom Shaw recently repaid by rewriting a play of his called *Jitta's Atonement*, which ran briefly in New York, and, to make an end of the catalog without completing it, Rudolf Kommer, Hungarian author and translator of many plays, together with a Dutch baron now promoted to the theatrical business, a young Viennese prima donna, and forty Russians, members of the Don Cossacks choir.

If you had come the day before you might have just encountered the ample form of Joseph Urban, who came to Ziegfeld's Follies as stage designer just about the time that the girl circus began to be spoken of as art rather than as legs.

Nearly all this assemblage of theatrical princes and princelings with the exception of the forty Don Cossacks who, one presumes, ate in their tents, was gathered a little later about the same hotel dinner table exchanging such repartee as there was in two or three different languages including the manual.

"You're going with me to Reinhardt's castle this afternoon," said Morris Gest, the American importer of the choicest theatrical goods and New York impresario—good theatergoers need not be told—for the Moscow Art Theatre and the Chauve-Souris, Eleanore Duse, and Max Reinhardt.

"I'm taking the Don Cossacks choir out there today and I want you to hear them. We'll eat luncheon at the castle."

As long as the whole choir was coming along, it seemed to me that one uninvited guest more or less wouldn't make much difference.

We went by automobile, Gest, Jacobson, Kommer, and sundry other artists and playwrights, the forty members of the Don Cossacks choir having apparently been delegated to move in another troop.

It was a trip of a few miles through a rough and beautiful country to Schloss Leopold Kron, the two-hundred-year-old castle in which Reinhardt lives in medieval spaciousness, attended, if one may make a guess, by fifty servants. Lying amidst an estate that seems to traverse half the duchy of Salzburg, the castle was built by a bishop with an eye for earthly as well as spiritual beauty and in quiet and unostentatious magnificence is not surpassed by the palaces that are the public show places of Europe.

We entered by relays, dropping out at the castle gate and taking a turn in the quaint, not too well-kept gardens that circle the main building. Dotted with odd, grotesque statuary, fantastic and strange pieces that look as if they might have been carved by some one of Adam's gifted descendants not long after the Fall, and wandering away to the edge of a clear, green lake, it was a charming landscape, as delightful in its haphazard medieval and Teutonic way as the more familiar and trimmer beauty places of France and England.

We met our host, Herr Reinhardt, in the garden. He shouted a greeting across an expanse of shrubbery and a few minutes later we were being introduced, as a sort of afterthought, to the lord of the surrounding magnificence, a quiet-looking man, not tall, with sharp eyes, dark and reserved as the suit he wore. They made a spectacular contrast, Gest and he, both emperors of a sort in different realms, the one voluble and expansive, the other contained and shy.

Our host we left in the garden to be conducted through the castle, a huge building with rooms as large as the average New York theater, beautifully fitted with old paintings and statuary, pieces from the seventeenth century, graceful sleighs, masks, candelabra, Venetian glass, fine crystal, rich murals. It was in one of these rooms that Reinhardt recently staged for an army of his friends a production of Molière's *The Imaginary Invalid*.

Taking in the quaint, spacious beauty of the place, fragrant of other and more highly colored times, filled with relics of the pomp and pageantry of religion, which were assembled in their most picturesque and characteristic aspect in the little chapel leading from one of the great rooms, you could understand the interest of its owner in bringing into being such a spectacle as *The Miracle* with its glorification of the sensuous color and sound of ancient religious ceremonial and legend.

Some time later we were being guided through a labyrinth of

halls and staircases to the relatively small dining room, exquisitely decorated in the Venetian style. There were eighteen or twenty of us at the table, though Herr Reinhardt had no reason to expect more than two or three guests, except that he knew that the unpredictable Mr. Gest was in Salzburg.

Mr. Gest had not told his host about the forty Don Cossacks singers whom he had invited to the castle, but when he did so, through Mr. Kommer a few minutes later, Reinhardt expressed more pleasure than surprise. To a man who lived like a sixteenth-century baron, forty unexpected guests was all in the day's work.

The talk such as drifted to my ears was of cabbages and kings, touching the subject with which these pages are concerned only fleetingly. Reinhardt complained good-humoredly that he couldn't go to a hotel any more without being buttonholed by some insistent fellow who thought that the hotel, or perhaps the city hall in his own town, would be a perfect place to stage *The Miracle*, and one got a picture of the patient listener giving ear to the delegation from some dingy hill town armed with a project for recouping the municipal finance by having the Herr Professor stage a grand pageant in the civic cowsheds.

Reinhardt is preparing to present Eugene O'Neill's *The Emperor Jones* in Vienna soon and I questioned whether that singular and defiant play, dealing in a fantastic yet acutely realistic way with a Negro porter, would be understood in Austria where the Negro is as strange and exotic a creature as an Indian yogi would be for us.

It was to O'Neill that talk turned later in the afternoon after Mr. Gest had considerately shooed away a dozen guests and left Reinhardt for a private word with the pilgrim from Ohio.

Reinhardt regards O'Neill as a pearl of the very first water, a playwright of unassailable international rank, and one of a very small band of world geniuses.

"O'Neill is a talent that will stand comparison with any in the theater today. He belongs to the new generation, expressing a thought and employing a technique that for us, who live in this age, is vital and important. *Anna Christie* we did not much care for here. It was, from our point of view, old-fashioned.

"What most interests me in O'Neill's plays is their curious rhythm. They all have a regular drumbeat movement that distinguishes them, and that seems expressive of something I sense, and like, in the spirit of America."

Reinhardt believes that the American theater is now the most important in the world.

"The capital of the theater used to be Berlin," he said, "now it's New York. Nowhere else can you see German plays, English plays, Austrian plays, French plays, plays from the Russian, the Czech, the Hungarian, and every other language. The French theater is closed to new ideas.

"The German theaters are hampered by financial conditions and by the spiritual changes brought by the war. Only American theater audiences have been improving and, with them, their plays."

It had been an unusual day for us, I thought, as we waved goodby to Reinhardt from an automobile, through a heavy rain that was doubtless somewhere on the road drenching the nice red boots of the forty Cossacks.

Brooks Atkinson and Irony

JANUARY 26, 1939

It is easy to overestimate the human capacity for taking a joke. Man is the only animal that laughs but you never know whether he will decide to exercise his unique privilege. He has an equally well-developed faculty of taking seriously what is presented as a jest. Orson Welles found that out in connection with the late invasion from Mars.

Brooks Atkinson, dramatic critic of *The New York Times,* is the latest victim of the delusion that Americans have an unfailing sense of humor and never miss the point of a pleasantry.

On the occasion of a recent revival of Oscar Wilde's *The Importance of Being Earnest,* he conceived the notion of freshening up a routine chore by speaking of Wilde as if he were still living. He treated his ancient play as a contemporary work and referred to Wilde's cleverness and promise, artificiality and preciousness, much in the manner of the Victorian critics who patronized Wilde in his own day.

It was an amusing pastiche, a skillful piece of fooling, and Mr. Atkinson went to bed with the easy conscience of a man who has contributed his day to the harmless pleasuring of mankind.

The next morning Mr. Atkinson's telephone began to ring. Strange and familiar voices wished to point out that he had made an unfortunate error in yesterday's column. Mr. Wilde was not among the living, as he had assumed. Mr. Wilde was long since gathered to his fathers. How could Mr. Atkinson have made such a mistake?

Such corrective telephone messages were so numerous and continuous that Mr. Atkinson felt obliged to issue a bulletin. The impetus which drove him to this action was probably a telephone call from one of his fellow critics who thought Mr. Atkinson should be informed of the vital statistics in respect to Oscar Wilde. If the brethren in his own fraternity had missed the point, the misapprehension must have been general.

So Mr. Atkinson printed a note which should rank as one of the curiosities in the history of theatrical criticism and remain an enduring testimony to the riskiness of literary irony.

He said, in effect, that he really knew that Wilde was not among the living when he penned his review and he offered irrefutable proof that he had long been in possession of such knowledge. His remarks, he pointed out, were "writ sarkastic."

Large letters in the headline of the review stated that the play was a revival. But aside from this tangible indication that the reviewer knew the piece was not the fresh product of a promising young man, there was the professional standing of Mr. Atkinson to clear up any fleeting misapprehension.

Mr. Atkinson is a scholar of the theater, a distinguished critic of long practice, a highly literate specialist. How could anybody suppose that such a man would be totally ignorant of the career of the most notorious English dramatist of the nineteenth century? It would be unbecoming to think such a thing of the youngest reporter on the Podunk *Sentinel*.

But such miracles of misapprehension are not uncommon, particularly in respect to what is written humorously or ironically. Every scrivener of long service has come up against these curious blind spots in readers, or what appear to him to be blind spots.

He forgets that you cannot reproduce a wink in print, you cannot point the joke by a tone of voice or a look.

Ordinarily, people do not read. They skip, they absorb what it pleases them to absorb by a process which does not involve attention to every word or sentence. No two readers will get exactly the same impression from the simplest, shortest piece of writing.

I had good advice on this point once, long ago, from an old editor. I had written an editorial in a vein of elaborate irony.

"What the devil is this?" he asked, looking up from my hard-labored piece with hostility and fixing me with a stare of displeasure.

"It's supposed to be funny," I said feebly.

"My boy," he answered. "Never try to be funny in print. It's dangerous."

He was right, but the cause he represented was hopeless. We vassals of his reign persisted in trying to slip a jest or a palely humorous attitude into the heavy solemnities of his editorial page, and if you were careful enough you could get away with it. But we recognized the danger of the practice.

When you write something that is not altogether seriously intended it is wise to follow the precedent of Artemus Ward and add, at the end, "N.B. This is rote sarcastikul."

Or better still, take a hint from Benjamin Franklin: "Strange! That a man who has wit enough to write a satire should have folly enough to publish it."

Bing Crosby's Radio Rehearsal

JULY 1, 1945

When I was in Hollywood some weeks ago something heady in the atmosphere prompted me to visit a broadcasting station for the purpose of attending a rehearsal of Bing Crosby's program. It was the first time I had been in a broadcasting studio since the toddling and primitive days of radio, when, believe it or not, I was a regular weekly performer on Station WTAM and used to arise every Tuesday morning at seven to describe the state of dramatic art at that moment to a breathless audience busily engaged in dunking doughnuts and preparing for the harsh realities of another day in a workaday world.

Few took the radio seriously in that innocent period, not even, I suspect, John F. Royal whose idea it was that a lecture on the drama would interest people at breakfast time and, if it didn't, no harm would be done and they could give their attention to the next performer, a lady gymnast who conducted a fat-reducing and health-promotion program and would tell her women listeners when to roll over and when to bend from the hips.

But my radio career was finished long ago and I came with innocent and wide-eyed wonder into Bing Crosby's broadcasting parlors. There was an astonishing kind of casual efficiency in the rehearsal. Bing Crosby, Gladys Swarthout, John Scott Trotter, and many others seemed to be walking about aimlessly over the stage and passing the time of day in idle converse, but, before you knew it, they had built up a show that was completely expert, well organized, and timed with the utmost precision.

The proceedings were interesting and they were also unforgettable and for a somber reason. No one present will fail to remember that afternoon.

Miss Swarthout was singing, the band was playing, the members of a Negro quartet were draped over the stage awaiting their cue and jesting quietly among themselves. Everything was casual and smiling.

Crosby ambled onto the stage from the control room. He looked distressed, but he had been looking distressed all afternoon. The music continued.

Without interrupting it, Crosby stepped to the forefront of the stage, cupped his hands to his lips, and whispered to the dozen or so people in the audience, "Roosevelt has just dropped dead."

There was no audible answer from the audience, only an expression of incredulity on their faces and then a look of being stunned as if they had been physically hit by a heavy blow.

For a few seconds, there was suspicion, or hope, that this was some kind of macabre joke. Then common sense told everybody that sane people do not joke on such matters.

A woman employee of the sponsoring firm left the auditorium and crossed the stage to the control room. In a minute she came out and signaled the audience by a nod and the expression of her face that it was true. With startling and unbelievable suddenness Roosevelt was dead.

The news passed in undertones to Miss Swarthout and the dozens of musicians and technicians on the stage. Their faces, so animated a few minutes before, solidified into a fixed glumness.

The performance did not stop. It was a rehearsal for the evening program and an interruption would have thrown off the timing. Or so I suppose.

Miss Swarthout continued her singing, the music played, and Crosby, in his turn, sang and went through his comedy routine. The show was finished at the scheduled moment and, if it had been broadcast, no one listening to it could have guessed that anything had happened to disturb the performers.

When it was over the musicians, actors, and technicians gathered in little groups on the stage to talk about the incredible thing that had happened. Roosevelt was extremely well liked by Hollywood and by the theatrical fraternity in general because, among other things, they have a generous attitude toward the underdog and they figured that Roosevelt was on the side of the needy and the undefended.

On the stage, it was like a funeral. Voices were muted, faces fixed in an unwonted expression of gravity.

Crosby finally announced to his company, "You might as well go home. Call up later. Maybe there won't be any show tonight." There wasn't.

I never thought of Crosby except as a pleasant minor troubadour of the radio who had chanced into enormous popularity, until I saw him in *Going My Way*. He was more than pleasant in that film. He was a skilled, tactful actor, an artist of taste, and a personage of no little power to charm and to move.

It was interesting to see him informally in his natural habitat, a broadcasting studio. He wanders around in his own rehearsals as if he was there by mistake, or had come in as an uninvited outsider and was expecting to be thrown out. His dissociation from the business of the proceedings seems complete except when his time comes to step to the microphone.

He wears a dilapidated felt hat, a probably expensive sweater which looks as if it came out of the ragbag, an old pair of well-tailored pants, and, altogether, he is the complete picture of the careless lounger.

His facial expression as he contemplates the stage around him is sober and saturnine and preoccupied, as if he were thinking of how nice it would be to go fishing instead of engaging in this foolishness.

He wears a pencil behind his ear and his clothes, his slouching manner, his lazy, abstracted air, and everything about him remind you somewhat of a clerk who is about to be fired from his employment in an unsuccessful suburban grocery store.

But don't let him fool you. Even in a single rehearsal you can see that this apparently slipshod, slow-moving man is one of the hardest-working, most conscientious of theatrical artists and one of the most efficient and intelligent organizers of entertainment.

Katharine Cornell

MAY 2, 1943

It has been said that the plays of Anton Chekhov are inconceivable outside the Moscow Art Theatre and the Art Theatre inconceivable without Chekhov. Katharine Cornell and Guthrie McClintic are proving that they are quite conceivable in the American theater if you go to enough trouble to get the right actors. Miss Cornell's production of Chekhov's *The Three Sisters* is without much doubt the finest ever made in English. In addition to Miss Cornell the cast includes Judith Anderson, Ruth Gordon, Gertrude Musgrove, Edmund Gwenn, Dennis King, Tom Powers, McKay Morris, and Alexander Knox.

All of these are not only players of individual distinction but most of them have acted together previously, and nearly all of them have appeared under Mr. McClintic's direction on other occasions, so that their performance as a group has some of that extraordinary harmony and perfection of rhythm which were the pre-eminent attributes of the Moscow Art productions.

I saw the Art Theatre's performances of *The Three Sisters* in Moscow and in this country and I saw the Cornell production recently in New York. At the risk of being liquidated by devotees of the Russian theater, who are a fierce tribe, I will say that the Cornell performance was superior in at least one important respect.

The women in the Cornell cast were better than their Moscow counterparts, as I remember them. Not that the men in the Cornell company are not good. They are excellent.

But the Moscow Art Theatre has, or had, an extraordinary number of superb men players. Stanislavsky, Moskvin, Katchalov, and Vishnevsky used to play in *The Three Sisters*. These were among the great actors of the world and it would be hard to match them.

The Moscow Art Theatre was relatively weak on the distaff side. Olga Knipper, widow of Chekhov, was the first actress of the theater and, in *The Three Sisters*, she played the role of Masha which Miss Cornell is now acting. Madame Knipper was an accomplished and intelligent actress but she did not have the personal distinction, the luminousness of Katharine Cornell.

Stanislavsky's wife, Lilina, played the role of Natasha which Ruth Gordon is now acting. I think Miss Gordon is the more vivid and exciting in the part.

I do not clearly remember the Russian actress who personated the eldest sister. If she had been as compelling as Judith Anderson is in the same role, I think I would have remembered.

The Moscow Art Theatre was and, I believe, still is the greatest acting organization in the world, but I do not think its performances on the feminine side in *The Three Sisters* were as individually distinguished or as memorable as those in the American company which will be seen here this week.

Moreover, Miss Cornell's production of the play is in English and that is a great help to the enjoyment and the understanding of those who neglected to learn Russian.

The Moscow Art Theatre existed before Chekhov started writing for it but he had a great part in molding its spirit. The great theater was conceivable without him but it would not have been the same theater.

His tranquil, richly textured plays with their curious quality of casual, haunting realism were exactly suited to the patient, disciplined art of the Moscow Theatre. The plays were not dramatic in the conventional sense.

They were delicate and evocative and flowing with implication. Their inner content was deep and rich, and the subtlest art of the actor was needed to bring it to the surface.

In the Moscow Art Theatre Chekhov found a medium which materialized his plays with extraordinary completeness and the theater found in him the perfect playwright.

Chekhov never saw *The Sea Gull* and *Uncle Vanya* until long after they were established in the repertory of the Moscow Art Theatre. He was tubercular and his illness sent him to the soft climate of Yalta in the Crimea.

He would not believe in the success of his first plays and when Stanislavsky and his actors asked him to write another he refused on the grounds that he couldn't write a new play until he had seen how they performed the old ones. So the entire company made the long journey to Yalta and played *The Sea Gull* and *Uncle Vanya* for their author.

He approved of what he saw and wrote another play. It was *The Three Sisters.*

A little later he wrote from Yalta, "I wrote four lines a day and those with intolerable torment." He was writing *The Cherry Orchard.*

A year after its completion he died at the age of forty-four. He had no predecessor as dramatist or short-story writer and he has had no successor, though he has had hundreds of imitators.

No man has had greater influence on the art of writers of the short story. From Somerset Maugham down they have paid him homage and experimented with his casual patterns of form.

Such self-consciously modern playwrights as Clifford Odets have imitated him and so has the old giant, the incorrigibly individualistic and the tolerably brilliant Bernard Shaw.

Even the unconformable and unpredictable William Saroyan has taken a number of leaves from Chekhov's chapters.

· Criticism

MAY 7, 1947

I wonder if we are not all inclined to stress the beauty and perfection of any piece of art in the form it had when we encountered it for the first time. When we read it or saw it, it made a deep and agreeable impression upon us. It has become pleasantly familiar. We do not wish it to change.

We feel that many things were better in the old days. Maybe they were not better. But we were younger then and more impressionable, and they seemed better.

When we see a revival of a fine old play that we found delight in many years ago, we instinctively expect to recapture the emotion we had on seeing it the first time. To some degree, we are judging it not for what it is now but for what it meant to us emotionally a couple of decades ago. If we find failure, the failure may be not in the stars, but in ourselves.

John Keats wrote a noble sonnet on the impression made on him when he first looked into Chapman's *Homer*. He felt "like some watcher of the skies when a new planet swims into his ken." But he could not feel that way on reading Chapman's *Homer* the second time.

The first impression we have of a fine work of art is unique because, to the individual, it is a discovery, and nothing can be discovered more than once. In the course of time, we may learn to appreciate it more completely or to understand it more thoroughly, but the rapture of discovery is missing.

When Maurice Evans or John Gielgud act Hamlet before any except the youngest and most inexperienced theatergoers they are competing against the memories their audiences have of Henry Irving, Forbes-Robertson, John Barrymore, and a dozen others. The ghosts of their predecessors are in the wings, and cold, unseen hands are laid on them in every step of their traffic on the stage.

It is a hard test for the contemporary actor of the classics, and, in a way, it is not fair. By a large part of his audience his performance is judged not for what it is, but for what it has been at the hands of another, or rather, for what it seems to have been in the memory of his auditors.

This involves a double standard of judgment. Theatergoers are comparing the current actuality of the actor's performance, as seen in their maturity, with the sentimental, emotional recollections they have of the impression that some other actor made on them in the same role years ago, when they had less understanding but a more excitable sensitivity.

As a critic grown old in practice, I am bound to attach some importance to the critic's training and knowledge in the matter with which he deals. But there are no absolutes in criticism, no rules that a great dramatist or actor cannot break.

Criticism is not a science. It is an art, and not often that.

Even what is called "objective criticism" can be objective only to a limited degree. Any play or book is, in one degree or another, an appeal to the emotions, and where emotion is so largely concerned true objectivity is impossible.

There is no extreme of nonsense which has not been solemnly expressed in the form of criticism, and the most extravagant nonsense has been proclaimed by critics who built their judgments on rules and felt that their standards were absolute and eternal. Even a genius, such as Voltaire, could make a fool of himself in this regard.

Shakespeare's *Hamlet,* he wrote, "is a coarse and barbarous piece, which would not be tolerated by the lowest rabble of France and Italy. One would suppose this work to be the fruit of the imagination of a drunken savage."

Voltaire was judging *Hamlet* by French eighteenth-century standards of unity, refinement, and elegance, and he assumed that these standards, because they derived from the Greek classics, had an unassailable and everlasting validity.

We have come to know better, or at least we have come to think differently. To Voltaire's objectiveness and dogmatism we prefer Anatole France's smiling and unassuming subjectiveness: "A good critic is one who relates the adventures of his soul among masterpieces."

That is modest enough, although there may be those who will think it an unwarranted assumption to imply that critics have souls or that enough masterpieces are being currently produced to keep them busy.

Judith Anderson in *Medea*

NOVEMBER 13, 1947

Within recent years I have taken more than one occasion to observe sadly that the era of acting in the grand style has passed and the giants are dead. I was thinking of what I had read of Edmund Kean and other great players of an elder day and how women fainted and strong men wept at climacteric scenes, so moving and so powerful was the effect created by the art and personality of the actor. There is very little fainting among the members of a contemporary audience.

I have read that when Kean was playing one of the Shakespearean tragedies a man in the first row of the balcony arose from his seat to obtain a better view of the stage. Instead of shouting for him to sit down, the audience, whose view he was obstructing, was so engrossed with the actor's performance, and so unwilling to lose a word of it, that one by one they got up from their chairs without uttering a whisper and the curtain came down with everybody standing in mute rapture.

Obviously, there was a quality of grandeur in Kean's performance which is not matched on the modern stage. Even in my own time, I have seen great changes in the style and effect of acting as exhibited by its most distinguished practitioners. There is less flamboyance, less wonder, less glory in the acting we see today.

The emphasis is on the play rather than on the performance. Reserve and realism have become fetishes.

John Gielgud and Maurice Evans are the best living players of Shakespeare's *Hamlet*. Their style is quite different from that of John Barrymore who played the role not so many years ago, and so is the effect they make. I was reminded of that with a sense of shock the other evening when a radio program put on a record of Barrymore's reading of one of the soliloquies.

In the final lines he seemed to overdo it so grossly that it brought a laugh. Yet, I remember him as the greatest Hamlet I have ever seen, and I suspect that he was great in an objective and absolute sense, if the absolute and the objective exist in respect to so changeable and ephemeral an art as acting.

People who attended his performances did not go to see *Hamlet*. They went to see John Barrymore play Hamlet. He let himself go in the part and he had the force and personality to dominate it.

Today's actors hold themselves in and they are overwhelmed by the play. Perhaps that is the fitting and proper attitude, but it diminishes the emotional effect of an individual performance.

One of the most famous criticisms of the actress, Rachel, was written by George Henry Lewes, and every theatrical specialist is familiar with it, or should be.

It begins: "Rachel was the panther of the stage: with a panther's terrible beauty and undulating grace she moved and stood, glared and sprang. There was always something not human about her. She seemed to be made of different clay from her fellows—beautiful but not lovable. Those who never saw Edmund Kean may form a very good conception of him if they have seen Rachel. She was very much as a woman what he was as a man. If he was a lion, she was a panther."

There are not many players on the contemporary stage who could be appropriately described as lions or panthers. But one whose art could justify such similes is now acting in the Broadway jungles. She is Judith Anderson and the play is Euripides' *Medea* as put into eloquent and poetic English by the California poet, Robinson Jeffers.

Here is acting in the traditional manner on a scale of splendor and magnificence. Everything about her performance is powerful, intense, violent, and spectacular. I have seen nothing like it in the theater since Sarah Bernhardt.

The remarks that Lewes made of Rachel would be precisely

applicable to Judith Anderson in this play. He said, "scorn, rage, triumph, lust and malignity she could represent in symbols of irresistible power; but she had little tenderness, no womanly caressing softness, no gayety, no heartiness. She was so graceful and so powerful that her air of dignity was incomparable, but somehow you always felt in her presence an air of indefinable suggestion of latent wickedness."

Lewes was talking about Rachel's performance of *Phèdre*, a play of entirely different quality, but the general tone and temper of his remarks are applicable to Miss Anderson's performance of *Medea*.

She has a wonderful power, an immense intensity, an extraordinary capacity for the suggestion of irrepressible, obsessed, and ferocious feeling. The energy that goes into it is tremendous.

It is a showpiece, a tour de force, but it is more than that. Though saturated with pyrotechnics, there is no false fire in it. The feeling seems to come from the heart and it is magnificently materialized in terms of the theater.

For once, we have again great acting in the traditional manner, and, what is more surprising, we have capacity audiences for it, who come to see, not a great Greek play, but a heart-tearing, deeply felt, superbly designed individual performance of its principal role.

Good Will

JANUARY 9, 1951

A few weeks illness is bad for the body but probably good for the soul. It affords a man leisure to contemplate his sins, which is always a wholesome employment, and it strengthens his faith in the instinctive kindness of his fellow creatures.

I had many evidences of the latter during a recent month's stay in a hospital. My room was so generously and continuously stocked with flowers that the total floral display would have done honor to a gangster's funeral. I had gifts of books and candy, and hundreds of notes and letters from well-wishers, many of them personally unknown to me.

I report these kindnesses not with any more than a normal spirit of vanity but with surprise and appreciation as an attestation of the amount of good will that exists in a supposedly wicked world.

The most spectacular benevolence visited upon me in this period of ill health was Katharine Cornell's gesture in bringing out her players and installing them in my living room to put on a performance of her new play, *Captain Carvallo*, which I was unable to see in its regular performances at the Hanna. It was an unusual occasion and probably unprecedented in American theatrical annals. You may be interested in a firsthand report of it. They brought the entire company of seven and they played in such costumes as the play required and quite as seriously as if they had been acting to a full theater and not to an audience of two.

If they were self-conscious at acting before so small an audience on a stage that frequently brought them within touching distance of the spectators, they did not show it. That requires art and discipline, but Miss Cornell's companies are always notable for these qualities.

I suppose I was the most embarrassed, as well as delighted, participant in the proceedings for, as Cedric Hardwicke observed, I would be obliged to pretend enjoyment when I did not feel it. There was no need for pretense. I thoroughly enjoyed the performance. I had the feeling the players did, too.

They preserved a complete seriousness of outward demeanor, but you could sense an inner wink. They were quite aware that they were doing a quixotic and extravagant thing, and this feeling added to the pleasure of watching the performance without in any way detracting from the illusion.

Miss Cornell cut up apples for the strudel she was supposed to be preparing quite as animatedly and realistically as she would have done on a public stage before a large audience.

Sir Cedric Hardwicke and Robert Emhardt had a little trouble hiding under the dining-room table, for it is an old-fashioned piece of furniture with projecting underledges which were not designed for comfortable concealment of the human body. But they made the best of it, and the inadequacy and discomfort of their place of refuge added to the amusement of their audience and fellow actors.

Nigel Bruce, excellent British comedian, who played Watson in the Sherlock Holmes movies and radio programs for years, was probably never funnier than he was on his knees on the floor of my living room shooting an imaginary gun in the form of a walking stick.

John Buckmaster, in his character as Captain Carvallo, spent no time under the table, but he seated himself on it frequently to the unexpressed anxiety and distress of Mrs. McDermott, who feared that he might break a table leg and injure his own. Hope Cameron, as an attractive maidservant, gave the living-room rug the most energetic sweeping it has had for years.

The stagehands were distinguished. They consisted of Guthrie McClintic, who was the director and chief property man, and Sir Cedric, Nigel Bruce, John Buckmaster, and Walter Starkey. They moved tables, chairs, and davenports from one room to another and put them into proper position for the requirements of the play.

McClintic spent some time in finding a suitable phonograph record to play offstage music for a love scene. He settled on something by Rudolf Friml, and it was perfect for the occasion.

It is remarkable how little the normal trappings of a stage, such as curtains and scenery, were missed. The imagination automatically supplied what was lacking.

It is true that it required a small wrench of the mind to visualize a doorway from the living room to the hall as a closet containing dynamite and hymnbooks, but Sir Cedric, who was supposed to be hiding in the closet during one scene, gave a lively impression of a man skulking in a cupboard.

There was some little difficulty with properties. The actors brought out a small antique chest in which the dynamite was supposed to be transported. But they forgot the geranium. Captain Carvallo is a philosophic and esthetic soldier who is pictured as carrying a geranium with him to the wars.

McClintic found a cyclamen plant on a window sill and pressed it into service as a substitute for the geranium. It did well enough, but, though I am no botanist, I know a geranium when I see one and it was a little disturbing to hear Captain Carvallo repeatedly refer to my cyclamen plant as a geranium.

Among the other properties needed for the play are several dozen hymnbooks. I do not have several dozen hymnbooks in my library.

But McClintic did pretty well. He found two Bibles and *The Bible Arranged for Everyday Reading*. I am afraid that he also palmed off as sacred reading a copy of Pierre Louys' *Aphrodite* and some of the essays of Anatole France, who was a pious man, but whose piety was highly unorthodox.

I do not know how McClintic missed Rabelais. It would have pleased him to include Rabelais among the hymnbooks.

Good Plays

JANUARY 17, 1952

I called *The Rose Tattoo*, current at the Hanna, a first-rate play. What makes a first-rate play? Nobody really knows. There is no such thing as objective and final judgment in respect to creative art.

Only very young and cheerful people or very old and tedious people believe that there is. A good play or a good book is simply a work which pleases and excites a particular category of people at a particular time.

Even the supreme geniuses of all time have had their ups and downs in popular favor and critical approval. Shakespeare was neglected for generations. The great eighteenth-century Frenchman, who wrote under the name of Voltaire, called Shakespeare a barbarian, though he introduced Shakespeare's plays to France. Voltaire was the most influential critic of his era, or perhaps of any era.

The greatest drama critic of our time was Bernard Shaw. Like Voltaire, he both despised and admired Shakespeare, but his general conclusion was that the Elizabethan dramatist was a pretty puny fellow as compared with Bernard Shaw. Neither Voltaire nor Shaw was jesting.

They were simply and logically writing what was dictated by their temperaments and, in Voltaire's case, by the fashion of the age, which was hostile to the romanticism and irregularities of Shakespeare's plays and insistent on certain classical rules of unities which are now obsolete and regarded as ridiculous.

There is no finality in life except death. Even taxes are not universal or eternal. Pleasant civilizations have developed without the imposition of taxes.

So far as I know, the American Indians never had any system of taxation, but they had a kind of civilization, and by civilization I mean a code of living which involves discipline and strict obedience to certain rules. We have rather less of that now than the American Indians had.

But to get back to plays and, more specifically, to *The Rose Tattoo*. What makes it a good play in the estimation of most professional critics? I suppose it is partly an intensity of feeling reflected in vivid writing. You may not like the characters in *The Rose Tattoo*.

The duchess says that they are horrible. I do not agree. Every aspect of human life is interesting. An obsessed passion for a man on the part of a sensual woman is legitimate and strong material for drama.

It doesn't make any difference whether or not you like the people concerned. What matters is the effectiveness with which they are presented.

I think they are very well shown in *The Rose Tattoo*. Serafina is a wonderful character. She is obsessed with love for a dead husband and, by ordinary standards, she is a little mad. But you can't miss the naturalness and inevitability of her feeling and conduct under the circumstances the author of the play presents.

One quality of a superior play is that it suggests more than it says. In another way, that is also a quality of great acting. That is to say, genuinely distinguished acting involves more than the superficial re-creation of character. It must give you a sense of the inwardness, the essential reality of the characters. Only the best players can manage it, and only the best dramatists can provide the opportunity.

One reason that Maureen Stapleton is so good in *The Rose Tattoo* is that she has something to work on. The character is set on a single key of intense and obsessed feeling, softened occasionally by a touch of humor. It is almost as difficult a role as Medea, and it has the same unity, desperateness, and savagery of emotional content.

Let us say that you don't like these people of the play because they are primitive and ignorant and moved by elemental feeling, not by intelligence or decency, as these words are commonly understood. Yet Williams did not think he was writing that kind of play. He thought he was writing a play which was essentially spiritual and idealistic.

His main idea, in the play, as he has said, is that the vital force of nature, regardless of its instruments, their pettiness or grandeur, retains its power and is always transcendent.

I don't know how many members of the audience gather that impression from *The Rose Tattoo*. It doesn't matter.

Any good play is subject to many interpretations, and the better the play the greater the number of meanings that can be attached to it, including those of the author, which are often wrong, or at least not projected by the performance and not shared by the audience.

Theatergoing

I spent last week in New York where I saw twelve of the most successful Broadway plays as a matter of professional duty. That sounds like a dream assignment for anybody who likes the theater, as I do. But it is not all beer and skittles. I wish I could tell you how it really is.

You go to four matinee performances. The time period between a matinee and an evening show is not sufficient to permit leisurely dining. You must change clothes and wash up. Meanwhile, your friends are coming to your hotel room for refreshments. There is always a sense of hurry and urgency. No conversation is finished. Nothing is settled.

Then you break away and reach the theater, about a minute before curtain time. The lobby is crowded. You must push your way to the box office through a brawling mob, some of whom are trying to buy tickets three months in advance. I heard one box-office man say to a prospective customer, "We have nothing until the last of June."

It is astonishing, and it is a testimony to the vitality of the theater that people will go through the ordeal they must endure to buy tickets, breathe, push, and crowd into a theater housing a Broadway hit.

The lobbies are insultingly inadequate to contain the eager mob which assaults them. During the intermissions they are incredibly foul with cigarette smoke. Some employee of the theater is always saying in a commanding voice, "Smoking in the outer lobby only." Yet a hundred people will usually be smoking in the inner lobby and dropping their burning cigarette ends on the valuable carpets.

New York audiences have no manners whatever. When you

are seated, they cross before you without so much as saying, "By your leave." You stand up to permit them to pass and they tramp on your toes with a kind of careless gaiety.

It never occurs to them to say "thank you" or "beg pardon." The duchess has been trying to reform theater manners in New York but I think the cause is lost. When somebody steps on her toes in passing to an inside seat she says "thank you" rather loudly.

That is supposed to remind the offender that the least thing he could do would be to say "beg pardon." It doesn't work.

These people are so callous and ill-mannered that they are completely unconscious of what they are doing. It is a state of mind. They are probably polite enough at home, but when they go through the preliminaries which are necessary to acquiring tickets for a Broadway hit, they feel themselves victors in a savage war and they think of themselves as an occupying force in a hostile territory.

You fight to get into a Broadway theater and you fight to get out. Then you fight for a taxicab to take you home.

Taxicab service in New York is ordinarily wonderful. The rates are cheap, the cabs large and comfortable.

So far as I have traveled, New York taxi service is second best to Paris. But when it rains there is no immediate and reliable taxi service anywhere in the world.

Last Friday night it was raining when we left a theater on West Forty-fifth Street. There were hundreds of people waiting for cabs. We thought it advisable to cross over to Forty-fourth Street. The crowds were even larger there.

After waiting an hour or so, we thought it would be sensible to visit Sardi's restaurant and wait for the crowd to clear out. So we had eggs Benedict, which I did not want. Eventually, we got a cab about two o'clock in the morning.

I love to walk in the rain but the duchess was wearing a new hat which would not submit itself becomingly to moisture. So we had to have a cab.

When I see a show in New York I usually know the star, or

some of the other actors. It is a polite and pleasant thing to go backstage and visit them. When you have finished and partaken of a light supper, it is around two o'clock in the morning. Then you must be up for breakfast and ready for a matinee at sometime after two o'clock in the afternoon.

It is fun, but it is not as easy and relaxing as you would think it might be.

Oscar Wilde

SEPTEMBER 9, 1954

In writing not long ago about the great talkers of the past I forgot to name Oscar Fingal O'Flahertie Wills Wilde. By all accounts Oscar Wilde was an incomparably eloquent conversationalist.

I am reminded of this in reading a newly published book, *The Epigrams of Oscar Wilde*, which consists of quotations from his writing and his talk. Any accomplished talker can hold a friendly audience. Wilde could fascinate his enemies by the wit and charm of his discourse.

He was apparently one of the kindest of men, but he had many enemies because of his affectations and his defiance of moral codes. George Moore, another Irishman of great distinction, hated Wilde, but he felt obliged to pay respect to the quality of his conversation.

Bernard Shaw, who was a great talker, gave way to Wilde. Shaw was a puritan and Wilde was a pagan. It is extraordinary that they should enjoy each other's conversation and respect the quite different viewpoints each represented.

Shaw was pretty good in the use of words conversationally. Wilde was probably better, since he obviously had warmth and charm and Shaw didn't.

The Marquis of Queensberry hated Wilde with an insane

intensity of feeling. Yet when his son, Lord Alfred Douglas, introduced them at the Café Royale in London, the marquis was enchanted by Wilde's conversation, and left the table in a high mood of admiration and enjoyment.

It didn't last. The marquis was a vengeful and extremely ill-tempered person, who in this day would have been recommended to the attention of a psychiatrist. So would Wilde for that matter.

But there was no real harm in Wilde, and there was a good deal of harm in his persecutor, who finally brought a great man to public degradation and complete ruin.

To some degree, I think that Wilde talked himself into imprisonment. Courts and juries do not relish wit and eloquence. At least they didn't in Victorian times.

He would have been imprisoned anyhow because of the feeling that existed against him at that time, but he might have got off more easily if he hadn't been so quick and nimble in his answers to the prosecutor.

The man who cross-examined Wilde was Edward Carson, a fellow student at Trinity College in Dublin. When Wilde was informed of this he said: "No doubt he will perform his task with all the bitterness of an old friend." And so he did, but Wilde's remark is derived from Rochefoucauld.

Wilde was a persistent plagiarist, but he added something to everything he stole, and you can say the same thing about Shakespeare, who was not a plagiarist, but a borrower of old tales and doubtful history.

In the first trial, Wilde was asked by Carson if a certain book was immoral. Wilde replied: "It was worse. It was badly written."

Wilde's attitude in the three court trials to which the English Victorian law subjected him was constantly flippant and contemptuous, but his answers were often witty and sometimes beautifully eloquent.

The records of these trials are exciting and wonderful literature. The prosecuting attorney asked Wilde whether one of Wilde's unsavory and illiterate young associates sold newspapers. Wilde replied: "No, I never heard that his only occupation was selling newspapers. It is the first time that I have heard of his connection with literature."

So it goes on. He could talk well and easily when his reputation and his life as an acceptable human being was on trial. How much better he must have been under the normal circumstances of a dinner conversation.

Desmond McCarthy, a distinguished and immensely knowledgeable Britisher, says that Wilde "was probably the greatest self-consciously deliberate master of the art of conversation who has talked the English language."

It is remarkable how many Englishmen of genius are Irishmen. Bernard Shaw, Dean Swift, and Richard Brinsley Sheridan are thought of as English. They were all born in Dublin. Sheridan must have been a wonderful talker.

When his Drury Lane Theatre was being consumed by fire he was taking a drink of port in a café across the street. Somebody remonstrated against his indifference to the calamity. He replied: "Can't a man warm his hands at his own fireside?"

Shavian Self-Portraits

FEBRUARY 24, 1957

A letter printed in this column a few days ago about Bernard Shaw argues that the characters in his plays are merely facets of Shaw's own personality. The letter also makes the point that Shaw's prefaces are "brilliant" and "magnificent." I cannot disagree, for I have often expressed the same opinions.

Shaw's prefaces probably represent the most forceful and luminous expository writing of our time. They are superb journalism, which means they are first-rate literature.

But it is only partly true that the characters in Shaw's plays are merely echoes of himself and that therefore his plays lack greatness. Oliver Goldsmith said to Dr. Johnson, "If you were

to make little fishes talk, they would talk like whales." Doubtless
they would, and it would be no loss to literature if they did, for
the talk of whales would be heard farther and doubtless be
brighter than the talk of minnows. Bernard Shaw speaks in his
own voice in many of his plays, and since he was a whale among
minnows his talk rings loud and is worth hearing.

It is Shaw himself who is speaking most of the time under the
name of Tanner in *Man and Superman* or Captain Shotover in
Heartbreak House or the Elderly Gentleman in *Back to Methuselah*. There are traces of Shaw's personal manner and attitude
in his Caesar, which is very unlike Shakespeare's, and in General
Burgoyne of *The Devil's Disciple* and even in Professor Higgins
of *Pygmalion* now masquerading on Broadway under the title
of *My Fair Lady*.

Shaw made no bones about admitting that he had used himself as a character in some of his plays. But many of them
contain characters which are quite unlike Shaw.

He often took one or another of his friends as a model and
though he distorted their images as his fancy dictated, or as
dramatic necessity required, the origins are still identifiable.

There is nothing unusual, or wrong, with an author using a
self-portrait in a play, or picturing his friends in one aspect or
another. Indeed, every author does so. The people in Wilde's
plays do not talk like ordinary people. They talk more brilliantly.
They talk like Wilde.

It is true that Wilde and Shaw put more of themselves directly
into their plays than do most authors. In the case of Wilde the
result is a sense of artificiality, in the case of Shaw it is an
impression of verbal brilliance and chop-logic argumentation
which is so continuously sustained that it sometimes becomes
monotonous. If these are faults they are the most admirable of
faults.

The complaint that Shaw is always putting himself into plays
is well answered by the fact that so many of his plays supply
fine roles for the most various types of acting. No modern
dramatist has provided a greater number of roles which more
richly display the art of the player and which are more eagerly

sought after by stars. Many of the great roles moreover are feminine and contrasting, such as Saint Joan, Candida, and Eliza Doolittle.

Shaw confessed that he made no attempt at realism in his plays, or at realism as commonly understood. He was striving for something better, something deeper and truer.

In one of his self-sketches he wrote: "My sort of play would be impossible unless I endowed my characters with powers of self-consciousness and self-expression which they would not possess in real life. You could not have Esop's fables unless the animals talked."

Something of the kind is true of all plays of any worth. Their characters are more articulate, more self-revealing than are the people you are likely to meet in real life. Shaw was a brilliant talker, but when he put himself into a play his talk was better organized, more to the dramatic point than it could have been in actual life.

Shakespeare was better than Shaw in disguising his own identity when he used it in a play, but his dramas are nevertheless an extension of his own personality as are the works of any artist.

Even in his greatest plays, Shakespeare sometimes spoke for himself through the fictional characters he created. Hamlet is recognized as perhaps the greatest and most original character in world drama. But he speaks some lines which are not true to character. In the "To be, or not to be" soliloquy he tells of "the proud man's contumely, the law's delay, the insolence of office and the spurns that patient merit of the unworthy takes."

These are not the words of a prince, second to the throne of Denmark, who could not reasonably be suffering from the law's delay or the proud man's contumely. They are the words of a property holder in Stratford who had some experience with the law's delay and must have suffered the proud man's contumely.

Nor is Hamlet's advice to the players suitable to the utterance of a royal prince. It is, however, quite typical of an actor and playwright.

Charm

APRIL 11, 1958

In a long service as a drama critic I have written about a great many exceptionally charming people and I have come to know some of them well. What I have never figured out to my own satisfaction is what makes them charming, and I have often ruminated on the matter.

It seems obvious to me that charm is essential to any art that aims at pleasing. But what is the nature of charm? Where are its roots, what is its form, how is it measured? I can find no light on these questions in the works of the wisest of men.

The most famous definition of charm occurs in J. M. Barrie's play *What Every Woman Knows,* in an often quoted passage which reads, "It is a kind of bloom on a woman." That is not a definition, though it is apt as a description. In the third act of the same play reference is made to "that damned charm."

How can a bloom be damned, you may ask. The answer is that charm is sometimes damnable or at least it is an attribute possessed by some people who are probably headed for enduring damnation.

All successful confidence men and swindlers have charm, for they could not ply their trade profitably without it. Politicians have it and great leaders of men, though they may be leading their followers to a catastrophe. On their way to power they must be pleasing to a multitude and it is impossible to please without some degree of personal charm.

This most valuable and mysterious of attributes is no great respecter of persons. It is possessed by great evangelists, revered saints, and by successful tricksters, charlatans, and impostors.

It blesses alike the ugly and the beautiful, though, since its source is partly physical, the comely are more likely to have it. One of the most charming men I have ever met was a professional pickpocket, who wore pince-nez eyeglasses attached by a black cord to his ear.

I read in some eighteenth-century book of memoirs about an atrociously ugly man who was quoted as saying, "Give me ten minutes alone with a woman and I will charm her as easily and thoroughly as if I were the handsomest man in England." I do not remember whether or not he was put to the test, but if possessed with as much charm as he thought he had he would have won.

The foregoing may seem an odd preamble to a conclusion I would like to suggest. The conclusion is that charm in most cases is a by-product, or a materialization, of simple moral goodness. It would be absurd to say that this is always so, but it happens often enough to be significant.

Charming people are invariably outgiving people. They are at pains to be pleasing, to give of their strength and vitality to others.

Most of them do it for no other reason than that it is natural to them and they can't help it. They are basically generous and fullhearted.

I am thinking at the moment of stage players in their professional capacity. To them the most important thing in life is to please audiences and they will tear themselves apart to do it, toiling day and night at rehearsals, going over the same scenes a hundred times, making any sacrifice to achieve perfection in every detail with the sole aim of pleasuring an anonymous mass of strangers who compose an audience.

This is a kind of virtue, for it is not essentially based on self-seeking, but on an ideal of dispensing pleasurable feeling to others. The reason that so many of our players are charming is that they genuinely enjoy giving pleasure. In the widest sense, the basis of their charm is moral.

That belief was strengthened by two visitors I had lately.

Both are stars in the world of entertainment, though they stand at different poles in the firmament. One was the night-club artist, Hildegarde, the other Katharine Cornell. Innumerable audiences have paid tribute to the charm they possess in such high degree.

Hildegarde's great popularity in her area of entertainment is founded on charm, and it is impossible to review her performance without using that word, or one of its derivatives. Since the quality she possesses is indefinable, a review of her performance is usually a kind of love letter rather than an analysis of her art.

While she was talking from an armchair in my library, I was trying to understand the source and nature of the charm she exudes in her public appearances. She was pretty and immaculately well-dressed. So are many other women who are not notably charming.

As she talked, I had the impression that she spoke from the heart, that her obvious wish to please was rooted in natural kindness and genuine good will.

She was not acting. The generosity, the enthusiasm, even the innocence and naïveté she evinced in some matters, all were part of her inmost nature. When she said she prayed to God for help and support she meant it. She is deeply religious and she carries her faith into her everyday activities and attitudes. I was taken with the idea that charm in her case had its essence in simple moral goodness.

Katharine Cornell has the same qualities. You cannot know her, or talk to her for any length of time, without being aware of her fineness as a human being. Everybody who has worked with her speaks of her kindness, amiability, and thoughtfulness. I can add much personal testimony to this general judgment.

She was preoccupied and overworked during the recent performance here of her new play, which was in constant rehearsal. But she found time to visit a house-bound critic who could not go to the theater, and to recite for his benefit some of the crucial lines in the play. She had planned to bring the entire company and put on the complete show, but that proved impractical.

That kind of benevolence is pretty rare in human life and I fancy that it has something to do with the charm Miss Cornell irresistibly emanates in her public performances.

TWO

Reflections on Politics

Oratory: The Radio and Politics

MARCH 7, 1936

The great scholar Havelock Ellis tells in one of his books about the remote island of Uvia, where the natives are so eloquent that they catch fish by oratory. A lot of fish are going to be caught by oratory in the political campaign ahead.

You cannot look on the prospect without misgiving. By grace of the radio millions more people will listen to political spellbinders than ever before. I doubt that it will aid sound judgment. Oratory is addressed to the emotions. The problems that face us ought to be met with the mind.

The printed word can be a jade and a trollop, but I trust print far more than I trust oratory. You can check up on the printed word. It lies there before you, cold, tangible, concrete. The spoken word is not so easily pinned down.

It gets its effect from several things that have nothing to do with reason. The sound of the speaker's voice, for instance, or his accent or the rotundity of his periods. You are attracted, or repelled, by these things which are extrinsic to the argument.

By the quickness with which he produces impressions, and through the emotion he generates, the orator can get away with half-truths and lame logic which would be immediately detected in a writer. Print ordinarily has to make some sense. It isn't so essential in a speech.

In my youth, I knew an old gentleman who never missed a speech on the occasion of Saint Patrick's Day. Coming from the hall one March day, he was asked about the speech.

"It was a grand speech," he said, "the finest I ever heard."

"What was the speech about?"

He was honestly annoyed by the question for he loved oratory for oratory's sake.

"How should I know what it's about?" he answered. "The speaker was an educated man and he used big words. I tell you it was a grand speech."

My ancient friend would agree with Macaulay that the object of oratory is not truth but persuasion.

It seems to me that there must be some connection between the current popularity of crackpot schemes and social panaceas and the ease with which millions of ears can be reached by radio oratory. No other country is plagued to the same extent by such an epidemic and no other country so freely offers orators the facilities of the radio.

Hitler and Mussolini, it is true, do not owe the radio much credit for their elevation to power. But they owe a very great deal to oratory.

It is probably not extravagant to say that neither Hitler nor Mussolini would be where they are were they not both orators of the first rank, nor would the history of Germany and Italy be the same.

"Let me persuade you to be hanged," says a character in Shaw's play *The Devil's Disciple*. Oratory has persuaded many a man to be hanged.

Well, since there is no escaping a storm of oratory in the forthcoming months, let us be prepared for it. Let us beware of the hypnotic voice, the cunning epigram, the sounding phrase that has no meaning. Let us look out for the unctuous flattery, the dazzling generalities, the crocodile tears for the dispossessed, the empty thunder against the well-heeled.

Pray, gentlemen, let us say, stick to the argument. Pay us the compliment of being reasonable creatures, do not ignore obvious facts, and do not make too many absurd promises. Shed your tears for your beloved people but tell us, at the same time, by what practical processes you propose to improve our lot. Do not treat us like half-witted children, even if the evidence seems to suggest that we are. Be clear, be simple, and, as God loves you, be brief.

Even then, I suppose we shall often have to ask with Shakespeare:

Nephew, what means this passionate discourse,
This peroration with such circumstance?

Roosevelt: Thinking in Terms of the Nation

APRIL 17, 1936

Every man has his prejudices and his loyalties. We are as God made us and, since He made us human, it is no use pretending that we are capable of pure and complete impartiality. But we can try to be reasonable and just after such lights as we have. Even in the emotionalism and nonsense of the current political campaign it may be possible to work out what is, for us individually, a fair and rational viewpoint.

Speaking personally, I am not conscious of any particular partisanship as between the Democratic and Republican parties. The difference between them has usually seemed to be the difference between tweedledum and tweedledee. I was for Roosevelt because I felt that he had a greater social awareness than most of the politicians who have sat in the White House.

That is, he was more acutely conscious of the widespread dislocations and injustices in the economic system, more sympathetic with the tragedy of the underdog, and flexible enough mentally to break with tradition in an effort to improve underlying conditions.

In a general way he seemed to me to stand against the greedy group of intrenched interests which have normally run the country and which are naturally opposed to any reform that disturbs their prestige.

I am still for Roosevelt as against any other candidate who has a chance of election. That is, I am for the aims and the principles which he, to my mind, represents.

It is something to have in the White House a man who seems to think in terms of the whole people, who is not afraid of experimentation in measures for social improvement, who is fresh and agile enough mentally to make needed adjustments to the exigencies of a dislocated economic order.

I do not know how long I can stick on the Roosevelt bandwagon. Good intentions, social sympathy, a warm heart may not be enough to make a better world or even to patch the holes in the world we have. The job needs great strength, wisdom, and farsightedness.

It seems to be apparent that the important, well-intentioned social measures of the New Deal, such as the NRA, were practical failures even before they were nullified by the Supreme Court. Popular as the AAA may have been with its beneficiaries, every disinterested citizen must look with misgiving on a policy of crop curtailment in a land where many have not enough to eat.

But though these measures may have been of doubtful wisdom, they represented a defensible experiment in attempting to restore an economic balance, and they may have been as practical as any that could be devised in the emergency with which the country was faced.

Better an experiment that fails than to sit twiddling thumbs while the walls are crumbling. It is no argument against the Administration that some of its experiments have failed. What we have to ask ourselves is: "How far were these experiments thought through, how sound were they theoretically, and how efficient and honest was the manner of their administration?" It is impossible not to have some doubts on these points.

Such misgivings multiply, and they enclose the heart of the problem which is: "Are the policies of the Administration, however admirable in intent, intelligently calculated to improve the lot of the majority of Americans, and is the personnel of the

Administration willing and able to carry them out honestly?"

Our unemployment situation is the severest problem facing the country and most people will approve, on principle, any effort made to relieve it. But even those who heartily commend the plan of work relief as against a dole must be conscious of the enormous waste, the frittering, the red tape, the contradictions that have accompanied its operation.

Can the Administration be charged with mismanagement in this matter or is waste and gross inefficiency unavoidable in such governmental enterprises? Every man must answer that question for himself.

There doesn't seem to be much doubt that politics has crept into both the WPA and the allocation of governmental funds to States. This is the most serious charge that can be made against the Administration, for the dangers it involves are obvious and it is apparent that they could be eliminated if the will at Washington to do so were strong enough.

It is a pity that the scheme of our government seems to require that the occupant of the White House be not only a powerful executive but a trained and adept politician. When a man has thought for many years in terms of partisan politics, when his career is based on the trading and conciliation that makes for party advantage, he is not likely to be able to free himself from political considerations in establishing policies or making decisions that have nothing to do with politics.

I have heard it said that a shrewd politician makes a good President because he knows how to get what he wants from Congress. A shrewd politician may make a good President, but he will not make a great President, for a great President will stand up for what he believes to be right against his own personal advantage and against all the partisan forces that can be brought to bear on him.

It is difficult not to feel, though you may not wish to, that President Roosevelt often thinks and acts politically rather than wisely in the larger sense. He ignores too many things that cannot be ignored. He is casual, careless, and cheerful in situations which warrant great thought and anxiety.

Nearly everybody, for instance, believes that a drastic inflation is inevitable, and informed people dread it as a plague that takes its toll of the great masses. A badly unbalanced budget involves the most serious threat of this thing that all men must fear, and yet we have no hint from the White House of any action looking toward the balancing of the budget, nor any indication of concern about it.

The presidential speech the other night was a careless pep talk. The best that can be said of it is the worst that can be said of it, namely, that it was good politics. Essential facts were wrong, the suggestions for meeting great problems were so airy that practical criticism runs through them as through a sieve.

This kind of thing must pain the President's friends and well-wishers, among whom I count myself.

Democracy

FEBRUARY 5, 1938

Democracy is like the weather in that everybody talks about it but nobody does anything about it. We wear our liberties like an old pair of shoes, which never need to be repaired or paid for.

That attitude will not be helpful to democracy in its fight for survival against the dictatorships. The latter have one advantage in the struggle. Their people are willing to make sacrifices for the system under which they live. They subordinate their own interests, as individuals or as groups, for the good of the whole.

They may be misled, they may be perverted by propaganda, they may be sometimes acting under pressure, but the fact observable by any traveler is that such countries as Germany, Italy, and Russia have achieved a unity of mind and purpose which is conspicuously lacking in the democracies of France and the United States.

A German asks: "What can I do for the Fatherland?" A Russian asks: "What can I do to help build Socialism?" An American asks: "What can the government do for me?"

Like most Americans, I believe passionately in the democratic system and I think its preservation is worth more effort and sacrifice than we are giving to it. We take it for granted, we talk about it with ardent sentimentality, and we do very little to make it work.

Our fundamental attitude is not "What can I do for democracy?" but "What can democracy do for me as an individual or a member of a group?" We want freedom of individual thought and action, but we are unwilling to accept the self-denials that make freedom possible.

Everybody wants something from our system of government and nobody thinks of giving anything to it. Big business wants to be let alone to serve its own interests which are not necessarily, or invariably, the interests of the country. Little business would like some loans and practically everything else that big business is asking, except the preservation of monopolies.

The farmers would like the government to assure high prices for farm products and low prices for everything else. Labor wants shorter hours and higher wages through government action. The unemployed want government jobs and the needy want government relief.

States, municipalities, individuals, organized groups of all kinds want something from the Federal government. Everybody would like to see the government giving out something if he is going to get his share of it, and nobody wants to pay the taxes by which these largesses eventually must be remunerated.

All this is natural, but it is dangerous to the democratic system in the new, hostile world which is forming about us. Unity, sacrifice, and some mainspring of selflessness is necessary to the preservation of any workable system of government or any political philosophy.

No government can function properly with every group of

its citizens pulling against another group, with labor divided against itself, with one branch of capitalism opposing another branch, with the Administration alternately petting and snubbing this group and that, with everybody looking out for his own interests and nobody thinking in terms of his country and the priceless heritages of liberty it represents.

Democracy cannot stand divided against itself, hampered and obstructed not only by its enemies but by its friends. It will not be destroyed easily from outside but it can destroy itself.

Democracy has disappeared in Germany and it was attacked in Spain not because it would not work but because people of democratic sympathies were divided and confused, unwilling to sacrifice their group interests for the sake of peace, order, and the preservation of the principles in which they all believed.

We need to be reawakened, to be reminded that this country and the liberties it represents are more important than any group, class, or individual it shelters. Democracy cannot live when its beneficiaries habitually act on the principle of take all and give nothing.

Mankind

APRIL 14, 1938

I am not a theologian, but if I were I should prepare a sermon on the affirmation that the fundamental trouble with this perplexed and uneasy world is a decay in spiritual values. What we seem to be undergoing is a destruction of ancient moral principles without the creation of any new values by which mankind can decently live.

These tyrannies that crush the souls of men, these barbaric wars that slaughter children from the air, this hatred and greed and stubborn self-interest which afflicts our own country are evidences of developments that lie deeper than politics or economics. They are symptoms of a moral revolution and a spiritual collapse.

Right used to be right. Its basis was justice, decency, consideration for the powerless. Now, in much of the world, right is might. Right is anything you can get away with.

Truth used to mean a patient examination of a reality from all its various aspects. Now truth seems to have no necessary connection with ascertainable facts. Truth is anything, however false and lying, that will serve national prestige, suit a political ideology, or help to promote a gang.

I suspect that truth cannot be mocked in that way without sowing infernal consequences. Men of many kinds may believe that they are warriors in a good cause, and, because they believe their cause to be good, they persuade themselves that anything which serves that cause, however dishonest and wicked, is also good. The end, they say, justifies the means. But a bad means often becomes an end in itself, or it defeats the end. In any case, such distortion of moral values leads eventually to chaos and barbarism.

Its consequences at the moment are shocking enough. Men are dying by the tens of thousands in China because right is might and a nation has been deluded into thinking that the end justifies the means. Races and religions are being harassed and brutally mistreated in many parts of the world by parties and factions who have the callous cynicism to invent moral reasons for what they do. Minorities are kicked around everywhere and the majority who do the kicking will give you sanctimonious justifications for the outrages they commit.

There is no justification, now or ever, for such things. They were wrong and wicked when man first emerged from the primeval mud and they will be so until the last cold star dissolves from a vanishing universe.

Nobody can thoughtfully read the world's news today without feeling that what it implies is a widespread moral retrogression. Wars have been made before, but never with such disregard for the humanities or with so callous an attitude toward slaughter of the civilian population. Treaties have been broken many times in history, but not with such an air of righteousness or so generally that no nation could trust the pledged word of any other. Tyrannies have grown up repeatedly through the ages, and men have lost their liberties, but these ancient tyrannies did not represent themselves as ideal democracies and men did not, as they do now, welcome the suppression of their individual rights and kiss the chain that made them slaves.

We need spiritual rejuvenation. We stand in desperate want of faith and good will, of truth, honor, fairness, and those trite, timeless measures of conduct which are the basis of a tolerable communal life.

We need to be refreshed once more at the tables of the philosophers and saints, to be told again by Francis Bacon that plain and simple goodness is the greatest dignity of the mind and that, without it, man is a mischievous and wretched thing, and —in this epoch of mental cocksureness and Messianic leaders who are on intimate terms with divinity—we particularly need once more to hear the accents of Thomas à Kempis when he says that faith and a sincere life are better than loftiness of intellect or deepness in the mysteries of God.

Europe: History Repeats Itself

APRIL 5, 1939

There is a chilling resemblance to 1914 in the current European crisis. You are depressed by the feeling that you have gone through all this before.

A powerful, strongly militarized Germany, intent on expansion, is faced by nations which cannot tolerate German expansion. Germany's spokesmen talk of being "encircled" and demand room to live. Britain and France are determined to stop German aggression by defensive alliances.

A dominant, ambitious Germany, lording it over Eastern Europe, is an intolerable threat to the national interests of Britain and France.

Hitler and Nazism merely complicate the issue. If neither had been born, the world would be faced with the same general problem had Germany grown strong again under another regime and preserved her prewar psychology.

The problem was and the problem is: How can a growing, vigorous, militaristic people obtain what it thinks necessary to its national existence and fulfill what it feels to be its natural destiny without taking what belongs to somebody else and without upsetting the European balance of power and disrupting the peace of the world?

That was the question in 1914 and it still is. We cloak the situation with modern ideological formulas but civilized life among the society of nations is not very different from life in the primeval jungle where the strong eat and the weak are eaten.

Fundamentally, it is not an ideal of democracy that is at issue but the interests and the lives of nations. Chamberlain was not willing to fight for the preservation of Czechoslovakia which was a real democracy. He has committed Britain to go to war for Poland, which is not a democracy but a dictatorship.

The reason is not that Chamberlain loves Poland but that Germany, since Munich, has grown so strong, ambitious, and unpredictable that she has become a genuine menace to Britain's imperial interests, and Chamberlain is taking help in stopping further German expansion wherever he can get help.

National self-preservation is the first consideration. Ideological issues are pushed into the background. A few months ago Britain was snubbing Russia. The present British government undoubtedly prefers the German system to Bolshevism, without liking either. It was commonly supposed and often said that Chamberlain's policy would not involve active disapproval if Germany were to expand eastward and precipitate a war with Russia which would destroy or weaken both Germany and Russia.

Within the last few days the relationship between Russia and Britain has changed completely. Britain is offering to hold hands with the Soviets in a military alliance and it is now Russia's turn to be cold and coy.

The prospective line-up on the democratic side is Britain, France, Russia, Poland, and possibly Romania, and some other Balkan or Danubian states. It is not the constitution of their governments which brings these powers together, for they differ radically in that respect. What unites them is fear of aggression and correlated considerations of national interest and national self-preservation.

It is not democracy that these allies will fight for, since not all of them are democracies. It is not the Nazi system that they will seek to destroy, for some of them are governed by much the same kind of system. It is not the brutal persecution of Jews and minority peoples which have aroused them, for some of the governments involved are themselves anti-Semitic and troubled with minority problems.

They are coming together, not to perpetuate an ideal but to defend their national lives, not to save the world for democracy but to save their own skins. The teams will be slightly reshuffled but it will be in essence a repetition of 1914 when the national interests of European countries came into irreconcilable conflict and the preservation of independence required that a stand be taken against terror and aggression.

If war comes it will not be waged on a clear issue between the ideologies of Nazi-Fascism and democracy, but between one set of nations trying to preserve their possessions and their independence against the covetousness and belligerence of another set of nations.

A Paradox

SEPTEMBER 19, 1939

Put it down as a nightmare. These things cannot be. The pattern of events is too complex for logical apprehension, the cynicism too savage to be real, the paradox too grotesque for human credibility.

For many years, until a few weeks ago, Russian Communism presented itself as the fiercest, most implacable foe of German fascism, and a corresponding hostility toward Communism was ardently and repetitiously proclaimed by the German Nazi hierarchy.

Soviet rulers have been shouting for years that they wanted no part whatever of any other nation's territory. The cornerstone of Russia's foreign policy was resistance to imperialist aggression and devotion to the cause of world peace.

Soviet Russia, said its spokesmen, was a true democracy in spirit, though they had not got around to putting it into practice, and its sympathies were naturally with the democratic nations against the hated fascist dictatorships.

The signing of a non-aggression pact with fascist Germany, the spokesman explained, was only a measure for guaranteeing peace, Russia promising to remain neutral in the war that was developing.

With this promise still warm on the lips, the Russian army begins marching into Poland and in one day penetrates as far as fifty miles on a five-hundred-mile front. In this swift and gallant advance against a small, defenseless foe, Russia is courteously helped out by the German air force.

The fierce, unappeasable enemy of German fascism is now the useful ally and loving helpmate of all that it pretended to hate. Nazis and Communists are brothers on the field of battle, and their union is sealed with a lasting cement composed of pulverized cities watered by human blood and held together with fragments of torn flesh.

Russia did not bother with the formality of denouncing the treaties she had with Poland before proceeding to violate them. Even Germany, not notorious in her respect for obligations, went through the forms of the diplomatic routine.

While announcing that no responsible Polish government existed, Russia was simultaneously recognizing the existence of such a government by telling its official representatives of the decision to send an army into Poland.

Faithlessness and betrayal are not new in international relationships. The commonest move in diplomacy is the double-cross.

But faithlessness and betrayal on the scale the world has witnessed in the past weeks is something for which civilization probably has no precedent.

The double-cross has evolved into the double-double-cross as an ordinary concomitant of dealings among nations. Solemn promises are a matter for obscene laughter, and lies are the warp and woof of official announcements and national policies.

Only a few months ago Hitler was piously declaring that he had no further territorial demands to make on Europe. Only a few days ago Stalin's agents were protesting the peaceful intentions of Russia and announcing a determination to remain neutral.

Today German and Russian armies meet in friendly handclasp on Polish soil and preparations are being made to divide the spoils obtained by a brutal aggression.

Duplicity and hypocrisy do not stop here. Molotov, Soviet premier, announces that the purpose of this armed invasion is to rescue the Ukrainian and White Russian minorities which were "without rights" and "to deliver the Polish people from the disastrous war into which they have been plunged by their unwise leaders." Shades of Austria, shades of Czechoslovakia!

Must every imperialistic grab for territory be disguised with the pretense of rescuing unhappy minorities, and must men be killed and nations destroyed to make them free?

I cite one more crowning irony. In 1920 Russia was at war with Poland, then under the leadership of Pilsudski. General Tukhachevski was the head of the Soviet forces.

In launching his campaign on the northern front he issued a proclamation containing this statement: "The destinies of the world revolution will be settled in the West. Our way toward world-wide conflagration passes over the corpse of Poland."

The corpse is there, the vultures are at it, but it is not the prophecy which is striking, but the irony. The same General Tukhachevski was executed by a Soviet firing squad.

He was tried and killed on a charge of being a "Fascist wrecker" who had become too friendly with the German army!

Presumably Soviet medals are being struck to honor the Russian soldiers who are now doing what Tukhachevski was killed for being suspected of thinking about doing.

Japan: War in the Pacific
Is Inevitable

NOVEMBER 28, 1941

If the United States and Japan adhere to their announced policies war in the Pacific is inevitable. Japan insists on the establishment of the "new order" and the "East Asia Co-Prosperity Sphere," which are euphemistic terms for Japanese military and economic dominance of the Far East.

The United States apparently demands as a basic principle of peace that Japan withdraw from China and Indo-China and give up her expansion program. Without extraordinary face-saving concessions no Japanese government could or would accommodate itself to these conditions.

The "new order" is the cornerstone of Japanese foreign policy and its justice and desirability has been drilled into the minds of the Japanese people by their leaders for years. We cannot make any real concession to Japan and the "new order" without betraying China and the principles for which we have historically stood.

National self-interest and the character of the Japanese people will not permit Japan to back out of the war in China and abandon her program of militarized economic penetration in Asia without making a last-ditch fight even if that fight is suicidal.

In a military struggle with the United States and Britain Japan would probably lose and be reduced to a third-rate power. But if she abandons her program she loses prestige and confesses to a defeat almost as humiliating as defeat by force.

If Japan neither fights nor withdraws from her program of expansion, but remains in *status quo* her position would still be untenable. Japan is economically weak and dependent.

To live tolerably she needs normal trade with the United States and free access to the raw products of Malaya and the Dutch East Indies. Japanese economy could not long stand up under the present restrictions and embargoes of foreign trade.

My guess is the current crisis will not long endure. If negotiations with the United States fail, as they apparently have, Japan will inch down toward Thailand and the Dutch Indies or begin some active expansion elsewhere, with the hope of entrenching herself before effective moves can be made against her. The question is how far does this government and its allies propose to permit Japan to go before taking military measures?

The nearness of war in the Pacific does not seem to have sunk into our national consciousness. We are still preoccupied with the war in the Atlantic, but that war is against submarines and an occasional raider. War with Japan would be a bloodier and a more destructive business.

Military experts say it would not last long. They were wrong about Russia, and they may be wrong again and for the same reason. They failed to take into account the morale of the Russians.

I judge that Japanese morale is equally high or higher. The Japanese are a fanatically patriotic people. They live and die fatalistically.

For years they have been existing, like the Russians, on short rations and in a military, disciplined economy, and these conditions, instead of weakening a people and dissipating their relish for war, seem to harden them and quicken the belligerence of their spirit.

In South America last year I met a number of American naval officers. They all seemed to think Japan could be easily disposed of and they were anxious to go about the job. My guess is that war with Japan would be no weekend picnic, but a long-drawn-out and destructive struggle.

Neither the Japanese people nor the American people want the war that seems to be forming. We need all our energies for the defeat of Hitlerism.

It is a tragedy that the Japanese and the world should be led to this pass by a group of foolish, war-mad leaders who instituted aggression as a national policy and are now in the way of reaping a whirlwind. They have made it nearly impossible for Japan to back down and they have made it suicidal for her to go on.

We cannot, either in honor or in consideration of our national security, do else than oppose Japanese aggression. The question is not whether we shall oppose Japan, but when and where. The next Japanese movement may decide.

The A-Bomb

JANUARY 29, 1947

In his authoritative, important, and dramatic account of the history of the atomic bomb, Henry L. Stimson touched on two points in which I had the most intense interest. He said, or implied, that the moral development of the world had not kept pace with its increasing and fabulous command of science and mechanical technique. That is the crux of the situation in which we find ourselves. We have the wonderful knowledge it requires to make an atomic bomb and we do not know how to control it on the moral plane.

So we live in dreadful fear of what should be a great boon to humanity. We have gained a world and we may have lost a planet simply because our spiritual evolution has lagged behind our marvelous inventiveness in terms of mechanics.

The other corollary point that Stimson made in his careful and reserved way was equally obvious and pertinent. He got to the meat of the matter when he emphasized the difficulty of establishing any kind of effective supervision of what is fundamentally beyond the scope of warfare as we have hitherto understood it. It is understating the problem to say, as he so honestly says, that "the control of this weapon will undoubtedly be a matter of the greatest difficulty and would involve such thoroughgoing rights of inspection and internal controls as we have never heretofore contemplated."

With our easygoing traditions of democracy and openness to the public view we would find no great wrench in submitting our armament manufactories to foreign inspection under such conditions as might be set forth by international agreement. But that would be much more difficult for Russia. It would require a complete and fundamental change in Soviet policy and attitude.

Latter-day Soviet Russia is secretive and isolated to a degree that Americans who have not been there can hardly understand. Not long before the last war, I was being escorted around Moscow by a government guide and we passed what seemed to be a manufacturing establishment.

It was guarded by numerous soldiers with fixed bayonets. I supposed it was a plant making war implements, or certainly a plant turning out something that needed to be guarded.

I found out later that the conspicuously policed factory was making leather gloves for civilian use. If an innocent glove factory in Russia must be so carefully screened from public view, what an enormous change must come in Russian policy if the most secret manufactories of lethal instruments are to be thrown open for thorough international inspection.

The truth, as I see it, is that the average Russian knows nothing about the outside world and the average American, so far as can be guessed by what you read and what you hear, doesn't know much more about Russia.

A few years ago, one of the girl guides supplied by the Russian government was taking me on a tour of the hospital facilities which had been newly set up in Moscow. We came to a hospital, which was outfitted with screen doors.

My cicerone pointed them out with an air of triumphant pride and said, "These are wire screens which keep out flies and mosquitoes from the hospital. They are a new Soviet invention. They do not exist in capitalist countries."

She really believed it. I disliked to injure a pride which was innocent and becoming, but I could not help saying that screen doors and even screen windows were not uncommon in America and that the houses of most workingmen were equipped with them. I could see disbelief in her eyes.

She was convinced I was a lying and somewhat ridiculous propagandist for capitalism as against the great system of Russian socialism which had invented screen wire and made it available, in small quantities, for the use of hospitals.

This was an intelligent girl who spoke several languages fluently and who could argue your arm off on such topics as the social philosophy of Marx and Engels.

She had a quick, well-stored mind, some of it filled with rubbish, and she was incredibly naive and ignorant about the world beyond the borders of Russia.

When I read the elaborate pinpoint arguments on the technicalities of the use of the veto in respect to atom power, they seem unreal, legalistic, and irrelevant. Any effective control of this fearful weapon will have to be based, not on the letter of written agreements, but on the spirit of common understanding between the peoples of this world and some shared and equal knowledge of what they are all about.

Germany

FEBRUARY 11, 1947

Yesterday's dispatches quote a Russian economist as charging that the United States and Britain have taken more than $10,000,-000,000 from Germany by way of reparation. The implication was that the Western Allies were picking more than their share of Germany's bones and deliberately denying to Russia a fair and proportionate indemnity. You would not expect a Russian economist to exhibit so much sense of humor. But our military governor in Berlin, General Lucius D. Clay, was not amused. He described the Russian accusations as "too ridiculous to be worthy of comment."

One of the charges made was that the American authorities had sent to the United States 95 per cent of the cameras manufactured by Agfa. The intimation was that this represented a lot of cameras, and it is curious that they are not conspicuous on the American market.

But even if we got the cameras the Russians are doing much better for themselves in the same line. They are taking the German factories which make the cameras.

Only a couple of weeks ago the Berlin press reported that all production had stopped at the great Zeiss optical works in Jena because the plant was now completely dismantled and removed to Russia. Many highly skilled German workers were taken along with the plant.

Zeiss was one of the world's most famous producers of fine photographic lenses. We may or may not have received some cameras out of current German production, but the Russians certainly got the Zeiss factory which made and presumably will continue to make an abundance of the best camera lenses for the new owners.

Window glass is terribly needed for bombed-out buildings in the American zone of Germany. There was talk in Berlin last fall of importing glass from America.

The Zeiss plant made window glass but Jena is in the Russian zone and little, or none of it, got out of that zone. With the removal of the plant to Russia, even the Russian zone in Germany will be deprived of this important source of window glass.

We have taken nothing from the productive facilities of Germany. The Russians have removed many large industrial plants in their entirety from both Germany and Austria.

Many of these plants were in the American zone. We are spending immense sums to feed the Germans, and one reason they cannot feed themselves is that factories which were the means of subsistence for many Germans have been picked up bodily and moved to Russia.

The Russian armies do not feed themselves in Germany and Austria. They live off the land.

The United States and the British supply every ounce of food consumed by their occupying forces, and a good deal of the food, clothing, and other commodities shipped thousands of miles to the armies of the Western powers leak out and find their way to German and Austrian civilians.

American soldiers in Germany and Austria are prohibited from eating in public restaurants because, by so doing, they would be taking food from the tragically short stock available to the local population. The Russians take the food, as well as the factories which manufacture the implements by which food can be produced.

In a way we are maintaining the Russian forces in the occupied countries. They eat German and Austrian food, and we largely supply to the Germans and Austrians the equivalent of the food the Russians consume or take away.

At the same time we have spent millions of dollars since the war's end in feeding and clothing the Soviet population in western Russia.

I am not primarily arguing that what we have done is more than fair, or that Russia's policy is less than just. But I am suggesting we have taken little from Germany as compared with what Russia has taken and that we have given a great deal more.

When a straight-faced Russian economist argues the opposite and implies that the United States is making an inordinate profit from the occupation of Germany one must conclude either that he has a weird understanding of economics, an irrepressible sense of humor, or an uneasy conscience.

The Air Lift

MAY 6, 1949

The Russian agreement to end the Berlin blockade is an official proclamation by a hostile referee of the success of a dangerous and magnificent experiment. It is the acknowledgment of an almost incredible fact, namely, that a great city can be fed, heated, and kept alive with supplies flown in by air.

Obviously, the Russians did not think it could be done. The essential purpose of the blockade was to force the Allies out of Berlin.

I know from conversations last year with American pilots and operations officers in Berlin that they did not think the air lift could succeed. They were worried about the damage being done to the delicate mechanism of planes by coal dust, and they were concerned about what would happen when the weather turned bad in the winter months.

In the first days of the air lift last summer they were tired and skeptical. For a military airman, it is not a pleasant duty to transport coal and food in a rather rigorous and tedious series of flights.

Such of them as I talked to didn't like it, and felt that the whole enterprise might fail of its purpose. But the boss, General Lucius D. Clay, was right. The air lift was feasible and succeeded.

Not without cost. Nearly fifty young airmen were killed in the prime of their lives, and the monetary outlay was enormous. The official calculation is that it cost American taxpayers $150,000,000.

I don't know the basis of the calculation and I suspect it is impossible to make a precise estimate, but the official figures are probably too low.

I have heard unofficial experts say that it cost about fifty dollars to deliver a ton of coal to Berlin, and some of them felt that around one hundred dollars a ton would be nearer to the real cost of freightage. What you can roughly but reasonably figure is that the cost of carrying coal in military airplanes is fantastically high.

It is doubtful that a great industrial city can be supplied with sufficient fuel to maintain its factories over a long period of time with coal carried by air. There has been serious unemployment in Berlin during the past ten months because of the shortage of coal and the consequent retardation of industrial activity.

Householders were limited to a few pounds of coal a week and all forms of heating were rationed with a severity not equaled in war. The only way for a Berliner to keep warm was to wrap himself in a blanket, if he had one, and go to bed.

So far as I can learn, or guess, last winter was one of the worst in Berlin's history.

Nevertheless the people were fed, and the food ration was a

little more plentiful than when supplies were coming in by train. Nobody died of starvation, nobody froze to death. That is the miracle and it is incredible.

Never in history has a populous community been fed and protected from disastrous cold and had its essential economy maintained by supplies exclusively delivered by airplanes. This fact is one of the great triumphs of a mechanical age and a mark in the books of the recording angels.

Of course the Russians can reimpose the blockade at any time, and they probably will if the meeting of the council of foreign ministers does not go to their liking. But for the moment they have made a concession of tremendous importance and they have done so, at least partly, because of the success of the air lift which they did not think had much of a chance. Neither did many Americans who were in a position to gauge the possibilities expertly.

The Russians could have stopped the air lift whenever they wished. In the beginning it seemed likely that they might. They were troublesome and wholly uncooperative.

In the early days of the air lift I spent hours in the Berlin control room which governed the operations of the planes using the corridor. You knew at every moment where the Allied planes were and at what height they were flying through information clearly recorded on the charts.

You never knew exactly where the Russian planes were because they wouldn't tell. The Russians would simply announce that their planes were going to use the corridor for practice maneuvers. They did not state the number of planes, or the height at which they would fly.

It was reasonable to suppose that the Russians were hoping for accidents and looking for trouble. Developments since have proved they were not.

One of the remarkable things about the air lift is the relatively few number of fatalities for an operation so tremendous and the fact that none of them was clearly precipitated by the Russians.

They talked ferociously and they acted prudently, and that may be a key to the next precarious and important step of our diplomatic dealings with them.

Jealous Nations

NOVEMBER 2, 1949

Yesterday's newspapers announced that the United States was urging Western European countries to form a unified trade area by abolishing quotas, monetary barriers, and all tariffs, and thus to create a great, free, mass market for manufactured products such as we have in this country.

It is a noble idea, but I suspect that most of us will be long dead before it is put into effect. There are too many conflicts of economic interests involved and too many psychological differences deeply entrenched in history and tradition.

It is natural for Americans to ask: "Why can't these European countries get together politically and economically in the way that the sovereign States of this republic have got together?" Only by such unity, I imagine, can the Marshall plan be made to work. I don't think it is working now except as a temporary crutch, and there is little reason to believe that the user will be able to walk alone when the crutch is taken away, as it eventually must be.

But European economic unity is not easy to achieve, even among those countries which share the same political philosophy and feel themselves members of the same family. There are, for instance, sharp differences of economic interests between a small country like Belgium and a populous country such as Great Britain. In some fields, both nations are rivals for trade on the world market and the prosperity of great manufacturing firms in each country is affected by changes in quotas and tariffs.

These manufacturing firms and the thousands of people they

employ have political power which is naturally exercised in support of what they believe to be advantageous to their economic survival.

Holland and Belgium are friendly neighbors. Yet Holland is, quite understandably, a little jealous of the higher living standard which now exists in Belgium, owing mostly to the fact that Belgium was not as hard hit by the destructiveness of war as was the Netherlands.

The Belgians, of course, are opposed to any measures which might conceivably lower their living standards. It would be politically impossible to put into effect any plan of economic co-operation between these countries which either of them thought inimical to their own interests.

The most dramatic evidence of this conflict is the British insistence on the demolition of industrial plants in Germany. It is a sickening waste economically and a political error of the first order.

Supposedly, the plants are being dismantled because of their potentialities in the manufacture of materials usable in war. Most factories can be converted to war use.

But the military availability of some of these factories being destroyed in Germany is pretty indirect and questionable. The obvious presumption is that they are being knocked down and carted away—in some cases to our possible opponents in another war—because the British are fearful of the competition they might create for their own peacetime industrial production.

In any case, it is a nonsensical policy to be spending enormous sums to build up Germany as a self-supporting country and, at the same time, to be destroying, at large expense, its means of self-support. As usual, the American taxpayers are paying the bill on both counts.

I spoke about the psychological differences among European nations, based on history and tradition. They are almost as great a barrier against real union as the economic conflicts of interests.

The President's Power

JANUARY 24, 1951

It seems to me that the cosmic columnists, the heavy political thinkers, and ordinary men of good will and common sense should give some thought to the technicalities of the American democratic system, with the idea of improving them if that seems feasible.

I have several things in mind. One is the tremendous power exercised by the Chief Executive. Another is the fact that in this country which is supposed to be ruled by the will of the majority, a regime that has ceased to represent the majority feeling can not be ended until its four-year term is up.

It isn't so ruled, of course. We have recently been reminded of that by published figures showing the shocking disparity in Ohio of congressional representation. Congressional districts with a few thousand population have equal representation with other districts containing nearly a million people.

In the United States Senate, a couple of Senators representing a heap of sagebrush, some gamblers, a few mineral mines, and not many thousands of voters have equal voting power with States holding many millions of people. I am putting it crudely, but that is about the way it is.

This system of democracy was created at a time when the individual States were jealous of their prerogatives, and with reason. The reason no longer exists.

Yet we go along with it. The majority does not now govern, except in a general and ineffectual way. Do we not need some constitutional change in this respect?

The Chief Executive today has a power which was not intended for him by the founding fathers and which, to some extent, nullifies the democratic concepts. I become a little ill when

I read that the President of the United States has often sent segments of the army outside of the country to quell troubles of one sort or another, and these precedents are accepted as authorization for the Korean War. There is no comparison.

Nothing in democracy, nothing in our history, justifies action by one man which would lead to a universal war. This is not a dogfight. It could be the prelude to policies and commitments which would wipe out most of the human race.

I do not know whether the Korean policy is right or not from the viewpoint of our own national interests. I feel quite strongly that action of the sort we are now engaged in should not have been taken without consultation with the American people and a complete and honest explanation of the reasons and the issues.

I know we are fighting communism but why should we choose to fight it in a place where we are at a tremendous disadvantage? Truman's idea of fighting communism wherever it shows its head in the remote reaches of the world seems to me appalling nonsense.

We elect a President by democratic processes and we proceed to kill him by equally democratic processes. He must be a leader of his political party. He must undertake administrative duties which would require the abilities of a superman, and he must make decisions in a crisis which would burden the shoulders of God himself. Is it surprising that he sometimes cracks and dies under this load of responsibility, some of it probably unnecessary?

But when his mind is gone, or when he is obviously incompetent to fulfill his functions as head of state, there is no way of transferring his power and duties to a successor.

Who knows how many of the last critical decisions of Franklin Roosevelt were made when he was no longer in the full use of his very great faculties?

I suspect that the British parliamentarian system might have some superiorities in the perilous age we are living through. It provides the mechanics for getting rid of the mistaken, the incompetent, and the unwanted at a time when their removal might be of some use to the state and to the world.

I suppose this will be taken by some readers as a tirade against the Administration, and God knows it is an administration that has made mistakes which shock the mind and tear the heart. But that is not my point.

The point is that we should think seriously about limiting the power and diminishing the responsibilities of any President and returning ultimate decisions to the people. I believe the word democracy is derived from a Greek word which means people.

The Declaration of Independence

JULY 4, 1951

The nation today pays homage not only to a historical event but to a work of literature. Much of the enormous influence the Declaration of Independence has had on thought and action in America is owing to the strength and nobility of its language.

The philosophic ideas it expresses are not original. The truth and logic of its generalizations have often been questioned. Few people, for instance, really believe that "all men are created equal."

But the persuasiveness and wonder of the language with which such ideas are expressed have given them validity in the minds of many generations of mankind, and acceptance in the heart.

Custom does not stale the Declaration of Independence as a masterpiece of verbal expression. Drill its words into the minds of school children, make a chore of it, repeat its passages until they become platitudinous and trite. It still has power to stir the feelings and evoke admiration when you read it for the hundredth time.

For the spirit behind it was ardent and sincere, and the writer who composed it had an exceptional skill in the use of words. He was appointed by the Congress to draft the Declaration, since his skill in the use of language was recognized because of a few public papers he had written and which had passed from hand to hand.

He became chairman of the committee charged with writing the Declaration and, like most committee chairmen, he did all the work. But when he had finished the document after a couple of weeks' labor he showed it to Benjamin Franklin and John Adams. They proposed some changes, which he made.

The Jefferson Declaration was reported to Congress on June 28. But Congress adjourned over the weekend and the Declaration was not taken up for final action until July 4.

It was fiercely debated and amended both in its language and its ideas. Jefferson had condemned the African slave trade and the British veto of the colonial laws hostile to it and the British incitements of the Negro to arm and to murder the colonists.

This was the longest paragraph in Jefferson's original draft of the Declaration. It was stricken out by the objection of some of the Southern colonies and the influence of Northern shipping interests.

Jefferson had denounced King George "for sending Scotch and other foreign mercenaries" to fight against the colonies. Congress struck out the word "Scotch" because some of its members were of Scotch blood.

Jefferson was only thirty-three years old at this time and just beginning as a writer. You can imagine his feelings when the writing on which he had labored so long and with such an intensity of effort was arbitrarily changed, amended, and added to by a body which, as an assemblage, had incomparably less facility than he as a writer.

Charles A. Beard, the great American historian, says that Jefferson twisted and winced when these changes were made in his copy. I don't know what historical evidence Beard has for this statement, but I am sure it is true, for it would be altogether human.

The Declaration of Independence is a collaboration. Its principal ideas stem from John Locke, the English philosopher, and indirectly from the Frenchman, Jean Jacques Rousseau. It was essentially an expression of the liberal philosophy of its day, the product of many minds and of years of discussion.

But Jefferson has inexorably and immortally put his stamp on it. His fervent faith is in it, his unique personal qualities, his magnificent and enkindling style of expression.

Among all the brilliant men in the Continental Congress not one, including Benjamin Franklin, could have written a document so serviceable to the needs of the time and so significant and flaming for future generations.

Foreign Aid

MARCH 14, 1958

The friends and proponents of a big foreign-aid program are numerous, diverse, and influential. Some of them met in Washington the other day to whoop it up for the current spending proposal which involves an appropriation of three billion nine hundred million dollars to be dispensed abroad.

The boosters included President Eisenhower, ex-President Harry Truman, Adlai Stevenson, Eric Johnston, Dean Acheson, some high-ranking churchmen, and a quota of Hollywood celebrities.

It was an impressively bipartisan and distinguished gathering, or gatherings, for President Eisenhower and Mr. Truman spoke on the same day but to different groups and from different tables.

The show of unity among such varied personalities, representing so many walks of life, was formidable and striking. It may have tended to create the impression that to favor an immense foreign-aid project was the sacred duty of all civilized Americans and that those who questioned the spending were lacking in intelligence, stony of heart, and not quite respectable.

That implication could be gathered from some of the speeches made in advocacy of the aid program. Millions of Americans will refuse to accept the suggestion that the spending of gigantic sums for subsidies abroad is a necessary and virtuous enterprise which should not be questioned by reasonable and well-intentioned men.

The obvious certainty is that our aid policy is questionable in many ways, both philosophic and practical, and that it is being questioned by perhaps the majority of ordinary Americans who are neither fools nor knaves. Advocates of continuous and grandiose spending would help their cause by answering some of the questions.

What assurance do they have that subsidizing foreign governments for an indefinite period will make permanent friends and allies of the subsidized peoples? Experience and common sense suggest that it won't. Money cannot buy friendship, but it can foster disappointment, enmity, and jealousy.

We are giving, or have been giving, monetary support to some fifty nations. It is natural that they should all want more than they are getting, and it is inevitable that those who are getting the least should be envious of those who are getting the most. We do not necessarily make friends of those to whom we are the most helpful, but we create resentment among those who feel they are not getting their full share of American bounty.

In the years since the end of the war we have given an enormous sum to aid nations all over the world. Any traveler knows that our government is today more unpopular and less trusted among the beneficiary nations than it was before the aid program was instituted.

Ironically, John Foster Dulles, who is largely responsible for the current aid policy, has become a kind of universal villain to the world at large and is made the personal target for resentments rooted in frustration and envy and intensified by our foreign-aid policy. For instance, France was angered by our gift of small arms to Tunisia and Tunisia was outraged when France used American gift planes to bomb a Tunisian village on a market day, killing a number of women and children.

Our foreign aid is divided into two categories, military and economic. It is not easy to dissociate the two logically. A sovereign nation is expected to provide its own military requirements from the products of its general economy. If it accepts military aid from other nations its general economy is relieved to the extent of the military contribution. On the other hand, if it accepts economic aid it can use that aid to build up its military strength. In the final analysis, economic aid and military aid are inseparable.

The theory underlying both forms of aid is that they make friends and allies of the beneficiaries, that they strengthen their power to fight communism, insure against the imperialistic ambitions of Russia, and help to guarantee our own security. If they did all that no price would be too high to pay. But there is no reasonable hope that they will.

Our foreign aid goes to governments and rulers, not to the people. These overlords change from time to time and policies shift according to self-interest, personal ambition, and fluctuating world situations.

The weapons that we give, the national economies we try to strengthen, the friendships we cultivate may one day be turned against us at the whim of circumstance or the caprice of personality. For example, Pakistan is our friend, India is a benevolent neutral, and we are helping both nations on a considerable scale. Either will turn against us and veer toward Moscow according to our attitude on the disputed province of Kashmir, an issue which is without meaning to most Americans.

There are times and occasions where foreign aid is wise and necessary either for humanitarian reasons or self-interest. But grandiose paternalism in perpetuity is likely to create more evils than it cures.

The foreign-aid appropriation currently demanded is three billion nine hundred million dollars, not a penny more or less.

It is impossible to measure the real needs with that exactness. It has been pretty well established that a substantial part of the aid money already expended has been wasted, some of it in obvious nonsense and absurdities. The least a reasonable American can expect is that the fat will be fried out of the new appropriation and that vigilance and common sense will be exercised in its distribution.

THREE

War

Slaughter

DECEMBER 1, 1939

I visited the capital of Finland once in the days when it was called Helsingfors. It reminds you of Akron. You feel at home in the Finnish town. The automobiles on the street are American. The people are like us in their manners and way of feeling.

Finland was the first nation in Europe to recognize that women were people by giving them the right to vote. The country even tried prohibition and the law was in effect when I was there. It was not enforced with any more strictness than it was here. A hotel porter reminded me of our spiritual kinship in this matter.

"You can get a drink anywhere," he said. "It's just like America."

Helsinki is a placid capital. People walk the streets of a summer evening to gossip and look and enjoy the air as they do in a small American town.

Or they wander to the grassy park in the heart of the city to listen to the music of a band. It is a brass band and the music sounds like German music.

They are a neatly dressed, clean people. You have the impression of a simple, honest, industrious folk who respect themselves, who are politically progressive, who have a high standard of private and public morality.

Yesterday, in the name of the brotherhood of man, aerial bombs were dropped on these inoffensive and defenseless people. Another nation, which boasts a population of 180,000,000 and can put an army of 10,000,000 afield, felt that it was threatened by Finland's 3,000,000 persons and an army of 300,000. Helsinki's population is about equal in numbers to the tenants that crowd a few government apartment houses in Moscow.

Yet Helsinki must be bombed because its power is a threat

to a nation that covers one-sixth of the earth's surface. Hospitals must be blasted, schools blown up, homes and apartments burned.

Women and children must be slaughtered and the entire population of a modern city terrorized into stupefaction by a rain of devastation which came without warning and without declaration of war.

"Workers of the World, Unite." Well, this is one way of getting them to unite. Death unites all.

The Finnish workers murdered on the street, or at the lathes, by the Socialist Fatherland can be comforted. They are "united" at last.

Another great blow is struck for peace and the progress of mankind under the beneficent banner of the hammer and the sickle. What are a few hundred lives?

What is morality, what is decency, what is liberty, patriotism, and honor? These are mere bourgeois catchwords when they stand in the way of Russian imperialism which describes itself as Communism. Kill, burn, destroy. Listen to the shrieks of children, watch terrorized women run and fall, and see men blown to bits with explosive bombs or trapped screaming in burning apartment buildings.

All this is necessary and good because the world must be prepared for the brotherhood of man and a wicked nation of 3,000,000 persons was provoking and menacing the life of a nation of 180,000,000.

There are no appropriate words for this latest triumph of Russian benevolence. The hypocrisy, the viciousness, the infamy are too complete for language to describe. The only proper comment is to step into the nearest bathroom and vomit.

Cassino Pulverized

MARCH 18, 1944

Fifth Army, Cassino Front—We stood on a hill a few days ago
and watched a scene of destruction the like of which no man
has seen before. It stunned the senses and wrenched the mind.
You have difficulty in believing the witness of your own eye. It
was sickening and terrifying, and it was magnificent.

While you watched not five thousand yards away a town was
being blotted out. At 8:30 in the morning Cassino existed as a
habitat for man. By noon it had practically ceased to be. Every
fifteen minutes all morning long waves of bombers of all types,
light, heavy, medium, came circling systematically over the town
to let fall their loads of destruction. The smoke and the dust of
pulverized buildings thrown into the air by one wave of bombers
was not cleared before another wave was overhead.

In relation to the size of the target the Cassino bombing was
the most intense in human history. The town is about a mile
square. In three and one-half hours it was struck by hundreds of
aircraft carrying more than 2,500 tons of bombs.

You could see the bombs as they hit and appraise the damage
done. They blew up a slash of red fire as they exploded. Then
came a cloud of black smoke. What you could identify a minute
before as a large building lost form and was unrecognizable.

The noise of the explosion was startlingly loud from the distance at which we stood. It must have burst the eardrums of
Germans in Cassino.

The bombers came wave after wave, hour after hour. It would
have been impossible for anybody in Cassino to catch his breath
after one bomb had exploded and before another had fallen.

The town was almost unceasingly wreathed with fresh con-
centrations of black smoke and the white dust of shattered build-

ings which spouted hundreds of feet into the air. The echo of
one explosion had not died down before there was another.

It was difficult to understand how human nerves could stand
punishment so violent and continuous, even if the physical body
survived. You could not help imagining yourself in the place of
the enemy. A half-dozen times I heard people in the little group
among whom I stood saying as they watched the inferno before
them, "I wouldn't like to be there," and you could sense a kind
of shuddering awe in their tones.

The tranquil stillness characteristic of the normal environment
multiplied by contrast the violence of the spectacle we were
watching. We stood on a high elevation in a pleasant grove. Before us was the lofty snow-covered Mount Cairo looking serene,
untroubled, and eternal.

To the left was Mount Cassino, crowned by the large mon-
astery which is the most conspicuous building in view and easily
dominates the prospect below. It was the town of Cassino, which
must have been before the war a sleepy, attractive, quaint place
of the type that tourists like to visit.

Except for the circumstance that Cassino was being blown to
pieces, the view was conventionally picturesque and charming
in the set panorama of picture post cards.

For hours we watched the great birds come and go with their
cargo of death and annihilation. It was a fine clear day and visi-
bility was good. There was astonishingly little flak and no
fighter opposition whatever. We could have seen it if there had
been any as easily as you see the action on the stage from an
orchestra seat in a theater. There was a little flak at the beginning but none later.

I was with William Stoneman and Edward Morgan of the
Chicago News. Morgan kept saying with nervous intensity and
a kind of puzzled irritation: "Where's the flak? I can't understand it, where's the flak?"

It is odd how people respond to a tremendous event such as
we were seeing. We had a first-row seat for a drama which involved the destruction of a city and the greatest display of
aerial bombardment in history.

You could see what was happening almost as clearly as you could see a fictional representation of the same event in a Hollywood movie. Some of the members in our little group of British and American officers and newspapermen said you could see people moving about in Cassino. I couldn't, even with the strongest glasses, and I doubt that anybody could.

Nevertheless you could follow the general trend of the action with glasses. You could follow the descent of a bomb from the time it was dropped. You could see when it was going to hit and what it hit. You could see the separate steps by which a town was being razed and pulverized. Your thoughts wandered to the fall of Pompeii or to Nero watching the burning of Rome.

The scope and drama of the event you watched were epic. Nevertheless after several hours your attention strayed. The fall of one bomb was much like that of another.

When somebody proposed that we have something to eat every eye left Cassino and was riveted on the prospect of food. The British had brought some hard tack, bully beef, and soybeans which they offered to share. We stood at a jeep or sat on the ground and ate.

There was a bottle of wine and a little whisky, and men who do not drink were glad to calm their nerves and settle their stomachs with a drop of alcohol.

Outwardly, it was like an outing on a spring day in picnic grounds, but the crowd was nervous and the jesting was feeble and self-conscious. Everybody was a little shaken by what he was seeing and nobody could get it out of his mind.

General Alexander was standing all this time a few yards from us. He was surrounded by other generals nobody could identify and somebody proposed that we ask them their names. Somehow it seemed impertinent to the point of the indecent to disturb a conclave of generals while they were watching a historic action they had planned.

A little after midday the bombers were finished and the artillery began. It was one of the most intensive bombardments of the war and the din was ear-shattering and nerve-racking.

There were guns all around us, in front, to both sides, and

in the rear, and some of them were only a few yards away. I had not been aware of their existence until they began firing. Thereafter I was fully conscious they were there. You could see the shells as they fell in Cassino. They came many at a time from various directions and they kept coming for hours. When we left it was hard to see how a single building could have remained undamaged in Cassino or how life could be lived except as men may live like moles and rats in the ground.

As we were leaving I stopped to pick up an exploded heavy-caliber cartridge on the hill before Cassino. Lying a few inches from it was a yellow wild flower whose name I do not know. Spring had come to Cassino.

Lava Annihilates a City

MARCH 23, 1944

Naples—The incredible goddess of nature does not lag far behind the hand of war in dealing a grievous blow to this area of Italy. A few days ago I saw an Italian town destroyed by the most concentrated aerial bombardment in the records of warfare. And now I have watched an Italian town being smothered and pulverized by one of the most devastating volcanic eruptions in Italian history.

Some say the current activities of Mount Vesuvius are the most disastrous in seventy-two years, other say in two hundred years. The figures mean little to the people fleeing by the thousands from their doomed houses, carrying their poor possessions.

We stood five thousand yards off while Cassino was being leveled. We were sometimes not more than fifty yards off from houses that were crumbling or were about to crumble at Mossa Di Somma and San Sebastiano.

As instruments of annihilation bombs are quicker, but lava is surer, more inexorable, more thorough. We spent most of the

day in the little town of Mossa Di Somma, or what was left of
it. At one side of the main street it was possible to get within
a few feet of the lava stream that was pushing against cement
buildings on both sides of the roadway and threatening to en-
gulf the rather imposing village church.

The lava crawled on inch by inch. After a while the slowly
increasing pressure of its weight became unsupportable and the
wall of a building would crumple and crash. First the side wall
would go, then the façade or the back wall. In perhaps thirty
minutes the two buildings on each side of the road which lay
nearest the lava stream would be gone. It was like a majestic
river overflowing its banks and taking everything before it.

We stood at the side of the stream. At the farthest part in its
forward movement, and there was not much in the immediate
path of its flow except orchards and farm lands. It was apparently the sidewise bulge that was slowly flattening and burying
the village of Mossa Di Somma.

There was no noise. The huge mass was like some fantastic,
fabulous monster that crawled stealthily on its way, chewing
away houses, wall by wall, and finally swallowing them. All that
you heard was the intermittent crack of walls at rather long
intervals and an occasional explosion which threw lava and
smoke and steam hundreds of feet in the air.

The explosions were alarming, and when they came everybody near by ran furiously to escape a possible hail of hot lead,
myself not lagging behind. In a few minutes they would be
back again.

The sidewalk explanation of the explosions was that they
were precipitated when the hot lava struck a well or a cask of
wine. I suspect that there was not enough water or wine around
to cause explosions of such force and that they must have been
set off by volcanic gases of some sort.

The lava stream pressing against the houses at the end of the
street, or what remained of the street, was only about twenty
feet high, but in perhaps an hour and a half it rose to about
forty feet. Farther out it reached mountainous heights. The lava

crumbled and pulverized a building, then buried it so that even the debris disappeared.

I always thought of erupting lava as resembling liquid lead and having the appearance of a full stream in motion. It is more like a slag group, and it rolls rather than flows. Lava thrown up by this monstrous and wasteful convulsion of nature might be mistaken for the massive by-product of some huge and orderly industry.

The mass as a whole is dark and ugly, but it breaks out here and there in a fiery glow. We were some distance down the mountain. The lava had so cooled that it was possible to approach within twenty or thirty feet of the stream without being made uncomfortable by the heat.

All the houses in its path were cement or stone, and nothing caught fire except the wooden framework and such furnishings as were left in the buildings. Small fires licked around the windows and doors.

But the destruction was wrought by the pressing weight of the lava, which crumpled a big stone wall as easily as a man's hands could crush a champagne glass. It was hideous, yet fascinating, to watch the irresistibility. The monstrousness of the force was awesome and unbelievable.

I turned my head away from the buildings at the end of the road for a second. There was a crash of falling masonry. A soldier standing next to me said: "There goes my ice-cream parlor."

The building nearest the lava stream on one side of the street had been a café. Its brick wall had toppled down the second my head was turned.

A dog wandered dispiritedly in and out of a house which lay in the immediate path of the lava. He was obviously searching for his master and finding it puzzling that no one was at home.

As the lava slowly came nearer the house, soldiers tried to whistle the dog out of danger. He paid no attention to them and ran into the house when they tried to catch him.

An American fighter pilot saw a chicken on the roof of a

house which had not long to last. He climbed up, caught the chicken, and brought it down to temporary safety.

The lava was passing near the attractive village church, whose destruction appeared inevitable and imminent. One of two adventurous airmen thought it would be interesting to ring the bells for the last time.

He went into the church, found the bell cord, and rang the bell. It was a pleasant variation to the sound of crashing walls.

The Anzio Landing

APRIL 27, 1944

The Anzio beachhead, where Fifth Army forces have not very comfortably ensconced themselves, is a fanlike wedge about eight by ten miles in size, and all of it is within range of German artillery set up on the hills. We were made aware of that disagreeable fact while our ship was still out in the harbor waiting to dock. You could hear the muffled roar of heavy guns and see shells falling in the dock area. It seemed remote and unreal, like a scene in a movie, but not so clear or loud.

Then you heard a more menacing explosion. A shell landed to the starboard of the ship next to ours. The ship was a comfortable distance off from us, and the shell had missed by a good margin. But it occurred to you that if the Germans could throw a shell that far they might accidentally hit the deck of the ship on which you were standing. I went to my cabin and put on a tin hat.

The sea was rough, and we stood out in the harbor for several hours waiting on the weather. You thought of the ship as a sitting duck waiting to be plugged. In reality there was not much danger. The harbor is just within the range of German guns, and their fire lacks accuracy.

While the German artillery was sounding and shells were

falling in the general neighborhood, the ship's steward and boy-of-all-work announced that tea was being served in the combination dining room and lounge. We drank tea and talked about the weather.

To one seasick correspondent the weather was of much more concern than was the random shelling. We were on an American-built LST, or Landing Ship, Tanks, but the crew was British. That accounted for the tea at ten o'clock in the morning.

The shelling died down to an occasional burst and then stopped entirely. When the sea calmed we docked. There was not a sound except the normal, pleasant noises of a ship unloading.

Most of the buildings around the dock were badly battered, and there was a great deal of debris scattered about. Otherwise the place seemed placid and rather attractive, not exciting, perhaps, but a good spot for a quiet and restful holiday.

I climbed into a jeep while we were still on the ship and at the dock. When we were at the ship's opening and ready to drive over some planks into the dockyard, I remarked on how quiet it was to the lieutenant who was acting as chauffeur.

At that moment there was a roar, and some shell fragments landed in front of us. I should say they landed less than twenty yards off, but I am not accustomed to judging the fall of shell-fire. Anyhow it was close, and the continued sound of guns suggested that more shells might be coming our way.

I ducked, curled up in my front-row seat so as to offer the smallest possible target, and said to the lieutenant: "Let's get the hell out of here. That wasn't the key to the city they were throwing at us."

He answered with what I thought was undue deliberation: "Well, I guess we better back up for a while." So we backed a few feet into the cover of the ship, where one had some protection from shell fragments and a good chance of being drowned if the ship should suffer a direct hit.

It was the first time I had ever been shot at or been within speaking distance of a falling shell. That sort of thing happens to millions, but nevertheless it continues to be interesting when it happens to you.

You expect to be scared and you are scared, probably out of all proportion to the actual risk. The strange thing is that you are also amused.

A shell that kicks up dirt and debris some distance away seems unreal and impotent. It reduces itself to a kind of malicious, but harmless, impertinence.

You say to yourself, "That's a pretty way of welcoming a well-meaning visitor to Anzio," and you ponder on the laws of chance which should have dropped that particular shell a few feet away at the moment you were driving off the gangplank onto the roadway.

Your heart beats faster, you are uncomfortably apprehensive about where the next shell will land, but you have a sense of exhilaration, a feeling of triumph in being alive.

After a few minutes there was a lull in the shelling, and we drove off into the exposed dockyard. A crew was standing in the yard, arranging planks so that the jeeps and trucks could make the descent from the ship to the ground. The men made you ashamed of the importance you attached to your feelings in a moment of risk.

These men stood here all day long under more or less constant artillery fire. They seemed unaware of their danger, or at least they seemed able to put it out of their consciousness. They arranged planks methodically, they beckoned traffic forward or back in the cheerful, imperious way of the corner cop on Easter Sunday.

A few minutes ago shells had struck a few feet from where they stood, and more might come at any second. You could not guess it from the demeanor of these men.

There were Negro soldiers among them who went about their work grinning. The dock neighborhood is the most constantly shelled and bombed area of battered Anzio, and these Americans, or others like them, work there in the open all day.

Without them, ships could not unload and Anzio could not be held.

They are doing the work of laborers and they are front-line soldiers in respect to the risks they take and the nonchalant courage with which they bear up and carry on under fire.

When the medals are being distributed these unpublicized back-of-the-line soldiers ought to be remembered. In a practical sense there is no back-of-the-line on the Anzio beachead. The whole area is a front, and it is under both artillery fire and aerial bombing.

We made our way down the main road of the town to the place where we were to be billeted. The road is overlooked by the Germans and is often raked by artillery fire. We heard some firing, but nothing came our way.

It is not healthy for a vehicle to stop on this road. We had hitched a ride to the billet from a lieutenant who was acting in the capacity of army baker. He told us he did not know exactly where the billet was but would stop to inquire of an MP. He did.

It was not much of a risk perhaps, but he need not have invited us to ride with him, need not have been bothered, delayed, and put to the smallest additional danger. That kind of spontaneous helpfulness and fellowship gives you a glow of pride in your countrymen.

Ghostly Berlin Ruins

SEPTEMBER 14, 1946

Berlin—You have read more than once about the devastation in the heart of Berlin and you have seen pictures of it. But no medium of expression can convey the inner quality of the scene, the spirit of ghastliness, and the feeling of something supernatural that underlie these ruined façades and this life crushed to earth and smashed into nothingness.

I walked last Sunday through the district that had its center at the intersection of Unter den Linden and Friedrichstrasse, as I had done on Sunday afternoons before the war on hundreds of occasions.

This corner and its environment are roughly comparable to New York's Times Square, or to the neighborhood of East Ninth Street and Euclid in Cleveland. Even on a Sunday afternoon this part of Berlin normally was crowded and lively. Now it is like a dead body which has not been buried.

Where thousands walked, there are a half-dozen aimless strollers. Where there were rows of sturdy buildings, busy shops, luxurious hotels, and cafés there are wreckage and rubble, ruin and void. The district is unrecognizable, or recognizable only in a vague way as familiar scenes appear to you in a nightmare.

I once knew every paving block on these streets. Now I could easily lose my way in them.

The old landmarks are gone, or so distorted that they seem weird caricatures of what they were. The famous cafés on three corners of the intersection of Friedrichstrasse and Unter den Linden and the buildings which housed them are pretty well smashed to the ground. They do not exist as recognizable entities. They are simply part of the general anonymous ruins of central Berlin.

The whole district is rubble and wreckage, with an occasional building left more or less intact to emphasize the general devastation. The panorama is not so horrifying at it is eerie, incredible, and unreal.

It is not like life. It is like Dante's *Inferno,* or some other poetic materialization of what human senses have not experienced and the human mind cannot comprehend.

All about you is bleakness and disharmony and gaunt, jagged ruin. You can hear your own footsteps echo like gunshots on the deserted thoroughfare which was once Friedrichstrasse, perhaps the busiest shopping street in Berlin.

Sunlight gapes through this rather narrow street for the first time in decades. The sun comes through the great holes left by the disappearance of building after building. You welcome the sun, but not as it shines over wounds and ugliness.

Unter den Linden resembles a barren and deserted field surrounded by rubble and ruin. I noticed that a single street café had opened on Unter den Linden near Friedrichstrasse in one of the few buildings that could provide shelter. Perhaps a dozen people were seated at its tables. In relation to the life that used to be lived on this street it was pathetic, and it intensified the prevailing dreariness.

I do not know how it was in the months immediately after the war, but it seems possible that the ruins of central Berlin might appear even stranger and more final now than they did then. Some time ago they must have resembled new wounds which were capable of being healed.

Now they look permanent, as if they had always existed and might always continue to exist. They have become accepted, like meager rations and all the other postwar deprivations, and people whose sad lot it is to live among them are probably little conscious of them except in a vague way.

Complete ruin has come to look neat, as if it were part of the ordained nature of the world. Very little traffic moves on these streets. But the streets are clean. Millions of tons of rubble still lie where buildings once stood, and it will be many years before it is cleared out. But the streets and sidewalks are passable and the wreckage of the structures that lined them is being slowly cleared out.

Miniature railways have been laid at the sides of the streets against the walks to carry off the rubble and this transferral is continuing constantly. But, so far as I could see, very little work of reconstruction is being done.

The task is so enormous that it seems hopeless and, with the best of fortune, it will take many decades. Meanwhile, the wreckage looks tidy, or as tidy as wreckage can look and that is one of the factors which gives an abnormal character to the scene. You think of war wreckage as being temporary and recent and removable. Here, in some districts of Berlin, it seems old and eternal, like the ancient ruins of cities long dead.

In the last few days I have passed several times through the Tiergarten toward the Brandenburg Gate. To one who knew the scene of old it is now one of the most fantastic and incredible in the length of Berlin.

You know the German passion for neatness and the Keep Off the Grass signs and the strict, clipped orderliness of its parks and open spaces. The Tiergarten is now a kind of weedy wilderness broken up with shacks and patches of vegetable gardens.

Sunflowers grow everywhere in this once meticulously tended park. I am told they are encouraged because of their oil and food value. But the homely sunflower, nodding wild and unrestrained in the Tiergarten, is something that I was not prepared for.

Nobody could anticipate the whimsicality of saturation bombing which destroyed nearly everything usable in central Berlin but which left standing, whole and untouched, statues and groups of statuary in the Tiergarten. They were much complained of from the viewpoint of art in prewar days, but now they deserve the respect that is owing to a capacity for survival in an uncertain and dangerous world.

They stare at you here and there from over the wilderness of the Tiergarten like some bizarre and indestructible monuments of man's will to create and preserve beauty in a hostile environment.

Some of them have not been touched. They stand out like white ghosts from another world, alone and detached, amid uncountable acres of barrenness and desolation.

One of the most vivid spectacles I have seen from the roadside in Berlin is an equestrian statue in the Tiergarten. Other than weeds and a few sketchy patches of vegetable gardens, nothing meets the eye except the sculptured man on a horse, riding nowhere, apparently for all eternity.

Normandy

SEPTEMBER 20, 1948

Falaise, Normandy—We are nearing the end of a trip of some six hundred miles through the battered towns and the littered beaches where the battle of Normandy was fought and won a little more than four years ago.

Do you remember how these names sank into your consciousness then, and what anxiety was in your mind? Omaha Beach, Utah Beach, Arromanches, Courseulles, where the landings were made, and Caen, St. Lô, Falaise, and a dozen other Normandy towns where Americans and British were slaughtered and the world held its heart in the mouth, fearful that they might be dying in vain?

Perhaps these names ring only vaguely in the memory now, for we are too close upon the events which gave them meaning. History will record a clearer remembrance, for what happened here altered the course of human life.

The residents of the little village of Chambois, a few miles from here, are anticipating the history books. They have erected a signpost at the village crossroads which reads, in effect: "Where the Canadians, the Americans, and the Poles made a junction, closing the Falaise pocket, thus ending the battle of Normandy and thereby deciding the fate of France."

More than 170,000 Germans were trapped in this pocket and captured, or annihilated. The fields adjoining the roadways are still grotesquely cluttered with hundreds of rusted German tanks and armored equipment of all kinds.

Standing sullenly in the lush Norman grass, they have an air of permanence, as if they were destined to remain there forever as ugly monuments to defeat and desolation.

The bones of Germans are still supposed to rest unburied in

some of these abandoned and rotting tanks. I saw none and I do not believe they are there.

The crazily battered equipment, the great holes in the armor, the metal parts strewn everywhere are sufficient testimony to the fact that death occurred on a wholesale scale. In these fields of rust and scrap, which meet the eye every few miles in Normandy, you do not need to see human bones to know that men have died by the tens of thousands in the rich verdure and under the apple trees now overburdened with fruit which they never lived to taste. Every pock-marked and rusted tank is a gravestone, every flowering weed is a funeral offering.

I visited the battlefields a year or two after the First World War. You could see no such dramatic evidence of destruction as you see now in Normandy, and the first war was more devastating to France than the second. They cleaned up more quickly after the first war and they rebuilt more rapidly.

Some of the Norman battlefields have the appearance of places which were combat areas only a few months ago, or just long enough ago to rust steel and iron.

The fields are rich with scrap iron. Why the thrifty Norman peasants do not gather up this treasure and sell it at the highest market in history I do not know, and I often asked.

I am told that many of these knocked-out and sorry-looking German tanks still have usable motors, and that some of the tanks are being made over into tractors.

But many thousands of them still remain on Norman fields, interfering with the grazing of the cattle, serving no useful purpose, and, apparently, having no market value even as scrap.

Hundreds of German tanks are stranded and forgotten on a single small field between Falaise and Chambois. Some of them are of tremendous size and their guns are of battleship dimensions. Nobody seems to be interested.

Even the children of the adjoining farms and villages do not do what you would suppose children might do anywhere under the sun. They do not play with the guns or pick up souvenirs.

At least I never saw them playing with the guns, and the number of souvenirs, such as German shells, gas masks, and a hundred other discarded or violently detached articles of warfare still remain on the ground.

The guns on some of the German antitank equipment remain in operation to the extent that they can be swiveled by a wheel in this or that direction. The only thing that was missing in one I tried was a wheel used, apparently, in raising or lowering the gun. We eventually found the wheel a few yards away.

It had presumably been taken off by a peasant who had no use for the wheel but was in dire need of the bolt which secured it to the antitank gun. Even without the second wheel the formidable gun could be moved around in a wide and alarming swath.

The greatest concentration of abandoned and ruined German military equipment in Normandy is between Falaise and Chambois. This is a vast junkyard.

But you see decayed and junked tanks and armored equipment almost everywhere in the Norman fields and sometimes in the most unexpected places. Riding along in a luxuriant and peaceful valley, you will be brought up sharp by the sight of a couple of tanks which have been knocked to pieces and left to the cows that graze contentedly beside them.

FOUR

The Writer at His Trade

A Newspaperman's Prayer

JANUARY 1, 1936

I never make New Year's resolutions. If a man cannot keep a resolution from day to day there isn't much chance of his keeping it from year to year.

There is egotism in every resolution. The resolver assumes greater strength of character and more impermeability to circumstance than he usually has.

Resolutions should take the form of a prayer and a hope. That kind of resolution might be all right on New Year's Day, or any other day.

A newspaperman's prayer at the beginning of a new year might go something like this:

Let me be clear and simple. Lucidity is a halo when it hovers over a typewriter. But let me be not afraid of a long word, or an unusual word, when it is the right word.

Nor fearful of an idea because it cannot be explained in primer English to eight-year-old minds.

Give me the grace to assume at least a modicum of intelligence in others as I am not loathe to assume in myself, and deliver me from the sin and the pestilence of writing down to adults as if they were half-witted children.

Let me remember that millions in this fruitful land are needy, and let me not try to appraise the hurly-burly of the passing show without considering their position and their viewpoint. Preserve me from complacence.

Give me the patience to inquire, the will to see all sides, the grace to be not more of a fool than nature ordained, the strength to hold fast to such truth and goodness as is in me to see and to understand.

Give me impartiality and detachment, but not to such excess

that the reason grows cold, the capacity for indignation is lost, and the eyes are dimmed for palpable phonies.

Preserve me from tediousness, from meddling in other people's business, from forcing personal opinions on another, or treating them as if they were anything more solid than personal opinions.

Let me not be so optimistic as to believe that this is the best of all possible worlds nor so cynical as to believe that nobody in it does anything that is not in his own premeditated self-interest. Give me, if it is not asking too much, the tolerant eye, the sympathetic mind, the luminous touch.

Above all, grant me the grace of humor, for there is no balance and little sense without it. I do not mean that I want humor every day. Five days out of seven is enough for humor.

No more grievous indignity can be put upon a man than to expect him to be humorous every day in the week. There are occasions on this imperfect earth when it is criminal to be humorous.

Finally, give me perspective on what passes in the little part of the world that I can see, and give me proportion in the view of my own relationship with it. Save me from any tincture of the Olympian manner, from any notion that I have plumbed the regions beyond the stars and learned there the secrets hidden from ordinary mortals.

Let me be clear about this: that I know nothing, that I am ignorant not only where we are going and why, but haven't the slightest special knowledge of the multitudinous and prosaic processes which are carrying us to the next corner.

There are already enough people in the world, don't you think, dear God, who have your private ear and speak with the assurance of miracle men, or great ventriloquists, on complex problems of life and art, politics and economics. Having learned the inner secrets of such mysteries by a kind of special divination, they hold forth in admonitory hands the simple, single key by which the world shall be saved.

Such grandeur is not becoming to a newspaperman and I do not ask for it. Amen.

The Press: A Man's Love
for His Newspaper

OCTOBER 7, 1936

They say that girls who work in a candy factory quickly learn to hate candy. By analogy, people who work for newspapers ought to hate newspapers. I imagine nothing could be further from the truth.

In my own case, I find that years of service in the galley only increase one's fondness for newspapers. I am not speaking of respect or admiration. In a moral sense, newspapers are no different from people. Some of them are honest, decent, and able, and some are not.

For the moment, I am thinking of newspapers detached from their policies, their strengths, or their weaknesses. I am thinking of them concretely in terms of the alive and pulsing pieces of inky paper that you pick up in the morning.

The pleasure that I get out of them is physical. I like the smell of fresh ink on paper. I enjoy the feel of the pages as I turn them over.

I revel in the sight of a newspaper that awaits reading. The fatter the paper the better. Sunday morning is the best time of the week. The newspapers are bigger. Their colors are livelier. They feel rich and glossy in the hands.

I find nothing formidable about their bulk. I delight in it. I know no pleasanter sight on a late Sunday morning than a huge pile of Cleveland and New York newspapers that threatens the breakfast table with its weight.

The papers, of course, must be fresh. I like a stale newspaper no better than a stale egg. Newspapers must not be mussed and disordered by another hand before they get into yours.

A plague on those people who cannot pick up a newspaper without rumpling and scrambling it until it is fit for nothing but the wastepaper basket. They have no order in their minds and no reverence in their souls, and they are a confounded nuisance.

Sometimes it happens that circumstances stand in the way of getting a fresh newspaper, and then you must do the best you can. I always had a great sympathy with a friend of mine from Iowa who has lived for many years in Paris.

He subscribed to his favorite Des Moines newspaper, for he was the kind of man whose breakfast is incomplete without the news of the world as reflected through the home-town paper. The trouble was that the Des Moines morning paper arrived in Paris about three weeks after the date of publication, and it came in bunches of six or seven issues.

My friend would collect them at the American Express offices, take them home, arrange them carefully in the order of publication, and permit himself to read one issue each day with his morning coffee.

It was an important matter in his life and I remember how angry and upset he was when the Des Moines papers didn't arrive on time, which was three weeks late and no more. He suspected the express company of some deliberate conspiracy against his physical well-being and peace of mind.

Then he figured that some clerical employee had a private grudge against him and was maliciously holding up the delivery of the Des Moines journals. But his resentment became rage one day when he collected a half-dozen issues of the paper and found that the wrapper on one of them had been broken and the paper rumpled as if it had passed through other hands before reaching his.

He was convinced that somebody at the express office was reading his newspapers before turning them over to him. It made him furious.

He conceived a hatred for a certain clerk whom he suspected

of being guilty. Normally a peaceful, kindly man he would gladly have seen that clerk boiled in oil.

The clerk, of course, was innocent. Why should a French mail clerk in Paris be interested in surreptitiously stealing a glance at the latest news, three weeks old, from Des Moines, Iowa?

My friend's suspicions were merely evidence of the disordered working of a man's mind when he finds that his newspaper has been tampered with before he gets to it. He had a fondness for his home-town paper that was partly physical in its essence. He disliked to be deprived of its companionship or to have it rumpled by a strange hand, in much the same way as he would have disliked to be separated from the love of his bosom or to have her pawed by a rude, interloping hand.

I imagine he was not altogether unique in that feeling about newspapers, for I have seen much evidence of the same sentiment among passengers on a ship when, after a long voyage, they are able once more to pick up a familiar newspaper. Their pleasure is patently sensual. They like the feel and the appearance of the newspaper to which they have been accustomed.

In their hands, the paper is warm and alive and slightly miraculous. James Russell Lowell had that feeling when he wrote, on picking up his weekly newspaper: "Behold the whole huge earth sent to me hebdomadally in a brown-paper wrapper!"

Invective

MAY 2, 1941

When people take the trouble to write a letter praising some piece I have written I am always as surprised as I am grateful. To me, the kindliness of the average individual never ceases to be pleasantly astonishing.

In a world fiercely beset by violence and cruelty it is a miracle that so large a proportion of mankind should remain well-meaning, generous, and forgiving.

I have had kindnesses heaped upon me by strangers in every part of the world, including parts of the world whose governments and ways of life we don't understand and cannot like.

At home, where the worst is known of any man, I am often touched by the patience of readers and the good will they express. I thank them, I wish them well, I pray that their indulgence will endure.

I cannot be expected to have the same feeling for those more censorious souls who write in to denounce in personal terms something that I have written or to express pointed doubts on such irrelevancies as the legitimacy of my ancestry.

I receive fewer such letters than might be expected, but they come every week, or every time I touch a hot potato, however gingerly. Some of them are pretty good, too.

I enjoy a going-over when it is well done and to the point. At least I don't resent it.

I genuinely welcome a disagreement which hews to the line and bases itself on fact and logic.

Indeed, I am not particularly displeased by the other kind which expresses itself in personalities and invective. All I deplore is the incompleteness and inadequacy of the reasoning.

I had a post card this week from an admiring but not especially articulate reader who answered in two economical words the arguments I had taken a column to express.

With extreme conciseness he wrote, "You stink." He did not even trouble to insert "confidentially."

That is compact criticism, but it is irrelevant as an argument and even as invective it is lacking in eloquence and variety. The expression of abuse, like the expression of love, must have some originality and diversity if it is to touch the mark.

Roxane, in *Cyrano de Bergerac,* quite properly complains of a lack of fluency in the protestations of love to which she is subjected.

"Play variations on the theme," she demands.

It is a reasonable request to make in respect to the phrasing of the tender passions and equally reasonable in respect to the wording of disapprobation.

A man who can think of nothing more than "You stink" to express what must be violent distaste is singularly lacking in inventiveness. It is hardly worth taking up the pen to write no more than that.

I sometimes wonder philosophically what does move a man to take up his pen for the purpose of dashing off a few words of personal vituperation, often obscene, to somebody he does not know in a letter which he does not sign.

Such letters are apparently prompted by the expression of an opinion with which the writer of the letter finds himself in disagreement. But there can be no intellectual satisfaction in writing them since they never attempt to meet an argument, to question reasoning, or to controvert a fact.

If you set down an analysis of world conditions as you see them, and as you believe they are from observations made over many years of travel, and you mildly conclude from this analysis that it would be better for the United States if the British Empire were not destroyed, you are likely to get an anonymous note the next day saying, "You warmongering obscenity," or "You paid hireling of the dirty, capitalistic press."

I don't mind. But I find such answers to fact and logic a little incomplete.

I suppose the writers are merely getting something off their chests. But they ought to have more on their chests than that.

We cannot have a healthy democracy with so limited a vocabulary of invective and so little capacity for the rational refutation of views with which we do not agree.

I please myself with the conviction that people who write in friendly and generous letters, however undeserved, are immensely more articulate and belong to an altogether higher order of mankind.

Censorship

MAY 25, 1949

An editorial in yesterday's *Plain Dealer* pointed out that the terms of a new city ordinance governing the sale of reading matter would, if rigidly enforced, forbid the circulation of Shakespeare's *Macbeth*. It would also stop the sale of practically all the great Elizabethan and Greek classics. The wording of the ordinance is not a supreme example of clear and exact use of the English language. But it seems to say that reading material which deals principally with any sort of crime, from murder to rape, arson, assault, and mayhem, must not be sold, or even shown, to any person in Cleveland who has not attained the age of eighteen years.

The ordinance seems to assume that the only corruptible element of the population consists of young people, and that wisdom and discretion descend on a man at the particular calendar moment when he arrives at the mature age of eighteen. Would that it were so.

The ordinance, or law as it is popularly termed, is designed to suppress the sale of comic books picturing criminal activities. But, as it is formulated, the ordinance apparently prohibits the distribution to young people of any book which deals principally with crime.

Hamlet deals with murder and murder is the whole point of the play. The crux of *Julius Caesar* is the murder of Caesar. *Othello* is a play about the murder of the pure and innocent Desdemona.

Crime is an essential element in nearly all great classics of literature. The supreme and final point of life and literature is death, and death is more exciting when it is accompanied by violence.

There is not a crime named in our new city ordinance which has not been made the basis of a good book, or an admirable play, with the possible exception of sodomy, and I suppose the lawmakers threw that one in just to be all-inclusive, since a comic strip based on that subject is unimaginable.

Violence is the natural and inevitable material of tragedy. I cannot remember a great work of tragedy which does not depict some form of violence, usually murder. In the letter of the law all such works are forbidden to the young people of Cleveland, although they are obliged to read many of them in high schools supported by taxpayers.

I know that this absurd ordinance is not going to be enforced according to the letter of the law. But some idiot could try to do so.

I saw a puppet show the other night, and it reminded me how perfectly natural it is for children and people of all ages to enjoy the fictional representation of physical violence. The show consisted in large part of puppets engaged in the business of slapping one another around.

Punch-and-Judy shows are no longer popular in this country, but they still have an enormous vogue in Europe. Some of the French Line ships put on a puppet show for children during the transatlantic crossing, and I have attended many of them.

They principally involve physical action and almost all of that action is concentrated on beating and slapping. The squeals of delight from the children in the audience when somebody was being thoroughly battered were utterly spontaneous and quite overwhelming. Children enjoy the representation of physical violence and it is quite normal and natural that they should.

Most of our nursery rhymes have some basis of violence, and that is one of the roots of their enduring popularity. The new Cleveland ordinance forbids the sale of books to minors which picture assault or mayhem.

The latter is a legal word for maiming and it means, in law, the maiming of a person in such a way as to deprive him of any of his members which are necessary to his defense or annoying to his adversary.

I am concerned about the effect of this ordinance on the circulation of nursery rhymes and fairy tales. The law forbids the sale of reading material dealing with assault and burglary.

That clearly prohibits the distribution of such childhood rhymes as, "Tom, Tom, the piper's son, stole a pig and away he run." Or "Taffy was a Welshman, Taffy was a thief, Taffy came to our house and stole a piece of beef."

Nor do I know what the law-enforcing officials will do about *Little Red Ridinghood.* As you remember, the wolf in that story committed an assault, and any assault is forbidden to be pictured for young people by the new local ordinance.

In the original legend, Little Red Ridinghood was devoured by the wolf. But in the adaptation made by a couple of Germans known as the Grimm brothers, a huntsman came along to rescue Little Red Ridinghood from the jaws of the predatory animal.

In any case, assault was intended. Perhaps young people shall still be permitted to read the expurgated version of Little Red Ridinghood.

Writing

SEPTEMBER 2, 1954

J. Donald Adams began his column in last Sunday's book section of *The New York Times* with a tribute to Ivor Brown of the London *Sunday Observer.* I shall begin this column with a tribute to Mr. Adams. He writes about books and literature—the two are not usually synonymous—with grace, liveliness, and good sense.

His general attitude is that novels and poetry are written to give pleasure, not to teach lessons or puzzle the reader with symbols and obscurities.

He winds up his column with this paragraph, which I heartily applaud: "We would all be spared a lot of dull reading these days if more of the boys would get things thrashed out either with their priests or their psychiatrists before setting pen to paper, instead of boring the hell out of us with whatever it is that ails them. And that goes for the poets, too."

That is pretty strong talk to emerge from the solemn temple in Times Square. But it is justified by a reasonable irritation provoked by facts.

Many of our most praised authors seem to think their mission in life is to present a sociological attitude, or to say what they have to say in a complex and long-winded way.

Their only real business is to tell a story in a lively, compact, clear, and interesting fashion. But sheer storytelling, as Ivor Brown observes, is supposed to be unfashionable, and young writers are discouraged because the long-haired critics put thumbs down on books which are merely narrative entertainment.

What else can they possibly ask? If you want philosophy you go to the books of philosophers, and if you feel in need of sociological information, you go to the specialists in these fields.

Our best fiction writers have had their wings clipped by the notion that story writing has to have some deep meaning beyond the depiction of character and the relating of a story.

William Faulkner's new book, A Fable, says Mr. Adams, is an attempt to set mankind on its feet. Faulkner has no business in trying to set mankind on its feet. It has been walking on its legs for many centuries.

Faulkner's real mission is to tell stories and he has a superb gift for this enterprise when he sets himself to it.

I suppose I shall have to read his new book, since he is one of the two or three genuinely important American novelists, but I approach the task with reluctance. I read a sentence from the book which ran for a full column. That is not genius. It is laziness.

Why should I do Faulkner's work for him? His business is

to be clear, readable, and illuminating. Nobody can do that by using sentences which take up a full page.

They put an unbearable strain on the reader and they defeat the essential purpose of a novel, which is to provide pleasure.

There is no shadow or subtlety or depth of thought and feeling which cannot be expressed in simple terms and in sentences which do not tire and irritate a reader of ordinary attentiveness and intelligence.

To paraphrase the chaste language of *The New York Times*, it is not necessary to bore the hell out of us by deliberate violations of the ordinary rules of composition and the suggestion of the obvious in terms of the obscure.

The critical response to Faulkner's book has been various and contradictory. Some book critics call it a masterpiece. Others call it tedious and confusing.

I am sure that it is not my kind of book. I like clarity and easiness of reading, and I believe these qualities are not incompatible with greatness.

Charles Dickens

SEPTEMBER 14, 1954

I have just finished rereading one of the works of a great journalist, who died many years ago. The name of the journalist is Charles Dickens and the work I am alluding to is *The Old Curiosity Shop*.

It has been more than forty years since I first read this wonderfully bad, wonderfully good novel. I do not remember what impression it made on me at that time. Probably very little.

Dickens was a classic author in that period and young people have a natural aversion to the classics, an attitude carefully nurtured by an educational system which requires them to read certain classics that they grow up to hate because they were

forced to read them at an age when they could not comprehend them. What should have been a delight was made a task.

I do not know how you avoid some kind of compulsion in
this matter. School children have to be introduced to the masters
of literature because, for the most part, the masters of literature
are dull reading for the young. But it seems to me that they
should be eased, not pushed into them.

I wince every time I hear some of the famous passages from
Hamlet, Julius Caesar, and *Richard III* because I had to learn
them by heart as a child and recite them, on demand, in a class-
room. I hope they have reformed this practice in our modern
schools and "not indifferently, but altogether."

To return to *The Old Curiosity Shop,* which was not required
reading in my schooldays. I said that I had just finished rereading it. That is not precisely true. It was read aloud to me by the
duchess, and that seems to me the proper means of deriving the
utmost pleasure from the novels of Dickens. He was essentially
an actor, and to enjoy the work of an actor you must have
company.

The book is absurd in some respects. Little Nell and her
prolonged death scenes are as corny as Little Eva in *Uncle
Tom's Cabin.* Both excited and moved profoundly the readers
and audiences of their time.

We live now in a different emotional climate. Edgar Allan
Poe once said, as I remember, that the greatest tragedy in the
world was the death of a young and beautiful girl.

Dickens' *Old Curiosity Shop* is based, more or less, on this
idea. Nell is an impossible symbol of sweetness and pathos.

No such creature ever existed in the world of reality. Yet she
seemed to have been thoroughly believed in by readers of more
than one hundred years ago and her death was a public calamity
which brought tears to many thousands.

Most readers of novels nowadays don't have that sensitivity of
feeling. They are emotional, but emotional in a different way.

Nell's death seems a triumph of bathos, not of pathos. Every
character in the book is overwritten and exaggerated, from the

old man to Dick Swiveller and the villain dwarf named Quilp. They have no roots whatever in ordinary humanity and yet they are picturesque and excitingly vivid.

As I have heard it read to me over the past weeks, I am induced to believe that it is one of the worst novels ever written and one of the best. There is no contradiction in that statement.

The crude and highly stressed emotionalism, which was completely suitable to the Victorian period, is no longer approved by a generation which counts itself more sophisticated.

But the skill of Dickens in telling a story and his characters have never been equaled in English novels.

FIVE

The Sportsman and His Dog

Squash: Health or Fun?

MARCH 6, 1936

Two or three presumably well-meaning readers have suggested, by letter, that I ought to write more about skiing, they having apparently taken some unbecoming pleasure in the recital of the discomfiture, the wounds, and lesions that attended my first experience with that noble sport of the Vikings. If these gentle readers do not mind, I prefer to talk about squash.

I perform at squash with no more natural facility than I have for skiing, but squash, while almost equally funny, is not so humiliating to the spirit or so damaging to the human epidermis. Not that a squash ball rudely propelled by a strong arm to the soft areas of the postern is not injurious to the feelings and hateful to the senses. Indeed, it stings bitterly.

But you can usually manage to keep out of the way of a squash ball by hiding against the back wall until your opponent has hit the ball, while I never discovered, in my small experience with skiing, that there was any way to avoid being hit by the snowy ground when your skis walked out on you.

I have been playing squash fairly regularly for about five years. For the uninitiated, if such there be, squash is a game played on an indoor court by striking a very hard rubber ball with a racket against four walls. That gives you the rough idea, and a rough idea is all that I ever had of it.

I have sanguine and elevated moments when I fancy that, after five years of practice, I know something about squash. At these times I am usually engaged in holding my own with an opponent who seems to me to be pretty expert.

I say, "Well, that was a good match. How long have you been playing this idiotic game?"

"Oh," says the young man, "I started last week."

An answer like that wilts the soul and freezes the marrow. When you hear it a few times the crushing thought dawns on you that you have no congenital talent for squash. I do not mind it as much as I once did.

For I have come to the conclusion that squash brings out the worst in man and that it can be well played only by people lacking the milk of human kindness and given over to low cunning and deceit.

I have seen mild men, my good friends and companions, turn into primitive and ruthless scorpions when they enter a squash court. Kindly men, sensible men, good husbands and loving fathers, men capable of being moved by music and the sweet beauty of a winter's night—these very men, once you meet them on a squash court, will change quicker than the chameleon into hard and pitiless atoms of energy, without soul, without grace.

They will overawe you with brute strength, they will move around like destructive tornadoes, they will maliciously hit the ball an inch out of your reach, they will contrive the most miserable plots to gain one small point, they will sting you in the rear with a ferocious lunge of the racket propelling the hardest rubber ball into your tender anatomy, and they will then ask, with crocodile tears in their voice, "Did it hurt?"

These squash players, who once were men, have become base, primitive creatures of a lower order of being, all cunning, wicked wiles, and murderous violence.

I am not myself immune to the baleful influence of squash. A simple, peace-loving man, bearing no grudge against my fellows and lacking the energy for any extraordinary villainies, I find myself on the squash court changed into a dissembling creature given to the lowest deceits, endeavoring to trick my opponent with a slow ball, or a hypocritical corner shot, then following this sly craftiness with prodigious wallops at a harmless ball and the wild, belligerent whoops of a red Indian at war with civilization.

There is an absurd rule in the iniquitous game which stipulates that if you hit your opponent with the ball on any part of his anatomy whatsoever, you play the point over again. That means that if you think you can't make the point by hitting the front wall you can avoid losing it by hitting your opponent's rear.

You can see how a rule like that leads to a certain carelessness among aroused squash players. In any respectable game you would lose a point if you damaged your opponent, as a baseball pitcher does when he hits a batter. But not in squash.

In squash when you hit your opponent you retrieve the point and get another chance to hit him. The result is that squash players are more or less continually picking squash balls out of their flesh, where they have been sunk by the force of a racket's leverage, and saying, with the greatest untruth, "It's all right, it didn't hurt." The ironic theory is that you play squash for your health.

Or that you play it to reduce excess poundage. These remain theories.

Squash players of my acquaintance take off a couple of pounds in a bitter and ferocious game of squash and the exercise gives them such a feeling of triumph and well-being that they promptly eat, or drink, twice as much as they would otherwise have done, with the result of taking on four pounds in place of the two they have lost.

It is certainly a wicked game, conducive to all that is evil in man, but I have no intention of giving it up. The eminent doctor and raconteur, Roubicek, who runs the club where I take my squash has selected as the slogan of his institution, "Gentleman, your health."

I am dubious about the health and nothing that I have seen in the practice of squash leads me to believe that it is effective in the promotion of gentlemanliness, but the fact is, it's fun, and that is something in an imperfect world.

Tennis: Perverse But Fascinating

SEPTEMBER 14, 1937

About this time of year, I habitually find solace in a remark that Kin Hubbard—God rest his soul—once made. It was "Supposing a man is a good tennis player, what then?" For it is at this season that I am annually deluded into taking up a tennis racket and marching onto a clay court with high hopes and heart full of good will for all mankind. A few hours later I leave the field, a misanthropic and broken man.

Each passing year confirms what was at first only an ugly suspicion, namely, that I shall never be a good tennis player. Indeed, the evidence in support of that truth steadily mounts in geometric progression and is now so irrefutable that it no longer hurts as it once did.

The wound is still there but time is easing the acuteness of the pain and soon only a faint scar will be visible. I can now manage a certain jauntiness of manner in the face of my triumphant and jeering opponents when I say, "Supposing a man is a good tennis player, what then?"

Kin Hubbard, who was known as the Hoosier philosopher, though he was born in Bellefontaine, Ohio, was not speaking from the heart of disillusionment as a frustrated tennis player. He never tried to play tennis and I am sure he thought it was a silly and infantile game. He was expressing more than an instinctive personal distaste. He was expressing an underlying prejudice of his time and place.

In Indiana of that period, tennis was generally regarded as too trivial and effeminate to enlist the interest of grown men or really sturdy boys. It was commonly thought of as a sport for sissies. In those days, pansies were flowers.

But whatever may be the social status of tennis in the new

world, I shall never be good at it. Did you say, "What's the difference whether you play a game well or not as long as you have fun?"

I answer, "Brother, a lot of difference." The enjoyment to be had from a game is proportionate to the skill with which you play it.

If you don't think so, examine your feelings when your opponent serves a hard one to the corner of the service court and you miss it, standing there sheepish and helpless, like a man suddenly confronted with the baseness and treachery of wind and weather. Then consider your feelings when, by some accident or misunderstanding, you yourself hit a fast one to your opponent's backhand and he misses it.

No, in this world it is better to ace than to be aced. The plop of the tennis ball makes the sweetest music when you hit inside the court. It has not the same sound at all when your opponent drives a hard one just beyond your reach.

The perversity of tennis is what makes it fascinating. It seems so simple and it is so complex. It looks so easy and it is so difficult.

Any man above the grade of a congenital moron ought to be able to serve a ball into the large area since he gets two tries at it. After twenty-five years of practice even Bill Tilden can't do it every time. The average dub can never be sure that the ball is going in.

Nine times out of ten he will knock the first ball into the net. The second ball is fairly likely to land in the same place.

It is a peculiarity of tennis that the height of the net increases and decreases through some capricious and inexplicable process not capable of being analyzed by science. Sometimes it grows to be about ten feet high.

It reaches out for the ball like some vast bird net and the ball is trapped at a great height like a struggling butterfly. That only happens when you are hitting the ball. When your opponent is hitting it, the net drops so low that a ball seems to go over it without leaving the ground.

Every inexpert tennis player is aware of the whimsical way in which the court defies nature by suddenly changing its dimensions. That side of the court which is opposite to you, and into which you are trying to hit the ball, will abruptly shrink in the middle of a game and the back line will move forward a couple of feet so that no matter where you hit the ball it falls outside the line.

Your own side of the court miraculously enlarges itself so that the ball hit by your opponent falls inside the line even when it is clearly directed toward the backstop.

I might do better at tennis if the height of the net and the size of the court would, respectively, remain the same for a few games. Of course, the fact that tennis is a polite sport and your opponents are permitted to decide whether the ball has fallen inside or outside the lines on their side of the net may have something to do with the apparent changes in the dimensions of the court. But since you are entitled to call the shots on your own side of the net, everybody ought to break even at the end of the tennis year.

I have one faint consolation in the matter of Sunday's game at Vermilion. A new hazard was introduced which might help to account for the humiliating result. The balls kept changing in size, weight, and color.

It rained faintly all day Sunday. The balls picked up the moist clay. Before nightfall they were as heavy as horseshoes and about the size and color of footballs. Tennis rackets were not devised to cope with such missiles.

It may be that I am a fair-weather tennis player.

Horses

OCTOBER 29, 1937

Every time I make up my mind to learn to ride a horse somebody falls off one. I was thinking of that the other day when I read of Cole Porter's painful accident.

Not that the idea of riding a horse ever gets much beyond the stage of a wishful reverie in my case. But it is enticing in the realm of pure ideas.

To take exercise without the struggle and inconvenience of furnishing your own motive power, to ride like a god in the air with the wind cutting your face and nature dropping her ordinary barriers to create a sense of exaltation and harmony in the universe—surely this would be pleasant. You think of the keen, wind-swept feeling in Browning's "Our Last Ride Together," of ancient romantic wars, and the solitary horsemen who were always winding their way down the road in the old novels and seeming to have a good time of it.

I have the highest respect for horses. So much, indeed, that I have been induced to climb to the top of a horse only twice. The first time hardly counted. I was in primary school, and the horse belonged to the corner grocer.

The animal had never been known to do more than totter senilely about his errands, but on this particular occasion he was seized with a dream of fire engines and the Kentucky Derby of 1890. He broke into a fierce gallop, slightly irregularized by rheumatism, and my contact with his unsaddled back was of slight duration.

It was years later before I encountered another horse on terms so personal. It was, in fact, not until last year, and the horse was Irish.

His name was Darby and I rode him, more or less, for four-

teen miles through Killarney's Gap of Dunloe. There is no other
mode of transportation through the rugged passes of the picturesque mountains. You ride a horse or you walk, and many
of the visitors who begin by riding end by walking.

You take the horses at Kate Kearney's cottage. There are
dozens of them there waiting, a little contemptuously I thought,
for whatever cargo might come to them. Each was held by an
Irish owner, who went along with the horse to see that it wasn't
damaged.

They call these Killarney horses "ponies." I suppose that is
Irish humor, for they seemed very large. You had the feeling,
indeed, when you climbed to the top, of having scaled a monument from which all the surrounding countryside looked infinitely small and remote. All horses must seem inordinately tall
to any inexperienced rider who finds himself on top of one
of them.

Aside from his height, Darby did not appear to be particularly
formidable. He had a tired and benevolent air, for which I was
grateful.

But fourteen miles is a long distance and the discomfort
after an hour in the saddle was excruciating to an unprepared
horseman. I tried to jog him on and get the agony over with.
When I did this he would stop altogether and tenderly contemplate the scenery.

He was right. The scenery was worth looking at. There
didn't seem much else to do except to climb down and look at
it with him.

We drank our fill of the Killarney landscape that day, though
Darby's attention, I must say, was occasionally diverted by the
green grass with which he toyed absent-mindedly. When he
seemed of a mind to move on, I followed him and awaited an
opportunity to work my way up on his back again by means
of a ledge or any other elevated object.

We were getting on so well together that I ventured to give
him a kick in the ribs when his walk became a crawl. There
seems to have been a misunderstanding for he suddenly lit out
in a gallop.

The sensation of having a huge animal jump out from under you, no matter where you sit, is interesting and most disagreeable. Darby had suddenly become unreasonable and elusive. Whether I sat near his ears, or on his tail, he seemed anxious that I sit somewhere else, and I was pitched backward and forward and from side to side with the utmost inconsistency and perversity.

It seemed a hundred times that I could not possibly keep sitting anywhere on Darby's back and I was in a mood to give it up and welcome the relative comfort of the green grass below when, for no reason at all, Darby slowed down, turned around reflectively and began to contemplate a fine mountain peak at his rear.

I climbed off his back, nursing wounds that have hardly healed to this day, and Darby and I made the rest of the trip through Dunloe Gap as friends and equals, both of us walking and pausing when the mood impelled, to share the beauties of the Irish scenery.

Hunting

DECEMBER 1, 1938

I have gone hunting only once in my life but I think I understand the feeling of these thousands who annually prowl over frozen fields, with a shotgun in their hands, looking for a rabbit or a pheasant.

Some time I may be tempted to try it again for I remember my one day of hunting not altogether unpleasantly.

If you could dissociate the aim and end of hunting from its incidental pleasures it might be wholly delightful. What spoils the adventure is the realization of its purpose in the unpleasant form of a dead bird in the hand or a mangled rabbit.

Or that is the way I remember it. I must have been about fifteen years old. At that age all boys, particularly if they live in a city, dream of hunting, though they often lack a shotgun and a place to hunt.

So I was enraptured when a man of my acquaintance, a red-headed Irish detective, offered to supply firearms and take me with him to a farm on which rabbits were rumored to lurk.

It was a train trip from the city and when we got off the coach we walked into another world. It was snowing and cold, and the woods seemed desolate and ominously quiet. Only the snow underfoot made a pleasant crunching sound in that emptiness.

It was piercingly lonely and forbidding but the strangeness of the environment and the sense of adventure you had were inexpressibly exciting. In the uneasiness you felt, there was mingled something wonderfully satisfying. You were at one with primitive man. You were fifteen years old and you were Daniel Boone and a whole tribe of rugged pioneers romantically and dangerously wresting the means of life from the overflowing resources of a hostile wilderness.

The wind numbed your hands. It didn't matter. The swift, long walk over rough ground set the blood pounding. You were in magnificent health and enormously hungry. You tasted the peace of the philosophers and the ecstasy of the conquerors, for you had got back to primitive nature and you were master of your environment.

We tramped all day. In the late afternoon we found ourselves walking very close together. The Irishman began to talk of banshees that haunted the night woods of County Mayo.

The rumor about the rabbits seemed to have been exaggerated. We hadn't seen one all day.

Denis was sorry and sympathetic.

"There's an empty bottle lying over there," he said. "You might fancy it was a rabbit and see if you can hit it. Be careful now, lad, of the backfire."

The backfire was disappointing. I had been led to believe that it would be paralyzing. There was only a slight jar and an explosion much less thunderous than I had expected. But the bottle was smashed and Denis was proud.

We were ready to quit when a rabbit appeared before us, about a hundred feet away. He sat there on his haunches, as if he had just walked over from a shooting gallery, or stepped out of *Alice in Wonderland.*

"Holy smoke," said Denis, "it's a rabbit."

The tone could not have been more thunderstruck if the animal had been a royal Bengal tiger.

We gazed hypnotized at the apparition. Denis was the first to recover.

"You take it, lad," he said. "It's your first hunt." I can hear the soft brogue now and the rolling of the r's in the word "first."

It was impossible for anybody to miss that conveniently fixed target at such a distance and the rabbit toppled as I fumbled with the trigger. We ran to retrieve the victim.

He was in two parts. The head had been completely blown off. It was a dismaying spectacle. I felt a little sick and ashamed.

So did Denis, though he tried not to show it.

"Fine work, lad," he said, but I noticed that he did not look at the decapitated and bloody creature, still warm, when he put it in the bag.

We walked silently to the train, close in comradeship, and further united with a sense of having shared in the reprehensible.

"It will be fine eatin', lad," he said, but when it was cooked he could not touch it. Except for the headless rabbit, it had been a perfect day.

Dogs

NOVEMBER 21, 1940

Today I intended to write a grave and grateful piece in the spirit of Thanksgiving, but something has just happened that drives me to write about a subject toward which it is difficult to maintain an attitude of either gravity or thanksgiving.

About a year ago in a moment of temporary aberration I acquired possession of a dog holding membership in a breed known as boxers. Since that day Gyp has been much on my mind. I have learned much from him. Again and again he has reminded me of the growing complexity of life and impelled me to ponder mysteries of existence which I had never previously considered.

When you were a boy and you owned a dog the dog slept on the floor of the kitchen and grew fat and hearty on whatever scraps were left from the table with an occasional reinforcement in the way of a nickel's worth of dog meat from the corner butcher's. Not the modern dog.

You buy him a bed, a metal bed that stands up from the floor, so he won't catch cold, and you pick out a collection of nice dog blankets to protect him from drafts. His feeding constitutes a delicate problem in dietetics.

Instead of table scraps he must have exactly three-fourths of a pound of ground meat twice a day. In the morning he gets a pint of milk and one egg, both fresh, and every day he must have a pint of cooked vegetables.

The meat must be carefully selected. There mustn't be too much fat in it.

My authority on modern dogs counseled me to buy top round steak and have it freshly ground, but I balked at that. If choice hamburger is good enough for me and my family it is good enough for the dog. As it is now, I consider it a break when the lady of the house forgets to order meat for dinner and we get a chance to share some of the dog's meat in the form of succulent and lordly hamburgers. If I could teach the animal to eat fresh-baked biscuits we would have hot biscuits every morning.

We don't have doughnuts any more because the dog doesn't like doughnuts. I don't know how much longer we will continue to have coffee since Gyp has shown a distaste for the beverage.

Now you would suppose that large and regular servings of meat, eggs, milk, and vegetables would be sufficient to maintain a dog in robust health. Not at all, if you listen to my authority.

The dog must have vitamins which are not found in sufficient quantities in a balanced diet of essential foods.

So, between meals, you give him a calcium lactate tablet or a Haliver Oil pill. God knows, few of us who are now men of fair-to-middling health ever had such fastidious attention paid to our diet when we were children.

What does Gyp do in return for this tender and lavish care? Damned if I know.

He is described in the books as a "working dog." If Gyp ever did any work around the house, I missed it. I doubt if he has any real capacity either for day labor or the more intellectual pursuits.

He was named Gyp the Blood, because he was born in Sing Sing and came to me as a gift from Warden Lawes. But his lack of mental distinction is so marked that I often call him, with ironic implication, Einstein.

One of my friends thinks that Gyp is an unsatisfactory name for a dog whose owner is a newspaperman and presumably of literary predilections. So he always addresses Gyp as Woollcott, after Alexander.

It makes no difference. Gyp will answer to any name or answer to none, as the mood impels him.

He has one neat habit. When you call him to come to you he will run as if pursued by the furies of hell, but in the opposite direction. When you say "go away" he will, likely as not, lie down at your feet and refuse to budge.

Even in the ordinary canine function of serving as a watchdog he is not particularly helpful. He loves tramps, peddlers, and suspicious characters. He runs out to meet them, licks their hands fondly, and practically invites them to come in and pick up the silverware.

But let a social acquaintance or a good friend come near the house and he will let out a bark that shatters the air and terrifies not only the visitor, but the dog himself, for he does not seem to understand where the bark comes from.

He is a great fraud, even in appearance. His face is the compacted image of ferocity, sadness, and wisdom while Gyp himself is shy, fainthearted, gay, and not at all wise. Naturally we love him.

But he does strain the limits of human affection. Just now they are strained to the breaking point. Gyp has a slight cold and I just telephoned the veterinary to inquire what could be done about it.

"Give him," said the authority, "a small glass of whisky mixed with corn syrup three times a day."

"What brand do you think he'd like, doctor?" I asked, sarcastically. "How about making it an old-fashioned, or a Manhattan?"

"Oh, any good Scotch will do," he answered.

I don't drink Scotch whisky. I keep it for my friends. Now I shall have to keep it for my dog and my friends will have to take what is left of whatever brand the dog appears to prefer.

There is some hope. We have just tried to feed him the mixture of whisky and corn syrup. He took a mouthful, looked pained, and walked away. He didn't like corn syrup in his whisky.

That is the first clear note of intelligence I ever saw Gyp strike.

Spring Comes to Gyp

MAY 8, 1943

I should appreciate it if the local authorities who are urging citizens to keep their dogs at home would talk with Gyp the Blood, my boxer. For months now I have been trying to persuade him that home is the best place after all and I have failed miserably. His unalterable philosophy is that home is a place to return to at mealtime.

Keeping Gyp in his own yard is a household problem more vexatious and insoluble than all others combined. It is not fair to a dog to tie him outdoors or to keep him in the house all day even if that were prudently possible. It is not fair to neighbors to permit your dog to roam their lawns and gardens.

We make the most earnest and laborious effort to strike a compromise and the results are not satisfactory. The difficulty first presents itself in the morning. His feeding time is at eleven and he has to be turned out hours earlier.

We used to send him forth alone. The yard is quite long, though not wide, and there is plenty of room for a run. He would run a dozen yards, then turn around to see if he were being watched from the window.

If he thought no one had an eye on him, he would take one longing look at the yard next door and then make a mad rush for it and the spaces beyond. If you could catch him with a reproving whistle in the instant between the look and the start of his migration, he would assume an injured air as if his intention had been misjudged. A few minutes later he would try it again, and if you took your eye off him for no longer than a wink he was gone in a whirl of astonishingly rapid motion.

In the winter months his migrations were fairly controllable. He got away only two or three times a week. With spring breathing its sweet messages he makes off for more inviting pastures every time he is let out of the house.

It has become necessary to accompany him on his peregrinations into the yard. Even that does not restrain him.

The other morning I walked with him in a spirit of trusting and amiable comradeship to the front gate. For a second I took my eyes off him to observe a bird which was shrilling in a tree above. In that unguarded second he disappeared as if by magic. It was as quick, as mysterious, and as inexplicable as a card trick by a master hand.

Of course, he could be kept on a leash. But that eliminates the romp in the open that a dog ought to have and it places an undue restraint on his liberty.

We have tried all sorts of devices to curb his vagabond sorties. One plan consisted in giving him half a dog biscuit when he was turned into the yard and putting the other on the doorstep with the plain suggestion, which he understood, that the other half was waiting for him when he returned.

The result of this bribe on an acquisitive and gluttonous nature was that he returned so rapidly he neglected to fulfill one of the purposes for which he was sent into the yard, with unpleasant consequences later for the rugs on the house floor.

We tried feeding him immediately if he returned to the house with reasonable promptness and delaying his meal drastically if he ran off from the home precincts.

We experimented with severe words and mild rebuke. We appealed to his better nature and we tried a vigorous crack over the back with a newspaper.

Nothing is effective. The spring winds issue an imperious call to the instincts and he is off for adventure in distant places every time you make the slightest relaxation in vigilance.

Usually we tramp after him over the neighboring yards and often we find him. But whether he is caught in his vagabondage, or returns home in a few hours on his own steam to eat, the spectacle he presents is one of intolerable humiliation and shame.

He is not merely crestfallen. He is abjectly embarrassed and profoundly penitent.

He will not look you in the eye. He will not stand up. He is limp with remorse and contrition.

You feel sorry for him. You are embarrassed by such abasement and prostration. He is a big dog and normally of a natural dignity, and this appearance of apology and servility is inharmonious.

He confesses in every line of his body and every flicker of his downcast eyes that he has committed a wrong of which he will never be guilty again. Ten minutes later he is on his way once more to forbidden pastures.

Gyp the Blood

AUGUST 18, 1953

Our house today is lacking some of the cheer and liveliness it has had for the last fifteen years. Gyp the Blood is dead. When an old and well-loved dog dies, the home where he passed his days is not merely bereaved and saddened. Its familiar routine is disarrayed. The rooms he used to inhabit seem unnaturally barren, empty, and still.

I miss the noise of Gyp's bark, the sound of his feeding, the animated presence of his body, which he habitually disposed in such places as required you to walk around him or jump over him. I even miss the murmur of his snoring, which he practiced almost continuously in his last years.

People who do not keep dogs, or other animal pets, are inclined to think that the sentimentality with which they are often treated is mawkish. They do not understand. But every child understands.

Dogs have character and individuality which are as clearly defined as the personality of a human being who sets himself above them by some peculiar process of logic which is not clear or provable.

Gyp was naive in some ways. It took him a long time to discover that birds fly and that he couldn't follow. He was also intelligent in his way and he had a singular nobility.

I never saw him beg or plead. He demanded his rights and he accepted them as his due. He was essentially affectionate, but slow to show affection. I never saw him lick a hand or ask to be petted.

Although he was exceedingly friendly he never bowed to a friend or succumbed to an enemy. Now and then he would get into fights with other dogs who invaded the home provinces, which he thought of as his own. He never bit a dog or a man.

In the case of dogs, he merely bowled them over with his legs and then looked surprised and disconcerted at their retreat. There was no ill nature in him whatever. He always seemed disappointed with the curious fallibility of dogs and mankind.

I watched his career for fifteen years, which is a very long life span for a dog. The last years were not cheering. It is disturbing to see a noble dog lose his nobility because of the stern and dreadful oppressions of time.

Gyp lost much of his hearing, which was so extraordinarily acute in his youth. He had no command of his legs, which often buckled under him. His hind legs were completely unreliable. Then he fell and broke one of his forelegs. That was the end.

He couldn't walk without being picked up and he was very heavy. When he was unsteadily on his feet he would break down, and he could not navigate the few steps to the yard without falling.

I know of nothing more touching than the sad eyes with which he expressed his shame and wonderment that he could no longer do what he had done all his life. His eyes will haunt me to the end of my time. They were not pleading or resentful. They were wondering, uncomprehending, and pained.

We had such fun in the old days. Bounce him a ball and he would attack it with delight and fury. The first real intimation I had of his age and illness occurred not long ago when I bounced a ball before him and he was not interested. The frolic had gone out of him. He had lost the capacity for play and nonsense. That is a good time to die.

But it is difficult to reconcile yourself to death. It is inevitable and it always seems so improbable.

I have written several columns about Gyp the Blood. I must remind you that he was born in Sing Sing Prison. That was the reason we named him Gyp the Blood. The name was extremely inappropriate.

He was a gentle dog, a sweet dog, a courageous and self-respecting being. His goodness was so evident that it was understood by the neighborhood children, who loved him, and his death will be mourned no less by them than by us who fed and nourished him from his youth to his decay and who now feel that the halls are dismally empty where he once played and slept.

SIX

The Fiber of Society

Charity: A Lesson in Sociology for Two Bits

JANUARY 4, 1936

When he approached me on Euclid Avenue, I knew he was a panhandler before he opened his mouth. He was a respectably dressed and well-shaved fellow of middle years, but he had the oblique and apologetic manner of a man about to ask a favor which he is afraid will be refused.

"Can you," he said, "let me have two bits for a room?"

The touch was a little unusual. Ordinarily a panhandler asks for a dime, or a cup of coffee, or streetcar fare to a destination where somebody has promised him a job.

I looked at the two-bits mendicant again. He had a bronzed, wrinkled face, very compact and almost chinless. The visage and the alert, nervous eyes gave him a birdlike appearance.

"Why do you need two bits for a room?" I asked. "You know you can sleep at Wayfarers Lodge for nothing."

His face became suddenly earnest and the restless eyes had a hurt look.

"I know, buddy," he said. "But you wouldn't like it there. They get you up at four o'clock in the morning and you have to sit around for hours waiting for breakfast."

I reflected that I wouldn't like it at all.

"But why," I asked, "do they get you up at four in the morning?"

The panhandler seemed pleased with the question. It was obviously a matter that perplexed and interested him and he started walking along at my side, his face furrowed with the intensity of his thought.

"Well, you see some of the fellows there work on the PWA.

They have to get up early. Some of the jobs are out in the suburbs, I guess, and it takes a long time to get there. So they
make us all get up at the same time. I don't know why they
do it.

"It ain't no place to sleep. Some of the fellows there is pretty
tough, too. I don't like to be around where they are.

"I was sitting there one day, drinking my coffee in the morning and there was a colored fellow sitting across from me, a
big fellow. He kept looking at me kind of funny and wildlike.
Then he says to me, 'Quit looking at me or I'll sling this coffee
cup in your face.'

"I wasn't looking at him at all. I was just sittin' there drinking
my coffee. I didn't say nothing, just kept on eating. Then he
slung his cup of coffee at me. Hit me over the eye, and the
coffee spilled down my face.

"They get funny, you know, them fellows at the Wayfarers,
just sitting around all day and thinkin'. Kinda goes to their head
and they ain't right and you can't tell what they're gonna do. I
don't like to go there. I can get me a clean room for two bits,
where there ain't nobody botherin' and wanting to pick a fight."

The lesson in sociology and psychology was worth more than
a quarter, and we parted friends.

I don't know how much of a fraud that panhandler was. He
was not drinking but the veins in his nose suggested that he
was no stranger to the bottle and he may have wanted the two
bits, not for a room, but for the varnish remover that brings
dreams.

It doesn't make much difference. For there was merit in his
argument, if not in him, and truth in the general situation he
depicted, if not in the incidents he cited.

Among these derelicts who find lodging on the bunks in charity hostelries, there must be many who have self-respect, who
are aware of the meanness of their surroundings, who have
hope and ambition and are conscious of a degradation which is
not of their own making.

Public charity makes no distinction between them and the

socially useless, between the fellow desperately down on his luck and the congenital bums, between the normally clean and the normally dirty, between the mentally alert and the feeble-witted who have just brains enough to keep out of institutions but not enough to be responsible members of society. When they reach a certain dire economic situation they are all listed in the same category.

I don't know which is the more pathetic, the man accidentally forced into these public lodgings who retains his sensitiveness and his hope, or the sodden, insensible, lethargic fellow who gets there by a combination of economic circumstances and his own nature and who has lost even such capacity for feeling as is involved in despair.

The first suffers the most, but the last may have more essential pathos because his lot seems so completely irremediable.

Law: Faith in Legislation

JANUARY 10, 1936

As a minor contribution to the current confusion, I should like to horn in with some reflections of a layman about the law. When the average citizen is not annoyed by traffic regulations or in the jug as a result of some misdemeanor, he is likely to think of the law as a cold and lofty abstraction.

He regards it more or less instinctively as something above himself and above the ordinary world, something framed im-partially and representing an indisputable wisdom. I am speak-ing of law as a whole, not of specific legislative acts.

An ordinarily reputable citizen may strenuously object to certain laws but his respect for law as a theory amounts to veneration. His trust in law is so complete that he habitually tries to correct any evil, no matter how essentially incorrigible it may be, by passing a law.

Lawbooks are cluttered with useless and unenforceable statutes which are a tribute to the naive and idealistic belief of the ordinary man in the power and virtue of law.

I don't question the social usefulness of that faith. But it seems to me that the premises on which it is based are not solid.

The law is neither a panacea nor a mysterious abstraction arrived at by cold and scientific processes, guaranteeing a kind of final wisdom and infallibility. It is, in practice, a compromise arranged by commonplace men and filtered through courts which are composed of other humans subject to the limitations, the prejudices, the environmental associations of ordinary humanity.

That goes for the Supreme Court of the United States. The justices of the highest tribunal are selected with the most scrupulous care from among the specially learned, well ripened in years and experience. They are lawyers of the highest repute, and their decisions are final.

Since they are such men, and since their power is so great, we surround them with the trappings befitting high rank. The new Supreme Court Building is palatially imposing. The processes of the court which sits there are conducted with singular and special dignity.

An aura of awe environs the elderly justices and their proceedings. The decisions they reach are received not only as absolute and unappealable, which they are; they are received as the pure distillation of law, arrived at by serene and immutable logic, freed from the personal equation and representing the utmost in human wisdom and detachment.

Now the fact is that no such distillation is possible and no such detachment exists, even in the Supreme Court of the United States. The decisions of the great and learned justices are governed as the decisions of lesser men are governed, by mood, by the sum of their individual experiences and sympathies.

The theory is that they reverse or approve laws according to a purely logical, impartial, and scientific interpretation of the Constitution. No such thing is humanly possible. The justices of the Supreme Court do not interpret the Constitution; they interpret their temperaments in terms of the Constitution, for they are men, not gods.

All this is obvious, in a way. Again and again the Supreme Court has split between groups that are usually recognized as representing the conservative and liberal elements in its membership.

Presumably they are all equally learned in the law. The division comes obviously not from disagreement about the law but from a disparity between the temperaments and natures of the elderly gentlemen who interpret the law.

The Supreme Court's decision in the AAA case found the often liberal Justice Roberts delivering the decision which invalidated the law, but Justices Brandeis, Cardozo, and Stone were in their usual corner.

If you read the majority and the minority decisions even halfway through, it was obvious that they were not so much coldly analytical interpretations of the rights of Congress under the Constitution as they were the reflections of the sympathies and emotions of men of varying natures and outlook.

The strongest criticism is that the Court's decision is likely to have come from its own minority membership.

"It is a contradiction in terms," reads the dissenting opinion, "to say that there is power to spend for the national welfare, while rejecting any power to impose conditions reasonably adapted to the attainment of the end which alone would justify the expenditure."

In different words, the decision of the Supreme Court is illogical and unreasonable from the viewpoint of three of the men who compose the court.

When that is the view of three members of the highest tribunal about the processes that finally determine what the law shall be, an ordinary citizen may be excused for failing to see the infallibility and the pure, solemn dispassionateness of the law as finally written.

Laws are made in haste and interpreted at leisure by old

men who take their ease in slippers and are subject to colds and all of the usual frailties and infirmities of mankind.

I have no moral to draw except to say that since laws are the product of individual temperament, we ought not to be satisfied to know that a candidate for the Supreme Court is a great lawyer and an honest man. We ought to know what he eats and what he reads, what view he takes of his fellow men and what, in short, he is as a human being.

Schools

MARCH 1, 1939

We are hearing a lot about education this week through the programs of the American Association of School Administrators. A layman hesitates to speak when the experts are talking but, after all, laymen are exposed to education and they constitute the raw material for its mills.

We can all speak with the modest authority of that character quoted by George Ade: " 'Whom are you?' he said, for he had been to night school."

Here are some of the questions that the teachers stir up in the mind of an old night-school boy: First, what proportion of the population is capable of education in any genuine sense? It has sometimes seemed to me that the capacity for education is as special, say, as a talent for playing the piano.

Real education requires a lively intellectual curiosity, a strong and unremitting interest in all that concerns human life. It demands industry, concentration, and a capacity for abstract thought, philosophic contemplation, and logical deduction. Out of 1,000 people what percentage have such faculties? Any teacher will tell you that he knows large numbers of students who have not the first elemental qualification for education, which is simply a desire to learn. Yet our educational system, so far as I am acquainted with it, proceeds on the theory that all people are educable and all of them are equally educable.

Of course, it is not necessary to the successful operation of an orderly and civilized society that every citizen be a triumph of the higher learning. But the kind of education that enables people to observe concrete political facts and come to wise and logical decisions about them is essential to the effective functioning of democracy.

Our founding fathers had great hope in this respect. Thomas Jefferson set more store on the value of widespread education in preserving democratic institutions.

"By far the most important bill in our whole code," he wrote, "is that for the diffusion of knowledge among the people. No other sure foundation can be devised for the preservation of freedom and happiness . . . Enlighten the people generally and tyranny and oppression of both mind and body will vanish."

We have made immense progress in popular education since his day, but is democracy any more secure? I pessimistically suspect that, as a people, we are misled by frauds and are duped by nonsense about as readily as we ever were, and the shadow of tyranny and oppression is still with us.

As democrats we must believe in the most widespread education, but it might be salutary to remember that the process is slower and more beset with difficulties than the founders of the republic supposed.

Another thought brought up by the presence here of the schoolmen is that our system of instruction seems generally to assume that education is something acquired during a fixed period of years in certain institutions devoted to pedagogy. Emerson expresses it rather too forcefully: "We are shut up in schools and colleges and recitation rooms for ten or fifteen years, and come out at last with a bag of wind, a memory of words, and do not know a thing."

Well, something does stick. A stimulating teacher shows us a sudden glimpse into an undreamed-of world of beauty. Or a curiosity is aroused that sends us delving for ourselves into some fascinating field of knowledge. Even if we are only faintly brushed by scholastic education we are not the same afterward.

But you cannot separate school from life. Education is not something in a vacuum that you touch reluctantly for a few school years and then forget about. It is a continuous process coeval with the life of an individual from cradle to grave. Or it should be.

Schools are a preparation for education. Their true function is not so much to impart knowledge as to create or encourage a capacity for independent thought and to lay the groundwork for understanding and reflection, which are the most enduring of human joys and the most valuable of the friends of human freedom.

Lost Duty

NOVEMBER 24, 1939

About twenty years ago, Kin Hubbard, the Hoosier humorist, made a joke which has stuck in my mind. I don't remember the precise words, but it went something like this: "Pinky Kerr's automobile broke down while he was taking his mother to the poorhouse."

In those days that was immensely funny. What made it funny was the absurdity and irony of the willingness of a man to haul his mother to the poorhouse while he was rich enough to own an automobile. People didn't do that sort of thing then. At least decent, normal people didn't.

Families were united by the closest moral ties. Parents cared for their children until the children were able to work and earn a living. When the parents grew old and were no longer able to take care of themselves the children repaid the debt they owed by supporting their parents, just as the parents had supported them.

There was no feeling of sacrifice on either side. People were proud and happy to do what was so obviously right and natural.

The family was a conception that involved reciprocal responsibilities for all of its members, and the first, most inescapable of these responsibilities was the duty of son and daughter to take care of the old folk when age and poverty set in upon them.

An automobile was a sybaritic indulgence. Certainly no normal son would dream of buying an automobile unless he had enough means left over to support his parents if they needed support. If he were to permit himself such an extravagance while his parents were in want, he would be an object of ridicule and contempt wherever he was known.

That feeling of family responsibility has largely disappeared from our social consciousness. Families which maintain automobiles include the poorest in the community.

Hundreds of automobile owners in every large center are people who are not able to keep themselves in food and clothing without the aid of the state, or without what used to be known as public charity, which every self-respecting man disliked and refused as long as he had a cent in his pocket.

Standards of living, of course, have changed in the last twenty years and mechanical progress has brought about certain shifts. But what has changed more than these, I imagine, is the character of our moral fiber.

People do not accept responsibilities as they once did. They frequently neglect so traditional and primary a responsibility as the duty of the family to care for its elder members in sickness and need, a duty which is recognized by the most primitive societies.

They will not make the sacrifices which normally accompany human life and which, indeed, even many animals make.

We live in times when millions are jobless and many of the young are not able to take care of their needy old folk. But millions of others who are quite able to do so don't wish to.

They could manage it, perhaps, by selling the car, or buying a cheaper one, or cutting down somewhere on cigarettes or beer or the various expenditures necessary to a "good time." They prefer to keep the car, have their fun, and let the old people shift for themselves.

Or they expect the community to support them. The money which they refuse their old folk is supposed to be gathered from the pockets of strangers, and the responsibility which they reject is saddled on the general public.

This procedure is viewed not as evasion of personal duty, not even as a public philanthropy, but as the materialization of a natural right which will somehow be helpful to the whole of society.

It is a comforting philosophy. The young are relieved of responsibility for their needy parents as a matter of justice and, somehow, to the benefit of the state which takes the load off their shoulders.

The Death Penalty

MAY 27, 1949

The Ohio House of Representatives this week passed a bill abolishing capital punishment. If the Senate concurs, the penalty in Ohio for first-degree murder will not be death in the electric chair but ninety-nine years at hard labor behind bars.

I am not altogether able to understand why it is considered more merciful to condemn a man to spend all his remaining days behind bars than it is to release him painlessly from a life which could only be unceasing drudgery, repression, and dreariness. But people have been debating the moral aspects of capital punishment for centuries and coming to conflicting conclusions.

In my high-school years, which were not yesterday, I was a member of a debating team which argued this issue in many school auditoriums with all the ferocious fervor and the sub-lime wisdom of sixteen-year-old boys.

The general tendency through recent centuries has been to-ward reducing the number of crimes legally punishable by the death penalty, and some of the most enlightened countries in Europe have abolished it altogether. No longer ago than the beginning of the nineteenth century, all felonies committed in England were punishable by death.

More than two hundred crimes were once capital offenses under British law. Men were executed for minor law violations which would now be punished by thirty days in jail.

The death penalty is now exacted in Britain for only four crimes: murder, high treason, destruction of dockyards, and piracy, with violence, on the high seas—the last crime not now giving much trouble to the authorities. Practically speaking, capital punishment in England is administered only to murderers, though Roger Casement was hanged for treason in 1916.

Murder is the only crime punishable by death in most coun-tries and States, or it was until the late war and the upsurge of Fascism and Communism and the general disturbances which precipitated some kind of martial law in many countries.

I suppose posterity will find our practice of legally killing murderers as barbarous as we now find the older custom of killing thieves or hanging prostitutes or burning witches. Yet there is something deep and probably ineradicable in the human make-up which demands a life for a life.

Some crimes are so shocking and ruthless and horrifying that they outrage the public feeling and give rise to an emo-tional state which is probably rooted partly in fear, disgust, and a desire for revenge, together with a feeling that some-how a wrong must be righted and it can not be righted without dealing out to the criminal the final violence he has inflicted on another.

We do not know what a more advanced civilization will think of this attitude. I hazard the guess that most criminals are mentally ill and that crime will one day be recognized as the product of an illness.

In my early days, drunkenness was thought of as a moral weakness and a habitual drunk was considered to be a bum who deliberately made himself what he was. It is now generally accepted that drunkenness is an illness which can be cured by medical treatment or psychological regeneration.

Will the same change of thought occur in relation to the habitual criminal? There is some evidence to suggest that it will.

That supposition does not necessarily mean that a better ordered society than the one in which we live will be softer in its treatment of habitual criminals. It may mean that the professional criminal will be treated as an implacable and irreformable enemy of society, as many of his kind seem to be.

As such, he might be quietly removed from a world to which he is a menace, but without incurring the moral condemnation which now attaches to him and without the involvement of the attitude of revenge which is now so strong in our dealings with criminals.

If he is mentally ill he is not morally responsible. But if he is ill and the illness drives him to do what he does, that illness is dangerous to himself and to society.

I can imagine a civilization which would be unhypocritical enough to say, "This man is a professional criminal and as such he is necessarily ill or dangerously abnormal. He is of no use to himself or the world. Let him be quietly removed. Don't make a living ghost of him by keeping him locked up the rest of his life. And don't think of him as a moral blackguard getting his just deserts and doomed to burn in hell, but remember that, but for a quirk in the mind, he might be you or me or any man."

None of us know, but it is reasonably possible that society someday will take that attitude.

It is not the death penalty which is so essentially unmerciful or barbaric. It is the assumption we make that we understand the reasons for crime and the undercurrent of revenge that underlies the punishment meted out.

Christmas

DECEMBER 27, 1951

Is it not possible that we overdo the Christmas spirit? I am writing this at about one in the morning following the Christmas holiday. I have listened to perhaps a dozen radio programs. Two or three of them presented Santa Claus as a criminal.

In one melodrama he was a killer who masqueraded as Saint Nicholas. In another he was a killer who got batted around and ended in misfortune.

The producers of these crime plays obviously felt that they had to make some use of Santa Claus as a contribution to the Christmas spirit. I think it is vulgar and absurd to lug in Santa Claus where he does not belong.

Practically all of the radio programs to which I listened during the eve and day of Christmas worked Santa Claus into the act, and the result was sometimes painful because of the incongruity with the general theme and because the programs so obviously represented a commercial use of the Christmas spirit.

We vulgarize Christmas. For the most part, we celebrate it in the buying and dispatch of Christmas cards and the presentation to our friends of more valuable gifts.

I used to have some resentment against the custom of exchanging greeting cards, thinking it silly and meaningless. I don't have that feeling now.

Christmas cards are a kind of apology for neglect of our friends during the months preceding the holidays. We don't write, as we should, and we make faint amends with a picture post card. These cards are getting more varied and attractive year after year.

I admit that the printed cards are more fluent and appropriate in expression than the words which would probably be used by an average person. Yet I prefer the kindly and informal messages which are often subscribed in handwriting to a Christmas card.

I think the general commercialization of the life of Christ at this time is regrettable and perhaps not far short of the sacrilegious. Nearly everybody who has something to sell makes use of Christ.

In the last few days I have heard many programs geared in a cheap way to the Christmas idea. Why would we encourage incompetence, vulgarity, and needless repetition in the radio presentation of the spirit of Christmas?

Christmas is a holy day in Christian theology and in the life of man almost everywhere. Why should it be used for casual commercialization in a radio program, and why should every producer think he must work into his program some reference to Christmas, no matter how absurdly irrelevant it is to the kind of entertainment he supplies?

In my mind our purveyors of popular entertainment overdo Christmas. In paying lip tribute to it with such incessant determination they overlook its essence. They make a commercial orgy of what should be celebrated in the heart. They are perfunctory and opportunistic about something which is deep and sacred in the mind of mankind.

But that is not chiefly what I have in mind. I am thinking of the intense emphasis we put on the Christmas spirit for a few days and then go about living our lives in the usual way, which, as Thoreau says, is a kind of quiet desperation. Everybody is a little uplifted by the Christmas holidays. The good cheer is real. Then we sink into our shells. Christmas should not exist for a day and the spirit it represents should not be temporary.

I imagine that the excessive emphasis we put on the celebration of the season is partly responsible for the decline and sourness in mood and attitude which we feel later.

Hospitals

FEBRUARY 26, 1958

They say that a long siege of illness strengthens the character. It may be so when the victim is of a naturally saintly disposition. For the generality of men, who are not composed of the stuff that makes cathedral sounding boards, the onslaught of physical disorders is likely to have an opposite effect.

They do not beget patience and fortitude. They shorten tempers, induce apathy, and tend to create a jaundiced view of the world and the goodly pleasures it affords. I hope that it is not altogether true in my case. But I must confess that I can see no improvement in my character.

While it can not be proved that illness elevates the character of its victim, it does seem to improve the character of his friends. Or, at least, it brings out the best in them. They are busy people, preoccupied with their own affairs. You may not have seen them for months, or heard from them. Yet when you are stricken with some disability, they come forward with all sorts of kindnesses.

They visit the sickroom where you are confined, and that is not an easy mission, for a sickroom is not a cheerful place. They telephone. They write. They send you books, flowers, phonograph records, and culinary delicacies. They wish you well in every possible way. There is nothing they will not do to insure your comfort and to give good cheer.

Friends are the greatest treasure that life affords and the treasure is multiplied when illness strikes. It is impossible not to be warmed and heartened by the revelation they make of human kindness and amiability.

I imagine that nearly everybody who has been seriously ill for any considerable length of time has been touched by the kindness his misfortune generates and discloses. He may be a lonely man with few friends. But illness will bring out people who wish him well and who are solicitous of his comfort.

If he is confined in a hospital he will have the attention of doctors, interns, orderlies, nurses, student nurses, and attendants of all kinds, from the technicians who draw drops of blood from his veins to the women who bring his meals. These people deal with the sick and the infirm day after day as a duty and a means of livelihood.

You would suppose that the unremitting procession of patients they see and care for would dull their sensibilities to the sight of suffering and cause them to lose awareness of the individual in the general flow of the nameless ill, changing every day but still the same. It has always surprised me to observe that the humblest patient in a large hospital is viewed and treated, not as an anonymous member of an ailing multitude but as a person and a fellow creature.

While I was hospitalized, the duchess had her dinner in the hospital restaurant. One evening she shared a table with a nurse we had known for several years. The nurse was weeping.

It seemed that one of her patients was suffering dreadfully and likely to die. She was so disturbed by the misfortune of this patient, whom she had known for a few days only, that she was unable to eat her dinner, and she had been a nurse for years and was well acquainted with the sight of suffering and the imminence of death.

I admire these people who choose to spend their lives ministering to the ill. It requires a sense of dedication, for the ill are not usually cheerful company, and succoring them involves some distasteful duties and the continuous observation of humanity in discomfort or pain. The mere presence of hospital ministrants helps to heal the patient.

For the sick unconsciously feed on the health and vitality of the people who attend them. The brisk, starched, and glittering nurse brings more than a thermometer when she enters the sickroom. She brings a vision of the outside world of energy and high spirits and she restores hope of rejoining that world. I have formed some good and lasting friendships among the members of a hospital staff.

I have heard of sick people who are loath to leave a hospital and would like to return if they could. They enjoy the sense of security, the attentiveness, and the freedom from responsibility which comfort a hospital patient.

I understand their feeling but I do not share it. The world of the hospital is not a normal world and too much of it is uncomfortable, distressing, or painful.

The days of feeding through the veins, which now seem to follow automatically after major surgery, are distinctly and memorably unpleasant. The liquid falls drop by drop from a receptacle placed at the side of the bed above the patient's body. It takes several hours to eat a meal in this strange fashion.

Another unpleasantness which hospital patients remember is the frequent use of the needle to draw blood samples or to inject medicament. You eventually have the false impression that you are being used as a pincushion and made to undergo the sufferings of Saint Sebastian, who was martyred by a shower of arrows shot into his body and who remains today the patron saint of pinmakers.

The only comfort you can extract from such hospital dolors is that you probably wouldn't be alive if you hadn't been submitted to them.

SEVEN

The Wandering Journalist

The Birthplace of Lenin

AUGUST 28, 1932

On the Volga—There was a stir of excitement among the three or four foreigners aboard the *Spartacus* on the morning when we reached the little town where Lenin was born. It is difficult for one who has never wiped the dust of Russia from his shoes to understand the veneration in which Lenin's name and memory is held among his countrymen.

He gathers up in his single person the worship appropriate to the founder of a state, to the first warrior, to the great martyr, to the creator of a new religion and a new world.

In a nation that systematically opposes the idea of the supernatural and the theory of the importance of individual genius Lenin diverts and intensifies the natural will of mankind to erect heroes and to create gods. It is true in a sense that Lenin is the new deity and the reformed gospel in Muscovy. He has already become a little fabulous and legendary.

His likenesses are everywhere in paint, bronze, marble, plaster, and they begin to become misty and contradictory. In one place you will see the image of the stern and vengeful Lenin, the warring, ascetic, unappeasable Lenin who drove the moneylenders from the temple of capitalism. In another image your eyes will be taken by the tender, benign, merciful Lenin, surrounded by children which he suffered to come unto him.

Idealization is manifest in nearly all these pictures and busts. Lenin has become not merely a national hero, but a symbol of leadership, of tenderness, of power, of spiritual renaissance.

With these reflections in mind, I was surprised that the Russians aboard the *Spartacus* showed no particular interest when docked at the town where Lenin was born and where he lived his youthful years. Among the several hundred passengers there

191

were only four of us who made the uphill pilgrimage to Lenin's boyhood dwelling place. All of us, with the exception of an interpreter, were foreigners.

The town looks bleak and shabby from the river valley, a collection of wooden shacks thrown up on a windy hill, surrounded by mud. We made our way painfully through winding roads thick with mud and cut by ravines. An intelligent man, you figured, would naturally become a revolutionary if he had to climb these wretched hills every day.

Once over the hill and into the town itself the prospect changes. Ulyanovsk, which is the new name of Lenin's birthplace, is much larger than it looks from the river. It is not the small village it seems, but a provincial Russian town, gloomy and poor in the dusk of a late afternoon, but sizable and evidencing some moderate comfortableness of living.

We passed row after row of square, yellow, wooden houses, all alike. A narrowly provincial air stamped everything. The desolation, the smugness, and the grooved respectability of the small life in such a place must have been conducive to rebellion. It reminded you of the little Norwegian town that produced another great dissenter, Henrik Ibsen.

We had a slight shock when we asked a small boy in a field to direct us to Lenin's house and he looked at us in wonder and answered that he didn't know. Later, we had to ask the same question of at least a dozen townsmen of Lenin's and it was evident that at least half of them did not know or had only the vaguest idea.

A young man and woman tittered mockingly when we asked the way to Lenin's house. It took us a moment to understand that they were not laughing at the question but at us, at our strange clothes and weird manners.

We were at least an hour in reaching our destination and we began to realize why the Russians aboard the steamer had hesitated to make the pilgrimage since the steamer's stay was short.

Lenin's house is a yellowish, wooden cottage, squat, substantial, edging a narrow sidewalk, bordered by trees. An electric lamp glows above the door distinguishing the house from its neighbors. Two men were sitting on the doorstep, unconcernedly smoking cigarettes. We aroused the caretaker who lived somewhere in the rear.

He took us through the kitchen into the living room. A Red soldier came out from nowhere. He was the sentry.

The house is preserved as it was when Lenin lived there as a boy.

A fine grand piano ornaments the spacious living room. The chairs and other furnishings are tasteful, solid, and almost rich. The large dining room, with its massive table, desk, and chairs, is comfortable and inviting.

It came over one with a start that this large, well-lighted, almost luxurious home was probably a typical Russian bourgeois background. It had housed the boy who lived to destroy the class of which it was representative.

Lenin is characteristically pictured as a workingman, loosely dressed, calloused of hands, wearing a cap. This was no workingman's home. It was the home of a well-situated, cultivated, intellectual or bourgeois family. The fine piano, the books opened on the dining room table, everything about the place attested to intellectual and cultural preoccupations of the people it once housed. I remembered that Lenin's father had been a high-school professor.

It was strange that a man produced from such a background should so intimately merge his personality with the toilers in factories and mines that he became not only one of them but their mouthpiece and their symbol. Strange, too, that the people he grew to suspect and distrust the most were the intellectuals, the people who came from precisely his own background, the people nourished by his own literature, his own ideas, his own kind of culture.

It was the same contradiction you saw in his hands as he lies in the Moscow mausoleum, the fine, sensitive, delicate, fastidious hands, the hands of an aesthete, of an aristocrat by blood and temperament. These hands when they are represented by artists of the regime are clenched and strong and blunt, as if they were made to idealize muscularity and manual toil.

But here in these rooms was the echo of the real Lenin, the pale intellectual, brooding over his books, listening to Chopin, drinking in the traditional culture of his day, overhearing the talk of his professorial father and his well-read mother.

We went upstairs to the whitewashed half-story rooms where the family slept. Books are scattered about as they were left. In Lenin's mother's room I picked up a volume of Shakespeare, a novel by Schiller, a work of Goethe.

Lenin's own reading was almost as conventionally classical. Well-bound books lie on his bedroom table. I could identify a novel by Dostoevski, a volume by Turgenev. There was also a book about hunting.

Lenin, like any boy of his age, must have wandered around in the neighboring countryside looking for rabbits with a gun. He lived to hunt bigger game.

We left by way of the kitchen. The Red soldier on sentry duty there was seated on a kitchen chair and not averse to accepting an American cigarette, which he didn't know how to light because, unlike Russian cigarettes, it contained tobacco at both ends.

It was late at night and Ulyanovsk looked more forlorn and oppressive than ever as we walked back to the steamer, got lost in the mud, and finally found our way down to the railway tracks to the *Spartacus* which had begun to shake her moorings.

We passed later through many villages and several large towns but they merge in memory without much distinction, hot, shabby, poor, busy, overcrowded.

Kazan, Samara, Saratov. What sounding, mellifluous names these are, singing remote legends of misty tribes! Today it is not the music of the past that comes from them, but the hum of a new industrial life trying impatiently to be born.

Samara is bursting with new manufactories for the production of asphalt and cement, substances of which its own streets stand in the direst need.

In Saratov the local interpreter blushes a little because Saratov's chief product is not airplanes or tractors but culture. There are four universities in Saratov, thirty-six schools, twenty-six technical schools, and illiteracy has been 100 per cent eliminated. A town must be proud of something, and Saratov is proud because its inhabitants have learned to spell out words and woo the demon that lurks in ink.

I remember vividly our few hours in Samara. We walked through the town to a park, had a swim in the Volga, and rowed back to the steamer in a flat-bottomed boat with six oars that became heavier every time they struck the water.

Our interpreter was an unusually intelligent young fellow of about twenty who talked painful but precise English. I was curious about his background.

"Seven years ago," he said, "I was one of Russia's thousands of homeless boys. I have no memory of either father or mother. They were probably killed in the revolution. I ran wild like an animal, picking up food where I could and sleeping in passageways or behind a fence. They caught me and put me in the Red navy. I served my time. They sent me to Moscow to learn languages. I studied English and I got this job as interpreter. It's only temporary. I don't know what I want to do, but I first want a good university education."

I have seen bands of these homeless boys, dirty, patched, half-starved waifs, living like alley cats, ready to beg or steal or run.

It was incredible that this well-mannered, cleanly dressed, educated, thoughtful young fellow could have come so short a time ago from that wretched condition of life.

This was a more important and promising miracle, one felt, than the creation of a new factory out of brick and steel.

We are one passenger less today. A peasant enjoying an excess of vodka fell overboard last night. Boats were lowered and they circled around for an hour before giving up to the river its victim. Somewhere a family is bereaved, but it is hard to attach an individual life to these massed millions of faces as they pass before you in a long Russian journey. They merge into the mystery and vastness of Russia itself.

War-Scarred Barcelona

JULY 13, 1937

Barcelona—The reality of the terror that shook Barcelona to its foundations comes home to you when you visit the churches. You read of these things in the newspapers, but they seem remote and nightmarish and hard to credit because they do not conform to what we know of human nature, or like to think of it. Whatever men believe, and however they hate, why should they expend their fury destroying the pillars and stones that other men have erected to honor what seems to them the highest truth and beauty?

Nothing that happened in Russia during years of bitter struggle is equal to the savagery and ferocity of what has occurred here within a few months. I hired an automobile the other day and visited about ten churches.

They were all gutted by fire, some of them totally destroyed, a few capable of being repaired. The doors of each, where there was enough of them left to matter, were walled up with bricks. A half block from my hotel was a fine church building. Its outside walls are still intact. They are covered with billboards advertising anarchistic meetings and other political activities.

The church looks as if it had been abandoned for years and had passed generations ago out of the minds of men. Only a few months ago it was warm with life, and the pious came by thousands on Sunday to worship within its walls.

Now its roof has been completely burned away and rain

drips down on the sacred paintings and what is left of the statuary. At the door of the church is a large sculptured figure of Christ with arms extended in welcome to the faithful. Somebody has put a red flag in His hands. "Death to the Fascists" is the inscription on the flag.

Nobody stops to stare, nobody notes the incongruity between the serenity of the figure and the belligerence of the banner, nobody bothers either to look at the flag or to take it down. The indifference, the neglect, the lack of awareness seems sinister and unnatural.

There is no evidence of resentment among the people who pass, nor any sign of interest. It is as if the mutilated church belonged to an era long past and half-forgotten and had no present existence.

I asked my interpreter the name of this once imposing church. He didn't know. He had forgotten or he thought it wiser not to remember.

If there is a church standing whole in Barcelona I have not seen it. They say that not all of them were burned, but I have seen none that are not blackened with smoke around the windows.

The roofs are off most of them. A few were so badly burned that nothing is left except an unrecognizable mass of debris.

I went up the winding road that leads to Mount Tibidabo, the highest point in the environs of Barcelona. The view over the city is magnificent.

A few years ago a great church was built on the top of the mountain. It was surmounted by a tall image of Christ extending his hands in blessing over the city that stretched out below. The sacred figure has been knocked down.

The church itself was burned but resisted the fire. It is now used as living quarters for the members of an anarchist organization.

When we passed the portals the other day a phonograph was playing from the nave of the church. My interpreter said it was playing the anarchist marching song. A dozen men could be seen inside the open doors of the church, sitting in their shirt sleeves and smoking.

They had installed a cookstove in the edifice. To provide a vent for the smoke they had rigged up a tin flue, cutting through the façade of the church just above the door. This wall of the church had been decorated with painted figures of Biblical characters. The flue was cut through the body of one of the Apostles.

By climbing on a ledge it was possible to see into the sacristy. It had been burned out but you could still see the blackened remnants of books that had been heaped up and fired but not completely destroyed.

A British newspaperman tells me that he saw eleven churches burning at one time at the height of the Barcelona horror. Many people who were here then will tell you monstrous tales of brutality and madness and you would not believe them except that the evidence of a world reverted to savagery lies before your eyes.

Priests murdered and mutilated, nuns stripped and made to dance in the streets, then burned; the bones of dead monks dug up from their graves and exposed to be kicked around and poked with sticks. These things are real and they happened yesterday, not two thousand years ago.

Friends of the government say the authorities did what they could to prevent these outrages. They say they were committed by irresponsible thugs and scum and the lunatic fringe among the anarchists.

Some say the churches were fortified and that there was firing from them. Such eyewitnesses as I have talked to believe that such charges are ridiculous.

In any case, everybody agrees that thousands were murdered who were not even guilty of so much as an attempt to defend their own lives.

Overt acts have pretty well ceased, largely because all the people suspected of fascist sympathies have been exterminated. But the passions that produced this murderous bestiality have not subsided. I asked my Spanish companion yesterday what would happen now if a priest walked the streets of Barcelona in clerical garb.

"He would be killed before he walked twenty steps," replied my little friend, quite simply as if he were saying something so obvious that it hardly needed saying.

Everywhere it is the indifference that is shocking, the callousness about human life and age-long spiritual values. In front of one of the smaller suburban churches I saw a stone cross that had been knocked from the steeple and thrown to the ground.

It must have been weeks that it had lain there undisturbed and hardly noticed. When I last saw this stone symbol of Christianity a group of children were using it as the base for a game of leapfrog.

Warsaw: City of Squalor and Luxury

JUNE 21, 1939

Warsaw—Even a few days in Warsaw gives you some feeling of the character of Poland which is illuminative of the present crisis. Books and statistics are eloquent about the poverty of the land. But it is its richness and magnificence which first strikes you. Hotels are not numerous, but the Europejski, into which I was ushered, is a model of ostentatious luxury.

It is a huge, tangled pile of ornate rooms, restaurants, tea-rooms, and bars, with a sidewalk terrace café that stretches out for a half block and must be one of the largest in Europe. When one comes in at night, and each of the hundreds of tables is illuminated and every chair is occupied, the café seems dramatically suggestive of luxury and gaiety. It faces a great square, flanked by fine public buildings.

You could easily imagine yourself to be in one of the fashionable quarters of Paris. People are smartly dressed. Jewels and furs are conspicuous. Prices are high.

Menus list every delicacy, including the mysteriously named Ohio cocktail which costs about seventy-five cents.

Everywhere about you in this neighborhood are splendid buildings, handsome boulevards, pleasant parks. Traditions of grandeur, graciousness of living are implicit in these urban scenes in every respect.

Then you walk a few blocks away through the old market and you are in the heart of swarming and squalid slums. There is nothing like them elsewhere in Europe.

People pour down these wretched streets in shoals. The congestion of human life is so great that individuality loses meaning and only the mass exists. It flows in a dark torrent past shabby little shops and holes in the wall where some merchant has set up business with a stock of a dozen loaves of bread or a few apples.

Traders transport their few boxes of merchandise in a horse cab or carry it on their shoulders. Commerce is carried on by the smallest units, divided and redivided until there can be no more than a few cents' profit a day for anyone.

Thousands of the pedestrians on these streets are accoutered in the traditional Jewish manner, long beards, black cloaks, and skullcaps. There is no ghetto here in the sense of a compulsory domicile but the mass of the poorer Jewish population tends to concentrate in particular sections.

With their gentile neighbors, they live in what is obviously the most extreme poverty. Congestion and want and squalor could not be more conspicuously and cruelly evidenced than here in these Warsaw slums.

When you take a horse cab back to the boulevards it is like passing from one world to another. The driver is a rag bag of patches and tatters. For a ride of more than a mile his tariff is approximately ten cents. It is clear that time and labor have little value in this overcrowded country.

It is really two countries. One is the pleasant land of luxurious hotels, fine buildings, rich living, Paris hats, delicate perfumes, high prices, music, and gaiety. The other is a land of shabbiness and want, of ceaseless struggle, not for comforts and success, but for the means to keep alive.

Of course, these contrasts exist in every country and in every city. Here they are sharper, more aggressively visible. Poland is nearer to the feudal age. There is a small class of gentry, much respected, which is the inheritor of the feudal lord's power and wealth.

This class carries on traditions of culture and refinement, fortifies the nationalistic spirit, directs the government, and lives in relative grandeur. Below is the great mass of the population, the peasants, the industrial workers, the petty merchants. They lead narrow and impoverished lives, perhaps without consciousness or resentment, because that is what they have been accustomed to and, in this arrangement of society, classes are more fixed than they are with us and men resign themselves more easily to their lot. If they do not have the comfort of hope they are spared its disappointments.

A newspaperman who spent several months touring the Polish countryside tells me the merchants in some peasant villages are content with, and can live on, a total gross turnover of twenty cents a day. Not twenty cents profit, mind you, but twenty cents in price of the goods sold.

He also tells that the peasants will split a match four times in order to multiply its usefulness. I have heard this story so often that I was impelled to test out its probable veracity by experimentation. I took a match and tried to divide it into four parts in such a way as to preserve the lighting end of each part. It can't be done.

Or if it is within the capacities of a Polish peasant, it is beyond mine. The story may be an illustration of a condition rather than the accurate reporting of a specific fact.

Americans and other foreigners who have lived here over a period of years like the Poles. They find in them a live sensibility, exceptional natural gifts, and a large share of the solid virtues of kindliness and hospitality.

Budapest's Beauty

JULY 9, 1939

Budapest—You may return to Budapest often but you always seem to be seeing the city for the first time. It remains strange and unreal, something dreamed and half forgotten. I was never here before so early in the summer. It can be as hot along the Danube as an Indiana cornfield in August.

Now the daytime weather is neither warm nor cool but so perfect that you are hardly aware of the temperature and every sense is quickened to exterior impressions. At night it is cool, but the air is soft and vaguely scented. It is the right season for seeing Budapest.

Idyllic weather is the only appropriate frame for these urban scenes. They have the character of poetry, of romantic painting, of an old-fashioned stage curtain, of something, at any rate, too lyric and well-ordered for everyday reality.

I am thinking of Margaret Island and, particularly, of the embankment along the Danube known as the Corso. Much of the social life of Budapest centers in these places and the fleeting visitor is hardly aware of any other quarters.

The big hotels are situated along the Corso and there are a couple of fashionable hostelries on Margaret Island. I should counsel the visitor to take a room overlooking the Danube.

It costs twice as much as an equally comfortable room facing the street, but it is worth it. There is no such view as this to be seen from a hotel window anywhere else.

The river at this point is lively with the traffic of ships. At night, the lights of dozens of craft pass and cross in intricate patterns of dancing movement. There is music on the larger passenger ships and the melody comes faintly across the water.

Below is the crowded street where people come to walk or to sit in one of the many sidewalk cafés that line the embankment for blocks without a break. The hum of gay, musical conversation comes up to your window from the street and mingles with the melancholy sweetness of Hungarian melodies played by gypsy bands in a half-dozen nearby cafés.

Across the river is the incredible panorama of Budapest, the lights that stream down the hills, the flaming white of the citadel, the magnificent palace, all floodlighted in such a way as to emphasize the line and form of the pageantry without revealing it entirely, so that the impression remains eerie, shadowy, dreamlike.

I have sung this song before, and I shall spare you further verses, but Budapest affects me as a piano affects some of my bosom friends. They can't look at it without wanting to play a tune on it and they are not satisfied until everybody within range is singing the same tune. I have done, except to add that Budapest makes sweeter harmony than I am accustomed to hearing, or would if I could carry the tune.

These Budapest hotels rate with the best in Europe. They are well built and well run. The atmosphere is friendly.

Americans and English are made to feel especially at home. All the employees of the Corso hostelries speak a few words of English and some of them speak it fluently.

Budapest has some extraordinary natural attractions for visitors and the Hungarians appear to have an aptitude for putting the stranger at his ease. They are like the Viennese in that respect, or the Swiss.

Because of the internal and international situation, many tourists are avoiding Austria and Central Europe generally. Hungary is getting some of this diverted tourist trade and might reasonably be expected to get more.

At the moment, the ordinary Hungarian currency is overvalued and prices are, consequently, somewhat high. The tourist who comes here a few days and exchanges his money within the country gets only five pengös to the dollar. If he sends outside the country for his Hungarian currency, or buys it before coming into Hungary, he may get eight pengös or more for a dollar. That makes a tremendous difference in the cost of living.

The Hungarian tourist trade would obviously benefit from a regularization of the present confused currency situation and the issuance of traveler's checks at reduced rates such as Germany and Italy find profitable.

That delightful garden in the middle of the Danube, Margaret Island, was not as crowded as I have usually found it later in the season. Only a few hardy sun-bathers were to be seen in the elaborate swimming baths where thousands come on hot afternoons.

But there were many people walking the flowered paths and a good crowd was listening to the dance music in the fine outdoor hotel café.

It was disconcerting to see the swastika flying from many of the pavilions on Margaret Island. What had that insignia to do with this peaceful Budapest garden? We learned later that the German flags were flying in honor of the German minister of the interior, Herr Frick, who was visiting Budapest and was scheduled to come to the island.

Over in another part of the city mysterious diplomatic negotiations were going on which might affect the destiny of Hungary and of mankind. Here in this green island there was a beauty and order which seemed deep and timeless, incapable of being touched by the exigencies of statecraft or the intrigues of politicians.

These contrasts impose on you in every prospect. Hungary is not a rich country. Budapest knows the meaning of poverty. Yet what richness of living there is in these fine parks, these pleasant cafés, this magnificent river, this unique and splendid pageantry of hills and lights and palaces and people who stroll by the thousands of a summer night under the trees, listening to music. There is more wealth here than richer nations can know or understand.

Hong Kong

AUGUST 20, 1939

Hong Kong—By daylight the harbor of Hong Kong is disappointing. The green hills of the island are disfigured with parched white splotches, bare and ugly. In the tropical sunlight the buildings along the waterfront look soiled and shabby and even the ships lack color and individuality.

But nightfall wraps the scene in fantastic beauty. The lights pierce the darkness just above sea level and they wind in immense tangled clusters to a mountainous height, following the circuitous roads from the valleys to Victoria Peak, nearly two thousand feet above the water.

These southern skies are thicketed with low-lying stars and the city lamps mingle with the heavenly illumination in a vast and inextricable pattern of flickering light. There is something prepared and artificial about the panorama. Everybody thinks of the resemblance to a mammoth Christmas tree and that is what it is like.

The lights dominate the horizon in every direction and they seem carefully arranged for pictorial effect. It is a conventional kind of beauty, as posed and retouched as a scene on a picture post card, but of its kind it is perfect.

Against this labyrinth of dancing lights, towering to infinity, the island looks rich and fruitful, the buildings have the appearance of castles, and the ships in the harbor are argosies of romance and delight. Hong Kong has what is commonly reputed the second most beautiful harbor in the world, following

Rio de Janeiro, and on a starry night you can not imagine how it can be surpassed.

The barman on the *Felix Roussel* was a connoisseur in departments outside the orbit of his profession.

"Take the ferryboat," he had said, "from Hong Kong to Kowloon on a fine night and you will see the most beautiful spectacle in the world."

I was glad to have followed such spiritual counsel, for if this is not the most enchanting seaport pageantry under the moon, it might well be.

However, there are thorns in the rose and serpents in paradise. I hope I shall remember the beauty of Hong Kong harbor as vividly as the noise in the island's streets, or the bugs, the smells, the heat, the plagues, and the poverty of an overcrowded Chinese city, so comfortable and elegant on one side, so wretched and despairing on the other.

The noise deserves a special chapter. I have never heard city noises in such volume or variety. Barcelona during the civil war period was the noisiest place I had ever known. It was a cemetery at midnight compared with Hong Kong.

The hotel in which I stay is in the center of the city, facing a narrow and busy street, flanked by moderately tall buildings which magnify sound like a megaphone. But even without this natural amplifier, the cacophony which comes up from below would be remarkable in power and diversity.

I have been trying, unsuccessfully, to separate and classify the noises which shatter the air morning and night. The predominant and characteristic note is the sound of wooden shoes on the cement sidewalks.

The Chinese here wear a kind of loose wooden slipper which creates an explosion when it hits the hard walk. It seems to be an indication of independence and manliness to slap the feet down in such a way as to produce a maximum amount of noise.

Young fellows, particularly, make a terrific bang with every step. Three of them walking along together make you think an old-fashioned Fourth of July is coming off. These streets are crowded day and night and the sound of wooden shoes hitting the ground in such numbers is deafening.

Above this steady roar you hear the queer guttural sound of the rickshaw boys warning traffic, or the calls of peddlers, or the voices of the newsboys, and particularly the newswomen, advertising their wares.

Most of the newspaper hawkers in Hong Kong are ancient and pestiferous Chinese dames who tug at your elbows, tickle your nose with newspapers, and split your ears with unholy soprano noises.

The streets sing and screech, they hum and blast. The talk is loud, the spitting, hacking, and coughing is universal and sonorous.

Every automobile horn has a different tone, each more raucous than the next, and they keep blowing without intermission in a weird and diabolic symphony.

Parking is permitted in the street below my window and when music from the hotel dance orchestra stops, it is almost immediately succeeded by the slamming of automobile doors, the shouts of hilarity, the noisy adieus, and usually some forceful if not eloquent profanity and a little minor scuffling and brawling on the part of the European guests.

Sometimes the ordinary noises of wooden shoes, singing, laughing, swearing, hawking, and honking are helped out by artificial aids. About five o'clock the other morning there came an interval of relative quiet which somebody apparently found intolerable, for it was suddenly broken by the sound of exploding firecrackers, small bombs, and toy cannon in the street below.

This world-war effect lasted for about an hour and, at its peak, was powerful enough to shake the plaster from the wall. I learned later that it was a somewhat more than mute testimony to a Chinese fete day.

But the noise is not so disturbing as some other Hong Kong plagues. I don't mean cholera, smallpox, dysentery, or malaria, all of which are epidemic here. If you have luck, these grave ills don't touch you, for they are chiefly confined to the refugees and the unfortunate mass of the Chinese population which lives in dreadfully overcrowded tenements or in the swarming streets of the poorer quarters.

But you can't put your feet down on the scrubbed and shiny floors of your hotel room without great risk of contracting a variety of ringworm pleasantly and euphoniously known as "Hong Kong Foot."

Nearly all Europeans here have, or have had, "Hong Kong Foot" and some of them have had it for eight or ten years.

The tranquillity with which they accept these plagues and nuisances are disconcerting to an outsider. The beds in one of the famous first-class hotels of Hong Kong, into which I was ushered, are infested by a most undesirable insect described as a sand flea. After a few nights on these hospitable mattresses, you are scarred and swollen by flea bites.

At first you try to adopt some defensive measures in the way of insecticides. Then you discover that the walls of the hotel are crawling with millions of the microscopic pests.

The only way to be rid of them would be to tear down the hotel and build a new one. This seems impractical and you resign yourself to the inevitable.

I made a polite complaint to the management in respect to the presence in the hotel rooms of so many uninvited and unwanted guests. He seemed pleased rather than surprised.

"Sand fleas," he said. "No harm. Everybody has sand fleas."

His Oriental face was wreathed in smiles. Sand fleas were something that you accepted gratefully as the bounty of providence.

Beautiful as the island certainly is, all the Europeans and Americans I have met here are looking anxiously forward to their day of release when they can shake the blisters off their Hong Kong feet in some more benevolent climate.

To live here comfortably you need wholly insensitive nerves, or a depth of philosophic resignation possible only to the wisest of men.

Memories

JUNE 20, 1941

They say this war may last for thirty years. I hope not. There are some places I'd like to see again and some pleasures I should like to relive when peace comes to a distracted globe.

I'd like to take breakfast once more in a café on the Ring in Vienna. The coffee "mit Schlag" there was the best in the world. The rolls called "Kipfel" or "Semmel" were of an inimitable tastiness and the boiled eggs, taken whole from their shells, were a high and delectable tribute to the industry of the hen.

But it was not the food, good as it was, which made breakfast in a Viennese street café so pleasant. It was the air of laziness, good nature, and amiability that permeated the place. You could dawdle over breakfast with an easy conscience for dawdling was in the essence of the atmosphere.

The first object the waiter brought you was a newspaper, attached to a holder, which made it no easier to read but prevented you walking away with the day's news. Usually it wasn't the day's news. It was yesterday's news or last week's news.

The English newspapers, printed in Paris or London, were always late coming in and sometimes they didn't come in at all. That was all right.

You read stale news with as much interest as if it were warm from last hour's presses. Time had no urgency in the Vienna that was.

Life was lived in a kind of half dream in which nothing was pressing and little was quite real. You read abstractedly as you drank your morning coffee or you looked out on the street at the passing panorama. It was never hurried and it was a little vague, as something seen in reverie.

I do not know whether Vienna will ever be like that again. But I should like to take breakfast again one day on the Ring when peace comes, or listen to the music in Stadt Park just as dark is falling and the waiters begin to light the lamps on the dining tables ranged on the terrace of the restaurant.

I'd like to be seated once more in a café on the Corso in Budapest, looking over the vista toward the castle, or watching the play of lights from the ships on the Danube, or taking in the lively parade of promenaders on the embankment, listening the while to muted, far-off music of a gypsy violinist.

Budapest has a twilight wonder and sweetness on a summer evening that touches the heart and rings in the memory like an old song.

I should like to walk again along the Champs Elysées of a Sunday afternoon with the street crowded by unhurried people taking the air, with the street cafés filled by chattering and smiling folk and the sun drenching the avenue and the Arc de Triomphe with a hazy golden radiance peculiar to Paris.

I don't insist on Paris of a Sunday afternoon. Weekdays are all right in Paris, or were, and so were the nights.

I'd like to walk again of an evening down the grand boulevards from the Madeleine to the Rue Faubourg Montmartre, passing the dozens of sidewalk cafés, mingling with the most animated street crowd in Europe, listening to that charming sound of commingled talk and music, feeling the strange quality of a Parisian night, mysterious, furtive, yet simple and open, gay and lively, yet sad and quiet and altogether picturesque, heady, and enchanting.

The Kremlin by moonlight has a kind of romantic, half-barbaric beauty which nobody ever forgets. I should like to see it again.

I should like to have tea on the terrace of Moscow's Metropole Hotel, see a ballet at the Bolshoi Theater, watch the proletariat dance on the night before a free day, and eat another dish of that distinctive Russian vegetable salad which precedes every meal served to the clientele of such Moscow hotels as are patronized by foreigners.

I wouldn't mind taking a rickshaw again to Bubbling Well Road in Shanghai, or visiting a Shanghai cabaret with its strange colorfulness and its odd commingling of humanity. Tokyo's Ginza is a unique and exciting thoroughfare and the alleys back of it play a queer medley of neon light signs, phonograph music, and the birdlike voices of Japanese waitresses who flock and flutter in every café on streets where every door is the entrance to a café.

I should like to visit a dance hall again in Saigon where the native women look like princesses of royal blood, and the tropical night has an unreal strangeness and beauty. I should like . . .

But there is no enjoyment of such scenes where there is no peace. Maybe thirty years is not too long to wait.

The Castle at Elsinore

SEPTEMBER 19, 1949

Copenhagen—I took a sight-seeing bus the other day to Kronborg Castle at Elsinore which is supposed to be the scene of Shakespeare's *Hamlet*. We went for thirty miles through beautiful countryside and we arrived in a mist of conjecture and misrepresentations which would have delighted the faddists who believe that Bacon, or somebody else, wrote Shakespeare's plays.

Our guide was not a scholar but he was intelligent and he was earning his money. His bus was standing on a central street corner and he vigorously waylaid all passers-by he suspected of being tourists and told them that he was offering the implied privilege of a trip to Hamlet's castle.

Of course, there is no such place as Hamlet's castle, though the movie experts who arranged Laurence Olivier's *Hamlet* seemed to think there was. But the illusion is particularly advantageous to the tourist business in Copenhagen.

Our guide buttonholed and sold one visitor after another with the inducement that the destination and chief point of the tour was Hamlet's castle. The official advertisements of the tour list Kronberg Castle as an incidental stop on the circuit. Our guide knew better.

He understood that illusion and sentiment are the guiding principles for human beings, including tourists. There must have been about fifty people in the large bus.

They spoke five or six different languages, but their whole concern was to see a castle which was associated with a play by a British playwright who lived more than three hundred years ago. It was extraordinary, and our guide made it more so.

He took us out on a rampart adjoining the castle and he explained solemnly that here was the place where the ghost of Hamlet's father walked and was met by the stunned prince of Denmark. This castle was built in 1585 and could not possibly have been known to Shakespeare when he wrote *Hamlet* a few years later.

Our guide had an explanation. He said that Shakespeare came to Elsinore Castle as a member of a company of traveling players, and he wrote his great play on the basis of that experience.

There is not the slightest historical evidence for that statement, and if the Danes have any facts in corroboration all Shakespearean scholars would be in an unimaginable dither of excitement. Of course, Danish scholars haven't any such evidence and they are a little ashamed of this good-natured fraud.

Hamlet is undoubtedly a mythical character and, even if he ever lived, he certainly did not live in any castle now existing in Denmark. The Elsinore castle is tourist bait. But, ugly as it is, it has a poetical and sentimental significance.

Our guide spoke a great deal of nonsense. He said that this castle was named in Shakespeare's play and he assured us that the platform on which we were standing was the plank on which the ghost of Hamlet's father had walked. The prosaic fact, and he undoubtedly knew it, is that the present platform is one stage above the old ramparts. If Hamlet met his father's ghost on either platform the ghost could be easily seen by his uncle, the king, since the windows of the palace were only a few feet away.

The play which Shakespeare wrote suggests much more amplitude of territory than is indicated by the physical environment of the present castle at Elsinore. If the king could not see what was going on at this distance he was blind, or drunk, and I do not overlook the possibility of the latter contingency which is implied in the text.

This so-called Hamlet castle is in Dutch renaissance style and it is to my eyes, very ugly. It is crowned with towers which are uneven in height and architecture. The cobblestoned courtyard is large and bleak.

Here is where Laurence Olivier and Vivien Leigh put on a performance of *Hamlet* a couple of years ago, and this was the place where a troupe of American players came this year to do the same play. It must have been very uncomfortable for the audience, but it could also have been sentimentally satisfactory for the players. They may have convinced themselves that they were playing *Hamlet* in his own environment and under conditions which existed in Shakespeare's time. They were wrong in both assumptions.

But sentimentally they were right. There is something poetically proper in playing *Hamlet* against the scene where he is, even mistakenly, supposed to have lived. The background is neither Elizabethan, nor Danish, according to the times when the mythical Hamlet is supposed to have been bearded by his father's ghost. But it is much more suitable to the play than painted and made-up scenery to which we are accustomed.

In the old days before the war when I was last in Denmark the Danes had erected a monument adjoining Kronborg Castle which was supposed to mark the grave of Hamlet. I asked the guide about this, because he did not show it.

He said, "We don't point that out to tourists any more. You know that Hamlet was a mythical character and it would be wrong to show his grave. I prefer to call it a monument."

For the previous half hour he had been referring to Hamlet

as a historical character and he kept constantly mixing up renaissance architecture with medieval architecture. Guides are the most influential of modern poets because they talk well and they have only an incidental respect for facts.

Yet nobody could deny the essential fact deducible on this trip, which was that about fifty people, who spoke different languages and were probably representative of their nations, had a strong and understanding interest in an English poet who lived more than three hundred years ago.

An Amusement Park
in Copenhagen

SEPTEMBER 20, 1949

Copenhagen—I suppose you could sum up the distinctive flavor of Copenhagen in the one word, Tivoli. That is the name of an amusement park. It may seem whimsical to seek the soul of a community in an amusement park. But everybody who knew Vienna, for instance, in prewar days, or even now, understands that the Prater, which is a vast amusement park, is the heartbeat of life for the average Viennese.

Copenhagen's Tivoli seems to mean even more to the ordinary inhabitant of Copenhagen or of all Denmark, for Tivoli is the first place provincials visit and the last they leave. It is situated squarely in the heart of the city. Imagine a park of many hundreds of acres in New York's Times Square, or in the vicinity of Cleveland's East Ninth and Euclid.

Tivoli is an amusement park, but it is different from any other I have seen elsewhere in the world. There are Ferris wheels, games of chance, merry-go-rounds, hawkers and peddlers, and all the other accompaniments of a commercial carnival.

But somehow it is not vulgar, or predatory, or cheap. It is idyllic, rich, and charming.

Flowers, fountains, and ponds give it a natural beauty. There are band concerts in the open air and first-class musical performances in an enclosed hall, often supported by distinguished international soloists.

Some Nazi collaborators blew up the old concert hall in one of the most senseless acts of destruction of a savage war, and Copenhagen has never forgiven or forgotten these insane hooligans.

But no breath of war hovers over Tivoli today. It is a retreat for young romantics, a delight for children, and a pleasure garden of memory for the old.

Restaurants of all categories are situated within its gates. One of the largest and most imposing restaurant buildings I have ever seen is an establishment called Nimb, not far from the main gates.

I don't remember whether I have seen anywhere a restaurant of this spaciousness and beauty. Certainly not in America.

You might find something like it in the Paris Bois de Boulogne or the Riviera, but, so far as I can remember, they are not equal to it.

But Tivoli is not for the rich, though the rich go there. It is for the average family, for the children, for the poor, for everybody.

You can dine there for practically nothing in American terms, or you can spend a very substantial amount for a de luxe repast.

You can eat in Chinese pagodas, in palaces, or in what could be regarded as the equivalent of American lunch counters. But everywhere, so far as I have observed, you will find good food and most of it is served in an environment of the liveliest activity and incredible beauty.

We had a meal the other day on a restaurant terrace overlooking a stage where a number of heavily muscled Danes were engaged in the business of lifting heavy weights. That seems to me one of the most unpleasant and meaningless of exercises.

But it was not disagreeable to drink coffee in comfort and simultaneously to watch the extraordinary exertions of the athletes.

From the same terrace, a little later, you could see a charming pantomime on a public stage. Officially, it was supposed to be an Italian *Commedia dell' Arte* performance, but it was essentially a kind of ballet.

Tivoli is the only place in the world, so far as I know, where they still put on pantomime shows in the old Italian tradition, with Harlequin and Columbine doing just what they did hundreds of years ago, and to the same music.

All Danes, I gather, think of Tivoli with a sentimental affection, and the older people and the visitors from the provinces think of it longingly and nostalgically. I suppose there is no other amusement park comparable to it in relation to its importance to the community where it exists.

But the Danes obviously love entertainment, and they pursue it with rather more persistence and vigor than most people. The other day I saw a long line in a street bordering the city hall square. It was composed of children, accompanied by their mothers, and an exceptionally miscellaneous assortment of people.

One of the most conspicuous members of the line-up was a man in riding clothes, carrying a whip and wearing a derby hat and all the proper accouterments pertaining to the exercise which he had presumably just completed.

From the varied appearance of the crowds and the general evidence that few members were rich, I assumed that they were waiting for ration coupons entitling them to buy some essential of life.

It turned out that they were lined up for a curious and rather antiquated luxury. They were waiting to buy tickets for the film, *Gone With the Wind,* and they were negotiating to travel to Sweden to see it.

The bookstore where they were lined up in early morning was selling tickets which entitled buyers to railway transportation to Malmö, Sweden, and provided them seats in a Malmö theater for *Gone With the Wind*. An enterprising Copenhagen newspaper had thought up the idea.

Gone With the Wind is too expensive a film to be shown profitably in Denmark. Its people were faced with going through life without seeing this popular American movie.

So the newspaper arranged with the Danish and Swedish railways and the management of the theater in Malmö for a joint excursion of filmgoers who would pay for their railway tickets and their theater admission fees in one contract. The results must have astonished everybody concerned.

I don't know whether it has happened before, but I find it a little unusual to see hundreds of people lining up to buy theater tickets and railway passage to see a film in another country. It is too bad that Margaret Mitchell did not live to hear about it.

Swedish Hospitality

JANUARY 18, 1950

We think of Americans as the most hospitable people in the world, and so do most travelers who visit these shores. But the virtue of hospitality is not confined to this country. It can be found to an incredible degree in other lands. I was sadly reminded of this the other day in reading of the death of Axel Jonsson. He was the president of the Swedish American Lines, president of the South Atlantic Lines, and a director of many other Swedish shipping and transportation companies.

I met him only once but under circumstances so pleasant and unusual that the occasion remains vividly in my mind. It must have been about twenty years ago. I was in Sweden for the purpose of writing something about the operation of the Swedish liquor-control law known as the Bratt system.

A day before leaving Sweden I found myself in Göteborg

from where I was to take ship for Antwerp. I knew nobody in Göteborg, and I was lonely.

I decided to present a card of introduction which had been thrust on me by the American ambassador in Brussels. It was addressed to a man named Folke Jonsson of whom I had never heard. It turned out that he owned most of the shipping business in Sweden which his brother, Axel, did not own and between them they largely controlled Swedish inland and foreign water transportation.

Folke was a friendly, beaming, roly-poly man. He invited me to dinner at his home which he said was in the suburbs of Göteborg, and I accepted. He called for me later at my hotel.

When we were seated in his automobile, which was a little smaller than a streetcar, I asked him how far it was to his home. He answered, "Only about five miles."

After riding for a surprisingly long time, I asked, "How far did you say it was to your place?"

"Five miles," he said. Then a smile of understanding descended on him. "I meant five Swedish miles." A Swedish mile is more than six American miles.

We eventually arrived at his home, a spacious mansion environed by trees and gardens. After a huge and excellent dinner, with the appropriate accompanying liquids, we retired for recuperation to the drawing room. In the ensuing conversation, the talk got around to tennis and I confessed that I enjoyed playing the game.

"I will have a partner for you tomorrow," said Folke, "a very good tennis player."

"I am not good at it," I said, "I just like to play it but I don't like to play with people who really know how to play."

"Oh," said Folke, "this fellow coming tomorrow is not a professional. He is the King of Sweden. He comes here every now and then for a visit and he is due tomorrow. You are sitting in the chair he usually sits in."

It would have been a novelty to have played tennis with a reigning monarch, but I was booked out the next morning for engagements elsewhere which could not be broken.

Later in the evening, Axel Jonsson came to visit his brother and guests, which included only myself and a traveling companion. Axel was a charming man, a widely traveled cosmopolitan who knew the world, understood it, forgave it, and enjoyed it thoroughly. Both brothers were wonderful storytellers, and I can still remember the gist of some of the tales they told on that evening so long ago.

We stayed up late, talking and laughing, and it was much after midnight before I bethought myself of the agony of getting up in the morning to take a ship to Antwerp at eight. I mentioned that I would probably feel very badly at that time.

Folke said, "What you will need tomorrow is some liver pills." He named a patented American brand of liver pills with which I had never had any truck and which I supposed were unknown outside the United States.

"I have not got any in the house now," said Folke, "but I will get some and bring them to your ship tomorrow morning."

We were sailing on a combination passenger and cargo ship which Folke owned. The skies were gray and life was drab as we stood against the ship's railing early the next morning idly watching the gangplank.

I had forgotten all about Folke's promise to deliver the liver pills. A few minutes before the ship was due to sail, I saw him come hastily puffing up the gangplank, tightly clasping a small object in his hand. When I met him on the deck he greeted me with an air of pleased triumph, extended his hand, and dropped what it held into my coat pocket.

"I got them," he said. "This is what you need. Liver pills."

I hold it as rather unusual in the history of hospitality that a stranger visits a city for one day, is invited to play tennis with the monarch of the country, and sails away on a ship owned by a man who, after a late night, sees him off with a gift of liver pills, a man he had never seen before and was destined never again to see.

Bali

NOVEMBER 11, 1952

Some years before the war I spent several weeks in Bali. It is, or was, an island of enchantment, unmatched anywhere, so far as I have seen the world. I don't know where else you would find an exquisite civilization mingled with the ancient and the primitive, or a life so naturally dedicated to art, beauty, and a quiet gaiety.

Every village in Bali has its group of dancers. Their dances are extremely varied, and they are often combined with a kind of drama. There is no word in the Balinese or Malayan language for "theater." But nearly all Balinese theatrical performances include music and dance.

The music is strange to the ears of a foreign visitor, but you can sense that it is systematized and disciplined according to its own rules.

The dancing is a curious combination of ancient ceremonies in propitiation of the gods and sheer art and entertainment.

Bali is the only place left in the contemporary world where you can see the ancient beginnings of modern drama and its evolution. It started with religious ceremonials and it developed into secular entertainment.

You have them both in the island of Bali. In a curious and unique way dancing and music have entered into the heart of its people as a duty and a delight.

No place else in the world do highly skilled dancers perform for the pleasure of dancing, or professional musicians play for the satisfaction of playing, year in and year out. Every night in Bali you can see a superb show by the roadside without payment of fee.

These people, of course, derive satisfaction from the approval

and applause of their fellow villagers, but they do not expect
to be paid for what gives them pleasure. I make an exception
of the players who perform for tourists in Denpasar. They are
paid. But the best shows in Bali are free.

You come across them on side roads almost every evening.
Your automobile is halted by a crowd in the road. You stop
and step down.

Then you are fascinated in watching what seems to be a
spontaneously arranged dance program of some skill and the
utmost strangeness. The native spectators are as interesting as
the show.

Women and children, bare of breast, and showing a naive
delight in what is set before them. Men holding hands. Men
and women with flowers behind their ears. A general air of
enjoyment, friendliness, and a childlike, smiling wonder.

One evening I found myself in the woods not far from Denpasar. I was startled to see a man eight feet tall emerging from
the night and the trees. He was dressed as the king in a pack
of playing cards. Then came the queen and the jack.

They were all eight or nine feet in height, and they resembled
a fantastic distortion of the nobility pictured on the pasteboards
that sophisticated people employ in the playing of bridge.

They went through some odd drama, or ceremony, which I
did not understand but found enjoyable in an eerie and inex-
pressible way. They were not doing what they did for the pleasure of others, but for their own enjoyment.

But they were trained and experienced performers. They
walked on stilts as easily as you or I would walk in shoes.

Bali is probably the most art-conscious community in the
world. The life of its inhabitants is built around dancing and
music and the creation of beauty.

They are wonderful silversmiths. I have in my possession a
beautiful piece of carved silver which was made for the holding
of tobacco and betel nut.

That is one of the contradictions in this strange and remote
civilization, caught between an ancient glory and the pres-

sures of modern times. Their beautiful women chew tobacco and suck betel nuts, which blacken their teeth. They anoint their hair with rancid oils.

Yet they have an exquisite perception of beauty and art as these are understood in the Western sense.

In their magnificent way they have achieved a good life.

A Baby Bull

NOVEMBER 1, 1953

Madrid—Yesterday we traveled about forty miles from Madrid to visit an estate where bulls are bred and trained for fighting. The estate corresponds in some way to a dude ranch in Western United States. But there are some interesting differences.

You are entertained here by Spanish dancers instead of singing cowboys. In place of rodeo performances, you are regaled in these Spanish precincts by a miniature bullfight with baby bulls and amateur toreadors.

This ranch is owned by a rich Madrid family which supplements its income by providing organized entertainment at a substantial fee for visitors to its country estate.

One of the privileges that visitors are offered is the opportunity to fight bulls in the small ring situated on the estate. I did not avail myself of this singular opportunity, and I had no intention of so doing.

But before I could be accepted as a guest, I had to sign a contract stipulating that the transport company involved would not be responsible for any injuries sustained in fighting bulls. It was the oddest contract to which I have ever put my name.

But there was reason and substance for the prudence of the transportation company. Some of its clients are misguided enough to imagine themselves in the role of bullfighters and they go recklessly into the ring to tilt against some small bulls with very sharp horns.

Their hosts, of course, take the precaution of warming them up beforehand with as much sherry wine as they can contain.

The performances of the neophyte bullfighters are amusing, but they expose themselves to some danger and, with the bravado and confidence of the innocent, they take unnecessary chances.

One of our party, who had certainly never previously looked a bull in the eye, hurled himself into the ring and proceeded to kneel down a few feet from the horns of the bull, flaunting the red cape which had been provided him.

The bull promptly knocked him down and his body seemed to go in every direction, but the body was fortunately in one piece and no damage was done except to his equilibrium and his vanity.

The bull was distracted by several other more adept toreadors, and our South American friend picked himself up and ran for cover. He was a little overweight and the exercise seemed a strain, though it was certainly advisable under the circumstances. A little later he returned bravely to the fray and was set back again on his heels by a baby bull.

I must emphasize that this is not a real bullfight. The walled ring is quite small, the bullfighters are young men, or small boys, learning their trade, and the bulls are about one year old.

No bulls are killed, no horses are wounded, no fighter is in any serious danger, though he might easily be hurt, or killed, by an unusual accident.

The one blindfolded horse in the arena is protected with coverings that are about as thick as a feather bed. In a way which seems stupid, the infant bulls charge at the horse and try uselessly to bury their horns in his body.

The horse stands impassive under these onslaughts and is apparently not much bothered except by the general strangeness of life to which he is subjected. He means no harm, he has no enemy, yet he is repeatedly rocked by an assailant he cannot see.

All this is supposed to be fun, and I must confess that I had many laughs in the course of the extraordinary performance.

Most of them were at the expense of the young bullfighters who suddenly were outwitted and knocked down by an infant bull they were tormenting.

These young and inexperienced bullfighters reminded me of amateur actors. They imitated their betters and their imitations were more comic than anything I have seen in the theaters.

I know nothing whatever about bullfighting, but I know a ham when I see one, and some of these actors in the bull ring were most dreadful hams. A ham exaggerates. He plays to the gallery. He does nothing naturally and gracefully. He imitates grace without having it by nature or training. Some of these youngsters are all right as performers and might succeed in what seems to me the miserable profession of bullfighting.

Even in this relatively mild and bloodless exhibition of bullfighting, there is an element of cruelty. These animals are tortured and frightened. One of them was driven into the ring with one horn torn off and the blood from the wound dripping into his eyes.

Nobody seemed to pay any attention to the probable fact that the animal was in desperate pain and in no condition to amuse the spectators by his savage lunges against enemies he had not made and could not possibly understand.

Ernest Hemingway can have the bullfights which he glorifies. I'll take a more moderate and less sadistic form of entertainment.

Don't tell me about the remarkable grace and the exquisite technique of bullfighters. I can find the same qualities in a show where horses are not ripped apart and where "brave bulls" are not murdered. I detest the whole business, but I recognize it as a Spanish custom deeply imbedded in history and tradition.

What I chiefly dislike is the glorification of this horror by writers who are not bred to the custom and who must be held in contempt by Spaniards who really understand bullfighting.

After the baby bullfights on the estate which I have mentioned, we were taken to a ranch house where about five girls danced Spanish measures to the accompaniment of a small orchestra. They were surprisingly good. All of them were professional, gay, and lively.

But what I most poignantly remembered was that infant bull, with one horn broken off and bleeding horribly.

He stood dismayed and frightened as all his companions did, looking for a way out and charging only when he was tormented by red capes, a loud voice, or a prod from a stick. The bulls were not much larger than goats and they could be fairly compared to bewildered and pitiful goats.

Vienna at a Waltz Tempo

AUGUST 4, 1957

Vienna—With the exception of a couple of playhouses staging operettas, Vienna theaters are closed for the summer. Little organized, large-scale entertainment of any sort is available. A few night clubs are open. They are mostly faint imitations of Parisian institutions, a subdued reflection of Montmartre without the raucousness and the swindling. Even their names are French, such as Maxim's and the Moulin Rouge, which are among the most popular.

There are a dozen others, some with floor shows and many are just bars with music and a few "hostesses." The emphasis is on sex in a placid way, though some of them feature an American import called the strip tease.

Vienna has no night life in the authentic Parisian sense. The principal streets are deserted after midnight, even in the central district where the night clubs are concentrated.

Vienna is not a gay city. But it is a friendly, fun-loving city, content with simple pleasures. Music is the cornerstone of its delights. Nearly every restaurant provides music of some sort, maybe only a zither strummer, a piano player, a gypsy violinist, or perhaps a small orchestra.

They all play the same kind of music. The foundation of their repertory is the Viennese waltz. Sooner or later they come around to a waltz melody by Strauss or Lehár, and they keep coming back.

The Viennese never seem to tire of these old, familiar tunes perhaps because the days of Vienna's glory are entwined with them and the memories of a colorful and gracious life. The music speaks of a romantic, irrevocable past and there is a hint of sadness in its gentle charm.

You feel it most in an ancient, candlelit restaurant such as Kerzenstuberl, where a single pianist plays the muted strains of old waltzes to the accompaniment of dancing shadows on the wall and the low hum of conversation among a clientele that preserves some appearance of a faded elegance.

It was much the same in other fine restaurants, such as Zu den Drei Husaren and Am Franziskanerplatz, the latter situated in a sixty-year-old building facing a quaint baroque square that breathes of an enchanted past. You listened to Viennese music, softly played, and lived for a time in a by-gone world where nobody hurried and reality was filtered through moonlight.

Even in the big, popular restaurants there is an echo of the past. The *heurige* musicians in the Grinzinger cellar of the immense Rathaus play Viennese waltzes and old folk songs occasionally interpolated with such importations as "Tipperary" for the benefit of American and British visitors. I found the food there abominable, but the atmosphere was pleasant and gay in the special Viennese way.

The guests joined the small, roving orchestra in the singing of familiar tunes and there was some mingling from table to table as the wine exerted its mellowing influence. One of the guests, a middle-aged woman who obviously had been a professional singer, lifted her voice so sweetly in an old Vienna song that the rest of the diners stopped singing and came to hushed attention. When she finished the song there was a general round of applause.

One of the most appreciative diners rose from his chair, bought a half-dozen roses from a flower peddler and gallantly walked across the room to lay them reverently on the table of the woman who had sung so well. It was a pretty gesture and, I thought, particularly Viennese in its old-fashioned, spontaneous courtliness.

The Grinzinger cellar in the Rathaus represents an attempt to transfer the rustic atmosphere of the suburban Grinzing *heurige* to the center of the city. It is not successful because the special quality of the *heurige* depends on the outdoor setting and the character of its clientele.

Originally, a *heurige* marked the festivities accompanying the drawing off of new wine at any of the suburban vineyards. Now it has been commercialized and goes on pretty much throughout the year at many dozens of places in suburban Grinzing, Sievering, Nussdorf, and elsewhere in Vienna's outskirts.

You sit on benches at long, crude, wooden tables. Wine is served in carafes, usually without food though a few of the establishments offer bread and cold meats and one or two will accommodate the more affluent with a hot dish.

Many of the visitors bring their own picnic food. All the vintner asks is that they buy a little new wine to wash it down.

There is music in all the bigger inns and gardens. It is called Schrammel music, consisting of folk songs and old Vienna tunes, played by a quartet, usually a zither player, a violinist, an accordionist, and a flute player. They lead the crowd in singing and they spur the festive, comradely spirit which is the soul of the *heurige*.

In the free interchange that passes across the tables we got into a conversation with a young, attractive Viennese blonde and her husband. It developed that she was the great-granddaughter of Johann Schrammel, the ancient musician who had composed and first played much of the music to which we were listening and whose name is still attached to that type of simple, Viennese melody.

In Sievering, another suburb, we visited the wine garden of Toni Karas, who composed and played the zither music in the film, *The Third Man*. It is an elaborate and beautiful place and apparently very successful, but Toni Karas did not seem particularly happy.

We talked with him in the intervals when he was not playing the zither for his guests. He is a stocky man with strong fingers, and his face is creased with worry.

For his work as composer and zither player in *The Third Man* he was paid 50,000 shillings, which is about $2,000. He made some additional money on an American tour. His acquirement of the handsome wine garden and its buildings and the success he had so far had with it he attributes to his share in the making of the popular movie. He calls his place *The Third Man* and in grateful acknowledgment of his obligation he plays the theme from the film four times nightly.

He was born in Sievering and for thirty-two years he roamed from one wine garden to another in suburban Vienna, playing the zither. He was a kind of wandering minstrel, a legend in the countryside, a man without care except for the zither and its music which he venerates.

Then the film impresarios came along and made him an international celebrity. The wandering musician is now a businessman, tied to his post and weighed with the burdens of the countinghouse.

The Orient Express

AUGUST 16, 1957

Paris—We came to Paris from Vienna by Orient Express, a famous train which has figured romantically in films and mystery stories and is supposed to be de luxe in its accommodations.

I had traveled on it a half-dozen times previously and found the trips comfortable and uneventful, except on one trip when I had my pockets picked by an amiable fellow traveler who removed a couple of hundred dollars in currency from my wallet but was considerate enough to leave me my letter of credit.

Nothing of the sort occurred on the trip I have just finished, but nevertheless it was an ordeal which I shall not willingly venture again.

The first-class compartment we occupied on this de luxe train was small and dirty. Blankets and sheets were a sickly gray. There was a washbasin in the compartment but no hot water and it was necessary to use it frequently to remove the grime accumulated on the hands from touching the furnishings.

Toilet facilities were primitive, consisting of a movable piece of old-fashioned crockery, the like of which I had not seen for a long time. Everything was shabby and antiquated.

I have traveled in better style on the Russian railways, though the Russian sleeping cars usually contain four berths and you are likely to have to share a bedroom with strangers of the opposite sex. Our compartment on the Orient Express was modestly limited to double occupancy.

When we boarded the train in Vienna, around 12:30 in the afternoon, our berths were already pulled out for sleeping. It seemed a little early to go to bed and we asked the sleeping-car conductor if we could sit in another compartment which was unoccupied and not yet made up. He replied that everything was sold out but that we could use the other compartment until we arrived in Munich.

Early in the evening, he tapped on the door and said we would have to move out and retire to our own nest because he had to make up all beds before we reached Munich. It was several hours before we were due in Munich and I asked him what the hurry was about getting the beds ready.

He replied that he had much work to do. An American Pullman porter could have made up the entire car in an hour. But our Orient Express porter, who was also the car conductor, was an excitable Frenchman, full of the cares and pride of office.

He always made the berths ready for sleeping several hours before they were needed and that was the way it had to be. Any suggestion that it didn't have to be seemed to put him in a state of panic and revulsion.

He was a shabby, fierce, anxious little man, doubtless well-meaning and desirous to please, but consumed with the preoccupation and the self-importance of the functionary.

All the berths in the car were put in place for sleeping by six o'clock in the evening. The passengers had to go to bed at that time, or else spend the evening standing up in the corridor. There are no lounge cars on the Orient Express, or anywhere else to sit down when the berths are pulled out in your compartment. You have the simple choice of lying down or standing up.

I was not ready for sleep several hours before sunset, but I had no wish to stand in the corridor, where the traffic back and forth is pretty brisk, so I lay down and watched the mountains and the castles fly by from a reclining position.

We arrived in Paris about nine o'clock in the morning. The conductor brought us two cups of coffee. He was still worried but amiable, because the time had come for the tipping ceremony. You pay a service charge of 15 per cent over the sleeping-car fare which is supposed to cover tips. Nevertheless the conductor expects an additional greasing of the palm.

I paid him the tariff of about ninety cents for the coffee and a tip of a couple of dollars. I judged from the manner of his acknowledgment that he considered it adequate but not liberal.

This odd functionary who collects tickets and also acts as a waiter and porter, performs an added and important service for passengers. He relieves you of getting up in the night to pass through the nuisance of customs examination when you cross the border into France.

When you start out he gives you a most formidable customs form to fill out. It warns the passenger to declare every dutiable article he is carrying and the dutiable goods are listed.

They include not only cigars, cigarettes, and spirits, but "all articles, bought or received as gifts and, notably, new clothes, furs, laces, textiles, fabrics, lingerie, glassware, leather goods, carpets, jewelry, wrought gold and silver articles, wireless sets, foodstuffs, perfumes, pharmaceutical products, etc., whether they are intended for trade or not."

There is not a passenger coming from Eastern Europe to France who does not carry some of this dutiable stuff in his luggage. You must also fill out a money declaration, stating exactly what you are carrying in dollars, traveler's checks, gold or any kind of currency, French or foreign. It takes a half-hour to fill out the forms as prescribed.

When you have finished making them out as completely and as accurately as possible, you hand the forms to the conductor-porter. That's the last you see of them.

There are no customs examinations whatever, or there were none in our case. The porter merely handed in the forms to the inspector in the middle of the night. That's all they wanted.

The formalities were complied with. It was not necessary to go beyond that. The formalities are nonsense, but they keep a horde of civil servants on the public payroll.

There was no real discomfort on this trip in a de luxe European train, or at least no inconvenience that a foreign traveler cannot accept as a matter of course. The point is that you pay too much for inferior accommodations.

The sleeping berths for two on this train cost about thirty-five dollars for an overnight journey. This, of course, was in addition to the train fare.

For the same money you can take an airplane and arrive at your destination in four hours. Why should anybody take a train?

The Lido

SEPTEMBER 1, 1957

Paris—The Lido proclaims itself "the most beautiful cabaret show in the entire world." It may be. This cellar night-box in the center of the fashionable Champs Elysées district is the largest in Paris and it is well equipped for spectacular displays, having both a conventional stage and a raised platform stage, together with a swimming pool and facilities for ice skating. You have the privilege of seeing more or less naked women in the air, on the floor, in the water, and on ice skates.

When I first visited the Lido in the 1920's it was a combination of swimming pool and Turkish bath, and the cabaret attractions were incidental. About ten years ago it was made over into a kind of ornate Venetian palace and a new policy was instituted of putting on costly and sumptuous spectacles. Since then, it has become widely accepted as the home of the best cabaret shows in Paris and an obligatory port of call for foreign visitors.

Certainly it is the most luxurious cellar in Europe. The environment is that of an antique and overdecorated royal banquet hall. The gaudy splendor of the surroundings does not afford much comfort to the spectator. I have never seen a show which put its audience to such disadvantage and inconvenience.

The Lido management boasts that its auditorium has a capacity of one thousand. It has, only if the tables are crowded so closely together that you can not move more than two inches without bumping your neighbor. The aisles between the rows of tables are so narrow that the waiters cannot pass except by snaking through and administering a sound shove to the shoulder or ribs of every diner they encounter on the way.

They don't seem to mind doing so and, indeed, they appear

to find a certain satisfaction in roughing up the customers. The nudging and bumping are excessive even in relation to the cramped and overcrowded facilities, and the scurrying and hurrying are remindful of a snack bar at a railway station.

You might reasonably expect a little more comfort and graciousness of manner at the prices charged. If you take the lowest-priced dinner, the charge is about twenty-five dollars for two. That includes two half-bottles of champagne of undetermined vintage and dubious quality.

The champagne is obligatory, whether or not you like champagne. The dinner, which is thrown at you rather than served, is simple and undistinguished. It consists of a consomme which tastes as if it were made of a bouillon cube, followed by meat, potatoes, and ice cream or pastry. The steak I had presented some difficulties to the knife.

But food and drink are not the specialties of the house, and you are deliberately hurried through the meal so that everybody will be finished at 11:15 when the first show begins. Unless you have a table facing the rear stage you can't see it very well.

We had a ringside table but it was at the side of the platform stage, and it was impossible to see all that was going on without corkscrewing your neck and even then one corner of the rear stage remained invisible.

The place has some aspects of the tourist trap in its overcrowding, its pressure, its relatively high prices. My feeling in this respect was intensified when I saw an Australian give a headwaiter a 10,000-franc tip, or about twenty-five dollars, to be seated at a not particularly desirable table. The Australian was feeling pretty good and I am sure he was not thoroughly familar with French currency and did not know how much he was tipping. The waiter knew, but kept the knowledge to himself.

I must say that the show was first-class and worth the pushing around involved in seeing it. The girls were lovely, dressed or undressed. They were a far more select group than the girls at the Folies Bergère or the Casino de Paris.

Some of them could even dance. All of them walked with

grace and wore beautiful clothes beautifully, when clothes were required. The costumes were magnificent and the whole spectacle was not only opulent, but quick-paced and pictorially splendid.

The formula for these Lido shows seems to be simple. They comb the international market for the best specialty acts and they work these acts into an integrated pattern, weaving them through a series of production numbers in which the girls and their costumes, or lack of them, are predominant. Everything is arranged with skill and a fine sense of color and design.

The shows are frankly sensual, but the sensuality is transmitted and disciplined through the imagination of producers who are both showmen and artists. The tableaux are voluptuous without vulgarity and, indeed, they represent good taste within the limited compass and intent of this kind of entertainment.

You do not need to have studied at the Sorbonne to enjoy the clowning of a burlesque orchestra which, I suspect, is American in origin, or to be amused by a very funny travesty of ballroom dancing in the style of Fanny Brice. A troupe of Spanish dancers is better than any I saw in Spain, and a juggler performs marvelously well in a frenzied and comic spinning of plates.

These specialty acts are incidental like hors d'oeuvres at a banquet. The real and substantial attraction is the girls and the fetching stage pictures.

EIGHT

The Daily Round

The Outdoors: Urban Aromas vs. New-Mown Hay

SEPTEMBER 27, 1934

About this season I like to think about getting out into the fields and the woods. I even toy vaguely with the idea of buying a farm. It is a kind of arrested juvenile romanticism.

When I was a boy I read a book entitled *Five Acres and Liberty*. It was an enthusiastic description of how health, independence, and all the blessings of a rich and happy life could be won by acquiring a small patch of land and growing something on it. There were pictures in the book of handsome tomatoes and delicately blushing radishes and fine red cabbages.

I hadn't read Voltaire at that time but I felt with Candide that the answer to life and the beginning of wisdom is "to cultivate your garden."

I experimented in a city back yard with radishes and lettuce, the only farm crops that came within the purview of my understanding and the limitations of the back yard. They grew, but the final harvest bore little resemblance to the splendid and brilliant pictures in the seed catalog.

I soon gave up gardening as one gives up other ideals that do not bear the shocks of a harshly practical world. But the dream lingers and I still find myself about twice a year looking up lists of farms for sale or gazing thoughtfully on tomatoes in the grocer's window.

Then I take a walk down Euclid Avenue and reason asserts itself. I am convinced again that I have no talent for a rural life. I like Euclid Avenue, even where it is in decay and a little forlorn.

The whirring of traffic, the changing brilliance of the shop-windows, the rich drama in parade of passers-by, with its mystery, its comedy—these things move and charm me and I would not willingly be without them.

The song writers talk about the smell of new-mown hay. Such fragrance is romantic but unsettling. For a steady diet, I prefer the smell of a city.

All cities have their distinctive general odors and, to me, all are pleasant. Berlin has an aromatic smell, like the sharp odor of new automobile tires. Paris smells like eau de Cologne and a woman's millinery shop, faintly diluted with spilled wine and sour beer.

Budapest has a sweetish smell of cloves and coffee and magnolia.

Cleveland smells of gasoline and oil and fresh textiles and the perfumes of the concentrated shops and movie theaters, the whole constituting a synthesis that Coty could not rival. I find it invigorating and agreeable.

Even the noises of a city are the attestation that the world is moving normally. Even the Cleveland streetcars, surely the noisiest in the world, are tolerable when they come regularly enough, and the steady whir of automobile motors in the night is a sedative.

A city man is at home in the city. In the fields he is lonely and ill at ease.

Not immune to the charms of rural beauty and peace, he knows there is beauty in the ugliest city and peace in the noisiest streets.

The towering skyline in dusk, or the blast furnaces at night, or a sudden apparition of neat prettiness out of a crowd—all this is enchanting beauty to a city lover.

Perhaps in the recesses of his being he feels that the throb of humanity is more intense in the city, that life is less static there, that all the troubles and wonders of living are accentuated where immense populations are centered, and he doesn't want to miss anything that life offers.

I should love to live on a farm if I could find one at the junction of Euclid Avenue and East Ninth Street.

Dentistry

MAY 17, 1935

America has made only three universally recognized contributions to world civilization: jazz music, cocktails, and dentists. Having had a tooth pulled yesterday, I am currently more conscious of the latter gift to mankind.

The grinding of teeth has the same effect on human nerves as dragging the paws of a cat over a tin roof, and the taking of gas for an extraction is much like being knocked over the head with a baseball bat while the end of your nose is being cut off.

But it must be said that these salutary human violences are perpetrated by the American dentist with a maximum of tact, indulgence, sanitation, and science. There is reassurance in the white walls, the chromium fittings, the gleaming instruments of the dentist's office, and there is comfort in his deft fingering and delicate solicitude.

If murder is necessary and inevitable this is the place, you feel, to have it committed with clean dexterity and the least of blood and pain.

You are solaced by the evidence that the dentist is conscious of the disagreeableness of the sensations he is causing. Not conscious enough perhaps, for pain is really vital and important only to the individual who is suffering it. Pascal devotes many pages somewhere to proving that no pleasure is equal in intensity to pain and, consequently, it is foolish to hope for much in this world.

Still it is mollifying to hear the dentist inquiring: "Am I hurting you?" It's a rhetorical question for he knows damn well he is, since you're sitting there to have your teeth ground, not to have your hair cut.

But a man in a dentist's chair is grateful for any kind word and for any evidence of recognition that he is an individual member of the human race and subject to the pangs of mortality. A good American dentist is a talented psychologist. He understands that men are babies. Some of these oral practitioners are so expert that they will have you asleep with soothing words long before the gas begins to work.

You will not find their like in Europe. At least I never have. I remember a visit to a Moscow dentist. There was no running water in the office, though the dentist, being the official operator for the Foreign Department, was presumably the best equipped in Moscow.

The instruments were few and created the general impression of a carpenter's toolbox, long disused. The dentist was a woman with large hands and an air of determination.

Our tête-à tête was incommoded by the fact that she spoke no English and I no Russian. What complicated the situation was that I insisted that a certain tooth was aching and she was convinced that it was another tooth, a friendly tooth which had never given me a moment's trouble.

We couldn't come to any reasonable agreement about which tooth ought to be extracted and I decided to call it even and walk out with such teeth as I had.

In North Africa, I was once overtaken with a slight toothache, while strolling in the native quarter. An interpreter suggested that an Arab dentist of his acquaintance would fix me up.

We went to the dentist's quarter. My interpreter's friend was sitting in his office, which consisted of a small piece of carpet, placed on the sidewalk, where he squatted hopefully. In front of him were a few formidable and stained instruments in the general form of pincers, and at his side was a dishpan full to the brim of brown and yellow teeth he had successfully extracted and which were apparently intended to serve as the badge of his prowess.

Do not believe that philosophy cannot cure a toothache. After a brief look at the turbaned dentist, the plumbing tools, and the full pan of menacing teeth wrenched from their sockets, my toothache abruptly subsided and I had no trouble for years thereafter.

Everywhere in Europe you will find evidences of three aspects of American civilization. One is the number of cafés that advertise American jazz bands, usually consisting of native musicians who never heard a jazz band.

Another is the universal blazoning in European cities of placards bearing the legend "American Bar." You can now see such signs over the doors of even the Parisian bistros, those multitudinous small cafés with zinc-topped bars where Frenchmen come for a drink of wine. "American Bar" in Europe means nothing more than that mixed drinks are served in the establishment.

Almost as numerous as the "American Bar" signs are the placards over dental offices reading, "American Dentist" or "Dentist-Surgeon, American Methods." There are very few native American dentists in Europe, though a number of them have worked up a good practice in Paris.

But American dentistry has spread all over Europe, by proxy, just as the jazz bands have spread, and for the same reason. In its particular field of human endeavor it happens to be the best.

Moving

APRIL 8, 1938

The spring moving season has ordinarily had only a remote interest for me. I understand very well the vague unrest, troubling yet blissful, which causes so many people to look with longing on a transfer van when the spring winds begin to soften the air. But I have seldom been able to do more than wonder about it.

This spring, for the first time in many years, I am moving, and I know at firsthand the pangs and the pleasures of the great army who pull up stakes each year and emigrate to another neighborhood.

It is a lesson in the transitoriness of worldly values and an eye opener into the recesses of the human soul. You have understood little of the cynicism of the world until you have seen the deprecating look in the eyes of a secondhand man as he surveys the treasures you are trying to sell him, and heard the tone of his voice as he dismisses them into the outer limbo of the utterly worthless.

Of course, as a personal favor he will take these things off your hands. The books you do not care to move he will buy for ten cents apiece, but he accepts them only with sadness and an intimation that he is being defrauded.

True, the books are not worth much or you would not be leaving them behind. But into the writing of each of them went months of labor and the heart of a man. Ten cents seems a small enough price to pay for so much sweat and blood, without hinting that any man who buys them at that price will surely lose money.

But the secondhand man is not interested in money. He wants to talk about art and politics and the future of the human race. He is sensitive and shy about the mention of money.

His manner assumes that such refined spirits as yours and his are not concerned with the dross that lines the purses of the vulgar. He will come to the money later as to a necessary evil of small consequence to enlightened souls, and when he does get to it he speaks of it casually, softly, and in extremely modest amounts.

He will offer you a twentieth part or a hundredth part of what you have paid for a piece of furniture or an object of art, and he will do so with an air of thoughtless prodigality. Maybe you rebel at the pittance offered for something you once cherished, a familiar possession of many years. The secondhand man dislikes bickering over small matters. He is hurt to find you so crudely mercenary.

"Well," he says, "you surely would not quarrel about a dollar? What is one dollar? I will give you a dollar more because I want to stay friends with you, but I am losing money."

He says it with so injured an air and his gesture is so generous that you are shamed and intimidated and you let him have the next item at several dollars less than he was probably prepared to pay.

Some of your stuff, including an article or two you might have prized, he will not buy at any price.

"There is no market for this," he will say. "I couldn't give it away. If you want I will take it but I wouldn't pay fifty cents for it."

You bow to an expert in the market, but it seems strange that in all this teeming world of varied and curious tastes there is not a single human whose heart would beat in rhythm with that ancient, painted bedroom suite, once the cream of fashion.

Bedroom furnishings seem to suffer the deepest metamorphosis on the brief road from new to secondhand. The dealer in used goods looks with especially disinterested and hostile eyes on a bedroom suite. It is out of style. It is disagreeable to look at. He can find nobody to buy it. In short, it is a nothing.

He hates to take it, but as a personal favor which his wife may never forgive and he will repent all the days of his life, he will give two dollars for it. The springs and mattress are worth nothing—in fact the dresser and the bureau are worth nothing—but he will take them all just to relieve you of so much trouble.

Then you go to buy a suite to take the place of the one of which you have been relieved. A bed suddenly bceomes an article of rare workmanship and the most delicate beauty. It is precious almost beyond price.

The springs, which you have just given away, are mechanisms representing the utmost in human ingenuity, and if you want a really good set, they are priced accordingly. The mattress is an intricate affair scientifically developed at great pains and study to induce sleep.

You pay for one of these accessories many times what you received from the secondhand man for an entire suite, and so persuasive are the arguments on either side that you are left with the impression that you have, in some mysterious and regrettable way, cheated both the secondhand man and the salesman who sold you the new suite.

Quartets and Snobbish Harmonizers

OCTOBER 3, 1938

Barbershop harmonizers are great snobs and tyrants. The won't let you join them unless you can sing. They expect you to stick to the key and carry a tune. They get mad if you don't.

They assume superior airs. They hint that you have no soul and had better go home, or at least get away from the piano. It has been my humiliating lot in life to attend many parties where the guests, at a witching hour, gravitate toward the piano and somebody asks, "Have you heard Cole Porter's new one?" and before anybody can say, "For God's sake, yes," he begins pounding out the tune.

Then some misguided soul demands another tune, something that everybody can sing, and before you can reach the door a quartet has been organized and they go through the entire repertory from "Swanee River," "The Bells of the Lighthouse," and "Good Bye My Bluebell" to "Joseph, Joseph" or "A Tisket, a Tasket."

I have been trying to crash a quartet for years. Often I get as

far as the piano and occasionally even succeed in sounding out
a few hearty notes. Immediately there is unrest around the
piano and soon downright hostility.

Somebody looks at me in a way that no friend should be
looked at. Then I feel a slight elbowing and what amounts to
a push.

If this does not work and my guests or my hosts happen to
be polite, somebody is assigned to approach me insinuatingly
to ask, "McDermott, wouldn't you like to sit down on the daven-
port? There's something I want to ask you about Czechoslovakia."

I don't want to talk about Czechoslovakia. I want to sing.
But does that make any difference to these Carusos and Martin-
ellis? No, brothers, no.

I am declared out on what seems to me a pure technicality.
They say that my voice is terrible, that I remember the words
of no song, that I am persistently off-key. They talk importantly
of key and pitch and harmony.

I argue with them. I say you do not understand the skylark.
Does the sweetest bird take music lessons from cracked baritones
and fat tenors, and does the bird prepare his songs with weary
toil? No, as Shelley understood, the skylark sings in "profuse
strains of unpremeditated art."

The important thing is not the song but the will to sing.
What really counts is not the tune but the soul.

Determination and loudness have their rewards in every other
department of life. Why should people who fancy they are
singers refuse to admit such values and say them nay?

The birds do not bother with the words of their heavenly
songs. Why should I put myself above the lark or the nightin-
gale and spoil a divine melody with mundane words, words
which are often remarkably trite, trivial, and meaningless?

If there was any sense or logic in mankind the best singer
would be that singer who could sing the most songs with the
fewest words. A succession of da-de-das is superior in significance and beauty to the lyrics of most popular ballads, and
these sounds have the valuable property of being adjustable

to any melody, thus eliminating considerable strain on the memory and releasing much human activity for more useful labors.

I have other arguments equally sound and unanswerable. But I can't get anybody to listen.

Quartet singers invariably consider my case not with their minds—or what they flatter themselves to be their minds—but with their emotions. They think they have settled the problems when they say, "McDermott, you're lousy."

I am thinking of hiring a lawyer. Or of organizing a quartet with one member.

Cravats

DECEMBER 21, 1939

Some millions of neckties will be bought and given as presents within the next few days. I fear that many of these purchases will be made too lightly.

It is my experience that the ladies, God bless them, have not much necktie sense. Or, to put it more politely, they do not approach the necktie problem with sufficient gravity and caution.

If they can't think of anything else to please a man they say, "I'll just give him a necktie." They don't concern themselves very deeply about what kind of necktie.

Evidence of this carelessness can be seen for weeks after the Christmas season in the weird draperies that hang around the necks of the male population with the disagreeable conspicuousness of an attack of measles. When you glimpse one of these Christmas cravats you know that the man wearing it could not possibly have thought of buying such a decoration for himself.

It doesn't look like him, it doesn't conform with his character or harmonize with his clothes. In brilliant and raging colors, or in meek pastels, it denies all that he is, all that he was, and all that he can hope to be.

A cravat is a highly personal adornment. It expresses a man's taste, prejudice, temperament, and mood. Some men will wear only such neckties as have a tinge of blue in them. Some men demand a touch of red.

Other men hate red and will not go near a necktie that has a glint of that color in its pattern. Likely as not an otherwise observant woman will give this particular man a gorgeous neckpiece of unashamed scarlet for a Christmas remembrance.

Neckties are related to a man's customary manner of general dress. If a man goes in for suits of sober gray and dark blue he wants neckties that will harmonize. If he affects fancy vests and dashing plaids he wants a cravat with some boldness and flash.

I fear some women—not you, of course, Dear Madame—are negligent and thoughtless of these matters when they approach the Christmas necktie counters. They think of a necktie, not in relation to the man for whom it is intended, but as something isolated and abstract. They like the color, the pattern pleases them. They select and buy what they like, not what they think, after due deliberation, that the prospective recipient would like.

I suspect their minds do not invariably hew to the point in these necktie transactions. They are thinking of an evening dress they are going to buy when they can lay hands on the money.

The dress is a charming number in a delightful shade of old rose. So the boy friend gets a necktie that blushes violently in a motif of old rose. He wears it, if he is loyal, but he would like to hide it.

His situation may be even more unenviable if the lady happened to be thinking of the new bedroom wallpaper when she selected his Christmas cravat.

A man has only one neck. It should be treated with respect. Of course, some men have no soul in their attitude toward cravats. They will wear anything around their necks that can be tied, and they are not conscious of the subtle and multifarious differences between one necktie and another.

It is the numerousness of these people that have made neckties so popular as holiday gifts. Any necktie is sure to please them.

But have a care, mesdames, for the others. These necktie-conscious men will spend an hour picking out one cravat. They fondle the materials, study the designs, and ponder the suitability of the color to that new gray suit.

They like rich and heavy silks and when they have found a particularly fine specimen they will exhibit it to their fellows with the pride of a connoisseur exposing his treasures to the elect.

It wounds such a man, it injures his spirit, it outrages his sense of decencies, to be presented with a sleezy, gaudy, ill-chosen neckpiece.

In the rear of his mind, I suppose, is the thought that a necktie is about all that is left to modern man of rich and brilliant raiment. He was once magnificently adorned in silks and velvets, laced sleeves, flowing capes, ruffs, and periwigs. Out of that ancient sartorial splendor all that remains to relieve the drabness of his attire is a colored silk necktie.

In the intervening years women have reversed the order which prevails among the animals and the birds, and the female of the human species has become the decorative sex. Without his necktie, man would be the dingiest male animal that walks the earth.

That is why the necktie is important. It is the attestation of man's essential manliness. It is a flaming banner of defiance flung against the onslaught of a progressive sartorial gloom.

Independence Days Abroad

JULY 4, 1940

This will be the first July Fourth I have spent in the United States in about twenty years. In that time I have not heard a single Fourth of July firecracker or seen the palest skyrocket.

My memories of Independence Day are bound up with busy foreign streets, hot asphalt pavements, writing in hotel rooms, or perhaps surprise and a kind of resentment for those occasions when I had forgotten the date and walked miles to the American consulate in quest of certain information and found the offices closed for the holiday.

The Fourth of July is celebrated by at least a few people in every large city of the world. These are the American consular officials and employees.

They observe every American holiday with scrupulous punctiliousness and they also celebrate every holiday fixed by the country to which they are assigned. Since native fete days are numerous in many countries, the American representatives abroad have frequent occasion for knocking off work, and if you happen to be in a foreign city at a time when the various holidays come close together you may get the impression that the American consulate is permanently closed.

I was looking over the record yesterday in a nostalgic effort to recall where I had spent the Fourth of July in the past ten years. In 1930, it was in Bombay, India.

In 1931 it was in Stockholm, Sweden. The record for 1932 is not precise, but I passed July Fourth either in Moscow or in a river steamer traveling the Volga to Stalingrad.

In 1933 I was in Berlin on Independence Day. The following year I lived through the hottest Fourth of July in my life. That was in Surabaya, Java.

On July 4, 1935, I was in Berlin, and the next year, same day, I went to what was described as a baseball game in Paris. The players, composed of American exiles, bulwarked by a few unhappy Englishmen, drank beer throughout the game and nobody ever ascertained the final score, though the general impression was that the total ran into the hundreds.

In 1937 I was again in Berlin on the Fourth. In 1938 I was in Budapest at that season. Last Fourth of July I spent in Hong Kong.

Time and catastrophe have changed the significance in these memories of Independence Days spent abroad. I used to think of the Fourth of July we celebrated in Bombay as something quaint and amusing.

The British ship on which I was traveling had docked in Bombay on July 3 and I went ashore with the other passengers. They were all British, and mostly men.

I believe I was the only American on the ship. After a day in Bombay, I came aboard again about midnight and went to bed. About two A.M. there was a clatter in the corridor outside the cabin.

I got up and opened the door. The hallway was crowded with about a dozen of my British fellow travelers.

They were yelling, "Get up, Yankee, and buy us a drink. It's the Fourth of July."

I managed to remember that the British had lost the war associated with Independence Day and the drinks should have been on the losers. There was no disposition to argue with that viewpoint and the barroom on the British ship was quickly and noisily reopened to celebrate American Independence Day.

My newly made British friends took the attitude that Britain had really won that war because it had rid them of America and Americans, and relieved them of governing a country that was not worth the trouble. It was all in fun and high spirits.

How impossible such an evening would be today! The independence of Britain itself is gravely endangered. No Englishman could have the heart at this time to joke about national independence or to make ironic, lighthearted pleasantries about the relationships between the United States and Great Britain.

What was the natural matter of jest has become an issue of life and death. I used to think of that Fourth of July in Bombay Harbor as one of the most amusing in my life. I now think of it not merely as pleasant, but as something remote, incredible, and touching, like an echo from a lost and better world.

Fourth of July is not what it once was anywhere in the world. You can be sure that American exiles in every corner of the globe are celebrating today with a solemnity of heart which they have not had before.

Independence Day is no longer only an occasion to commemorate an old, half-forgotten blessing. It has become an occasion to celebrate a living American reality, which is vanishing elsewhere, and to renew faith and the strength by which it may be kept.

"I Give You—"

OCTOBER 10, 1941

John Mason Brown has an article in this month's *Atlantic Monthly* magazine on the boners that people make when they introduce public lecturers and the embarrassment they cause the speaker. Mr. Brown, who is an authority on the theater and one of the most popular lecturers in circulation, intimates that he is tired of being introduced as Heywood Brown or Maxwell Anderson. That isn't so bad.

When Ramsay MacDonald visited New York at the zenith of his career as a statesman, Hector Fuller absent-mindedly introduced him over the radio as the prime minister of the United States. That was a real triumph of misidentification, though I suppose the isolationists would argue that Hector was not really wrong but merely a little premature.

Mr. Brown writes about the nervousness, trepidation, and agony produced in him by some of the people who have introduced him. I can speak from the other side of the rostrum.

In my chautauqua days, happily long since passed, I used frequently to misgrace the public platform and it was frequently my pleasant chore to introduce John Mason Brown. I suppose I have introduced John Mason Brown as often as any living man has introduced anybody outside of the fat lady's barker in a circus.

The introduction was made before much the same crowd which attends the Town Hall lectures here year after year. There didn't seem to be much sense in it.

When a man is introduced to the same people eight or nine times they ought to remember him the next time. They do, of course.

They know the man who is introduced better than they know the man who does the introducing. Nobody is forgotten with such merciful quickness as the man who introduces a public speaker.

On the occasion of Mr. Brown's last visit here I insisted it was only fair that we reverse the roles. He would introduce me for a change and I would make his speech. This plainly equitable scheme fell through because of a suggestion of discontent on the part of the audience.

Mr. Brown thinks he has trouble while sitting through the introductory remarks which precede his speech. How about the troubles of the introducer?

After all, Mr. Brown talks about the current Broadway shows and they change season after season. He has a fresh theme with every new show.

But Mr. Brown does not change. At least he does not change in ways that concern the people who introduce him.

He still continues to be born in the same place, to be educated in the same institution of learning, to work for the same newspaper, and to hold his firm and exalted place as an authority on the drama. If you stick to the essential and vital facts, there are not many variations to be played on the theme of John Mason Brown.

Besides, the members of the audience have heard all that stuff before and they don't want to hear it again. Indeed, they don't want to hear any introduction.

They paid their money to hear Mr. Brown and every word the introducer speaks cheats them of their rights, for the more time the preliminaries consume the less time remains for the speaker.

I sympathize with the lecturer Mr. Brown tells about who was preceded by a chairman who talked for forty-five of the sixty minutes allotted to the speaker and who concluded by saying: "Mr. So-and-So will now give us his address."

"You bet I will," said the speaker, who had a train to catch. "It's 575 Park Avenue."

Then he abruptly quit the platform and ran for the railway station.

I had an idea for simplifying the preliminaries attendant on Mr. Brown's Cleveland appearance as a public speaker. Since he has spoken here with such faithful regularity it seemed that it would be sufficient to say to his assembled admirers, "Here's that man again," and let it go at that.

But observing the eagerness with which his Southern charm is habitually regarded by an almost exclusively feminine audience, I thought it might be more appropriate to say, "Here he is, girls. Come and get him."

That would have been enough. But there is a fixed and inexorable convention which rules that speakers have to be introduced and that at least several minutes of time must be wasted in doing it.

I don't know why this custom arose or why it endures. But I suspect Mr. Brown hints at the reason when he says he is lonely and half paralyzed with fear when he is obliged to speak at a meeting without benefit of an introducer.

The introducer exists because lecturers want him. They like to have their wretchedness shared by somebody and any shivering soul will do.

A Snow Shovel

MARCH 19, 1946

An editorial in the *Plain Dealer* last week made a slighting reference to my aptitude for the manual arts. The basis of the aspersion was that I had once bought a disassembled lawn mower, and when I had succeeded in putting it together it operated perfectly except that it worked backward and had to be pulled instead of pushed over the lawn before it would consent to cut grass.

The conclusion arrived at was that if my efforts in assembling a lawn mower resulted in a machine that functioned in this curious fashion, it was a lucky thing that I was not included in the G.I. Bill of Rights, for I would surely make a mess of it if I had to put together one of the packaged houses which are shipped complete, but in separate pieces, to veterans and must be fitted into place. How right that editorial was.

I was appalled when I read the announcements about the packaged houses and contemplated what would happen if it fell to my lot to try to put one of them together. I know that many people find such problems simple and even pleasant to work out.

To me they are as complex as spherical harmonics, and the people who are at ease with them live in another world and excite my wonder and admiration.

The other day I ordered from an out-of-town dealer a snow shovel which was advertised as offering the advantages of having wheels, making it easier to push and eliminating bending. It has always seemed to me that there was room for improvement in the ordinary devices for removing snow from sidewalks. They require an expenditure of energy which is wholly disproportionate in an age when so much tedious labor is performed swiftly and easily by machinery.

I looked forward to the new shovel as an improvement comparable to Leonardo da Vinci's invention of the wheelbarrow in the fifteenth century. A snow shovel is a simple instrument, and I supposed it would arrive in one piece, or, at most, two or three pieces.

When it finally came it was in about fifty or a hundred pieces, I should guess, including handles, crossbars, blade, washers, cotter pins, bolts, screws, axles, brackets, and wheels. Even the rims of the wheels came in two parts and had to be bolted together.

I took a dismayed look at this formidable assemblage of disconnected and, to me, unrelated and hostile machinery, and said to the female branch of my household, "Return this mess to the senders and tell them to send us the parts for two Swiss watches. They would be easier to put together and probably just as useful in removing snow as this chaotic collection of irreconcilable pieces of metal."

But the distaff side of the house has a turn for mechanics and likes to puzzle out their mysteries. At the end of about eight hours' unrelenting study of diagrams, hammering, bending of metal, turning of bolts, fitting and refitting of pieces, she finally got the thing together and capable of moving on its own wheels when pushed.

I stood around holding this or that piece in place, or handing down a cotter pin, and offering advice while she did the work, completing it without casualty other than hitting her finger a few times and cutting some holes in the kitchen linoleum by a misdirection of energy.

When assembled it was a beautiful machine with a comforting appearance of practical efficiency. It may be the perfect instrument for removing snow with the least possible effort. But we do not know. The day the snow shovel was assembled it stopped snowing and it has not snowed since.

The lack of a facility for mechanics or a deficiency in manual aptitudes may relieve you of some chores which you do not like to perform, but there are times when the absence of such faculties is a distinct and disturbing disadvantage. That was often true overseas under war conditions.

When you rode in a bomber you were required by regulations to wear a parachute, or, at least, to have one with you. On occasions when I was going for a free ride in a combat plane it was no comfort to know that, if anything happened, I could not possibly operate a parachute and would probably choke myself with it before making a beginning toward getting it on.

While waiting in Scotland several days for a military passenger plane to North Africa, I listened to a young lieutenant explain the operation of the life preserver you were supposed to find useful if the ship crashed in the sea.

It was the type of preserver outfitted with a gadget which you manipulate at the proper moment and in the proper way and the preserver inflates itself. But if this device didn't work you were expected to find another gadget, put it in your mouth and use your own breath to bring about the desired state of inflation. You do this while being knocked around in the sea.

I paid but scant attention to the lieutenant's careful instructions. It would be far easier for me to drown than to understand what he was saying, or, if I could understand, to put that understanding into practical use.

Accents

MARCH 28, 1946

I was fascinated and startled by an assertion in a Saint Patrick's Day speech that William Shakespeare spoke with an Irish brogue and expressed my wonderment in print. It seems that I should not have been surprised.

The English poet undoubtedly did pronounce certain words as they would now be pronounced by an Irishman who speaks with a brogue. Ted Robinson pointed out that the vowel combination *ea* was pronounced in Elizabethan times as a long *a* and that Shakespeare would have said "raisin" when he used the word *reason*.

Come to think of it, the same thing is probably true of *either* and *neither*. In early English usage they seem to have been pronounced "ayther" and "nayther," and it is likely that Shakespeare pronounced them that way. It was not until the end of the eighteenth century that the pronunciation as "eether" and "neether" was generally established.

The pronunciation "eyether" and "nyether" is a relatively recent innovation. It is apparently an affectation without the blessing of scholarly authority.

I have no specialized knowledge of phonetics. My information on *either* and *neither* is taken from H. L. Mencken's *The American Language*, an extraordinary book which manages to be sprightly for 450 pages on an academic subject and maintains its liveliness for an additional 700 pages in a supplementary volume.

I never liked the pronouncing of *either* as "eyether," and I was pleased to have my prejudice confirmed by Thomas Lounsbury, a great fellow in these matters, who is quoted by Mencken as saying: "All of us are privileged in these latter days frequently to witness painful struggles put forth to give the first syllables of these words (either and neither) the sound of "i" by those who have been brought up to give it the sound of "e." There is apparently an impression on the part of some that such a pronunciation establishes on a firm foundation an otherwise doubtful social standing."

Another pundit, Richard Grant White, says the use of "eyether" for *either* is no more than "a copy of a second-rate British affectation."

I have often heard Irishmen in Ireland pronounce *neither* as "nayther." They had a good deal more authority for it than the fastidiously correct people who pronounce it "nyether."

One of my uncles was born in Ireland. He had nothing that could be called a brogue—the common impression that all Irish-born people speak with a brogue is an illusion—but he had one peculiarity of speech. He always pronounced *cook* to rhyme with *Luke*.

We kidded him about that pronunciation, which we supposed to be peculiarly Irish. But it was probably good sixteenth-century English.

I want to make a few remarks, subject to discount, for they are based on casual reading and individual observation rather than on systematic study. The standard English speech of today is really a south-of-England speech. It is what is popularly called an "English" way of speaking and it is now pretty generally used by educated people in all parts of England.

But it was originally a local accent and intonation. It is now more or less a manner of speech which is distinctive of a class rather than of a locality.

The majority of Yorkshire-born Englishmen, for instance, speak very differently from their compatriots in the south of England, but a Yorkshire man of the so-called upper classes who is educated in the public schools speaks about the same as an educated Londoner speaks.

I had dinner once with a London-born English couple in Paris and, during the course of the conversation, warmed up by a bottle of wine, the English wife turned to her husband and said of me: "Doesn't he speak like a Yorkshire man?"

It was not intended as a compliment, for a typical Yorkshire accent seems somewhat barbaric to a Londoner. But it is not only possible, but rather likely, that an average American, or an average Yorkshire native, speaks in rhythm and accent which is closer to sixteenth-century English than does the upper-class Londoner.

The Elizabethans pronounced their *r*'s clearly. So do the Americans and the Irish; and, certainly, the Scots. The educated Londoner sounds the *r* only before a vowel.

In the English of Shakespeare's time, such words as *fast* and *path* were sounded with the short *a* as in *hat*. They still are so sounded in America. But in cultivated modern London speech *path* has become something like "pawth" and *fast* is "fahst."

These pronunciations and many others in so-called standard London English are deviations from early English habits of speech. Somebody could write an amusing essay on the way in which the accent of a class in London has imposed itself on the world. I have heard Germans, Scandinavians, and Russians who talk English in that accent.

The most highly regarded of our own stage players approximate that way of talking. I mean people like the Barrymores, the Lunts, and Cornell, and all the great players in my memory from John Drew to Otis Skinner.

Mencken is wrong, I think, when he talks about the great differences in speech between American and British stage players, at least in drawing-room comedy as acted by leading players. There is not much difference, and you can be sure that the American players are doing their best to eliminate such slight distinctions as might remain.

John Barrymore spoke as clear and musical English as has ever been heard on our stages, and it was extremely close to standard London English, but before he played *Hamlet* in London he was worried about possible complaints against his accent and set himself to acquiring what, for average ears, he already had, which was a standard London English way of talking.

Hats

DECEMBER 6, 1946

Our legislators never matched the great State of Kansas by passing a statute regulating the size of bed sheets provided by hotels for their guests. But we seem to have enacted our share of trivial and curious legislation.

However, when someone intimates that a statute providing a penalty for theaters which permit hats that obstruct the view to be worn in their precincts is an antiquated and useless law, I rise with a wail of dissent. People attend a theater to see a play. The very word *theater* is derived from a Greek word signifying "to look at."

The Greeks did not mean to look at hats. They meant to look at the stage and the performers.

Hats worn by some members of an audience are capable of blotting out the stage, or of making it a difficult exercise in gymnastics to see what you have come to see.

You cannot reasonably assume, as some women do, that a hat, like the six-foot rabbit in *Harvey,* is invisible. When a woman in the *fauteuil* ahead of me, wearing a monstrous concoction on her head, turns around coyly and inquires, "Does my hat bother you," I wish to say, "Madame, it is apparent that your hat is not made of glass, and you should assume that I find some difficulty in seeing through it, and take the damned thing off."

But I usually content myself with a meek and polite, "Yes, madame, it does bother me," and I receive in return a look of shock and bewilderment, as if the wearer of the hat had suddenly discovered, with distaste and apprehension, that Genghis Khan was sitting behind her.

The law against wearing obstructive headgear in a theater is perfectly sensible and I am grateful for its comfort. I supposed it was a city ordinance and did not know that it had the full and impressive authority of the sovereign State of Ohio.

I hope the legislative committee which is engaged in studying the modernization of Ohio statutes will not be so henpecked and mousy as to recommend its deletion from the lawbooks. Some amendments might be acceptable.

Hats that impede the view could be permitted to be worn at lectures. With notable exceptions, including, of course, all women among the exceptions, the lecturers are not much to look at.

Some operas are better enjoyed with the eyes closed and a big hat in the foreground might be more convenient than annoying. But, for full enjoyment, a good musical comedy, or a first-rate play, ought to be seen as well as heard.

I imagine that the Ohio law which threatens a fine for theater owners, or managers, who permit hats to obstruct the view of their patrons was passed in the years when picture hats were in style. As I remember, and the women will check me on this, picture hats were something elaborate and spectacular, topped by towering ostrich feathers, such hats as Gainsborough liked to paint.

Women who wore them were naturally loath to take them off when they attended a theater for the purpose, among other things, of exhibiting their highly pictorial headgear. But they discommoded theatergoers who had to sit behind millinery that blotted out not only the actors but the stage lights.

Complaints, I am sure, were numerous and furious. But there was chivalry in those days. Theater managers hesitated to ask their most fashionable lady patrons to remove their proudest hats, and likely as not, the lady would refuse the request, if it were made, as unwarranted and impudent.

Theater people were in a jam. I should not be at all surprised to learn that they were instrumental in getting the Legislature to pass a law fining themselves for permitting obstructive hats to be worn in their theaters. That gave them legal warrant and gentlemanly excuse for asking their female patrons to uncover.

You remember the signs flashed long ago on the screen in the nickelodeons, "Ladies are respectfully requested to remove their hats." Such pleas used also to be printed in the programs for stage plays.

But the convenience and comfort of theatergoers, or their ability to see what they have paid to see, should not be subject to the whim or the good will of patrons who insist on wearing big hats to the playhouses and keeping them on. Like the hotels in Kansas which fail to provide their guests with seven feet of bed sheet, they are law violators, or accessories to the violation of the law.

Let the hat law, section 13411, remain on the books. I can think of newer laws which make less sense.

Smoking

SEPTEMBER 7, 1950

An editorial in the *Plain Dealer* the other day said that the cigar manufacturers were planning practically to double the sale and use of cigars by a publicity campaign. It quoted a publicity release from the manufacturers as saying that "women are being impressed with the meaning of the cigar to their menfolk and the men in turn are being cautioned in the etiquette of smoking so as to win the further approval of the other sex." The editorial writer then went on to suggest that the usual feminine caution to a cigar smoker was: "Get that thing out of here and get it out fast."

As a habitual cigar smoker, I suspect that the quoted command represents the attitude of many women toward cigars. I regret it, and regard it as a deterioration of good taste and delicacy of understanding in our republic, largely manifested by our female population.

I remember the time, not so very long ago, when it was usual for a man in a woman's company, who felt the urge for nicotine, to inquire of the lady: "May I be permitted to smoke?" That polite question is still sometimes asked in France, but I have not heard it in this country for years. The women do not even ask the men for permission to smoke, and there was a time when smoking by women was thought of by men as highly reprehensible.

But what I am wondering about is the curious decline in fairly recent years of the popularity and respectability of the cigar in relation to the cigarette. In the fair times gone by when you took a cigar from your pocket and asked your female companion if it were permissible to smoke, the standard reply was: "I hate the smoke of a cigarette, but I love the smell of a good cigar."

Of course, the dear lady could not recognize the difference between the smell of a good cigar and the cabbage that is sometimes sold in cigar form. But her heart was in the right place and her respectability was assured. For in those days cigars had a much higher social and moral standing in the community than cigarettes.

The young and innocent will not believe this but the great State of Indiana, where I was born, once passed a law banning the sale and smoking of cigarettes. Of course, the law was not enforced and it was soon repealed.

But there were a few fanatic females who went around on the public streets snatching cigarettes from the mouths of the miscreants and debauchees who were engaged in puffing one of the forbidden articles quite commonly described at that time as "coffin nails." Since that era the practice of smoking cigarettes has grown enormously and, strange to say, the average human being lives longer now than he did then.

While cigarettes were often regarded as pernicious and somewhat disreputable forty or fifty years ago, the cigar was in good social standing. No morally incensed woman ever snatched a cigar from a man's mouth and warned him that he was on his way to perdition. The cigar was relatively respectable, a badge of manliness and maturity, and it was more popular than cigarettes.

When Vice-President Tom Marshall made his famous quip, he did not say: "What this country really needs is a good fifteen-cent pack of cigarettes." He said: "What this country really needs is a good five-cent cigar," because most men smoked cigars habitually in his days.

A habitual cigar smoker is now a relative rarity as opposed to the number of people who are addicted to cigarettes. I attend many social parties at which everybody smokes cigarettes and nobody but myself smokes a cigar.

It is a little embarrassing, particularly when the hostess apologizes because there is not a cigar in the house, or produces a dried rope which has been lying around the house, concealed and forgotten for years, and has long been dead.

How did the cigarette come into its present eminence at the expense of the cigar? I suppose one reason is that women have learned to smoke cigarettes and few of them have taken up the delights of a good cigar. Another probable reason is that the cigarette manufacturers have been much more active and spectacular than the cigar makers in promoting the virtues and attractiveness of their wares.

You never see a picture of a pretty woman in the magazine or newspaper advertisements, portrayed in the act of puffing a cigar.

Yet pretty women in the Scandinavian countries do smoke cigars, and so do a few Americans. On a transatlantic voyage, I once offered an attractive woman one of my best cigars, as a jest. It was a mistake. She liked it so well that she smoked up half a box of my cigars before we reached Le Havre.

I should think the cigar manufacturers might find it profitable to take the hint. They have untold opportunities for improved salesmanship, and the building up of the prestige of their incomparable wares.

How about a double-page advertising spread showing Winston Churchill smoking a cigar, with the caption: "Distinguished men smoke cigars," and on the other side a picture of Hedy Lamarr smoking a slightly smaller cigar, with the underlines: "So do beautiful women."

Of course, Miss Lamarr would first have to be introduced to the pleasures of cigar smoking, but that could probably be arranged, and it would almost certainly increase the total sale of cigars.

Canes

MAY 29, 1953

What has become of the men who used to carry a cane or a walking stick when they promenaded the boulevards? I don't see them any more. It is regrettable. A man's cane, when he uses it as a swagger stick, is one of his last vestiges of glory. It is the faded symbol of a sword which his ancestors carried as an attestation of manhood and gentlemanliness.

The use of a walking stick leads to decorum and care in dressing. Nobody ever used a walking stick who was not very careful in the way he dressed. You must live up to a walking stick, and practically everybody does, or did.

Most London tobacco shops sell walking sticks. The tobacco is usually so bad, as I have said before, that it is better to smoke the canes than to smoke the cigars.

Canes are still used quite generally by Europeans and they are almost extinct in this country. We have apparently come to think of a walking stick as an affectation. It is not so at all. It is a dying affirmation of manhood, and at one time it was a signal of distinction.

When I was a very young man in Indiana, I remember only three or four men who carried canes to the general approval. They were Booth Tarkington, James Whitcomb Riley, and a theatrical critic named Hector Fuller.

Tarkington wore his cane lightly. He was a very great figure in Indianapolis, and he was extraordinarily modest. So far as I know Tarkington never had an enemy, and everybody in his neighborhood admired his art and loved him as a fellow man. If he wished to strike out with a cane, that was his business, and it had the appreciation and indulgence of the general population.

James Whitcomb Riley was another sort of fellow. He wore

eyeglasses with a black ribbon. In the words of Robinson's poem, "he glittered as he walked."

When he took to the sidewalks he was a spectacle of enormous propriety and elegance. He never really liked children, but he wrote beautifully and lastingly about them, or so I gathered from my childhood, which was spent a few blocks from his home in Lockerbie Street.

Hector Fuller, the theater critic, was an unusual and distinguished man. He always carried a cane on his expeditions into the streets. But he was born an Englishman, and that circumstance of birth always excused his use of a cane, which he often waved and employed to make his points in various barrooms.

I have owned and carried many different kinds of canes. Some included a sword in their interior. Some concealed an umbrella. Some had a torchlight in their top. I have lost most of them, but I still remember them with affection.

The editor of the *Plain Dealer*, one Paul Bellamy, once presented me a cane which we selected at the Galeries La Fayette in Paris when we were visiting that place of delight. It was a beautiful cane. The handle was enclosed in snakeskin.

I lost it in a very strange way. I was on a train in Austria riding to the pleasant mountain resort of Semmering. The light train was lurching and staggering on the roadbed toward the mountains. When we neared the destination, I pulled down the suitcases from the racks above. On top of them I had placed my precious cane.

When I pulled down the luggage, the cane sailed out the open train window and landed in a field.

I have often wondered what the farmer felt when he saw that cane in his domain, so like a snake, and if he shot it before he picked it up and found that it was harmless.

Bellamy has never believed that story. He has thought that I lost it in any of several more likely places. But it is true as I tell it.

The Death of a Friend

APRIL 16, 1956

Last Saturday all that was mortal of Paul Bellamy was consigned to the grave, and his friends are put to grief that this lively and endearing man will no longer walk among them. Yet he will live in the sunshine of remembrance. The words are poor that we can speak of him but the feeling that underlies them is rich.

I knew him well. So well, indeed, and for so long a time, that we were as much a part of the same whole as men can be. When he died I had a sense, not only of bereavement, but of my own diminishment.

He was not made of cathedral sounding boards. We frolicked together at his home and mine, sipped the nectars in Parisian street cafés, walked in company along the boulevards, and climbed the hill to Montmartre. Many a time we have heard the chimes at midnight. Like Dr. Johnson, he was always ready for a frolic and, like Johnson, he was essentially a thoughtful man of serious interests.

His outstanding personal characteristics were high spirits, quickness of mind, kindness, and good humor. He was a bracing and stimulating companion who talked fluently and whose conversation sparked listeners into an articulateness they did not customarily possess.

We used to play squash together. Our game was a farce for we did not take it seriously and spent most of the time sitting on the gymnasium floor, often talking lightly about the eternal verities and trying to pluck off the garment of truth to discover its naked essence.

A few years ago Paul was taken with a serious, chronic illness which impeded his speech and made his talk hesitant and difficult. He also lost the normal use of his legs. Though he could get about, his legs sometimes faltered.

These would be calamities for any man. For Paul Bellamy they were the severest of tragedies. For he had a special relish in the pleasure of talking and he had been accustomed to talking with exceptional briskness, for his thoughts ran ahead of his utterance. He also liked to walk at a hurried gait, and this was denied him.

I never heard him complain. Instead, he consoled others.

When I was in a hospital, following a surgical operation, flirting with death and not much concerned so far as it affected myself, he sent me a worried and bracing letter urging that I must will to live because of my responsibilities.

He and Mrs. Bellamy were my first visitors after several serious bouts with the Grim Reaper.

I speak personally of my relationship with the Editor Emeritus of the *Plain Dealer*, because that is what I know best. But I believe that practically every old-time member of the *Plain Dealer* staff has benefited at one time or another from the unfailing flow of his sympathy and his kindness. He was devoted and generous to his family in a rare degree.

Thousands of his friends in Cleveland and elsewhere must be indebted to him for his counsel, his sympathy, and his help. They will remember not only his beneficences but the glowing personality with which they warmed themselves as they would at a hospitable fireside.

The poets echo the idea that death is no more than a long sleep in which men find repose and a release from the tensions and tribulations of life. That may be. But selfishly I would exchange this tranquillity of death for the living presence and a single spoken word from my friend.

Let me quote from the Biblical Ecclesiasticus:

"A faithful friend is a strong defense: and he that hath found such an one hath found a treasure. Nothing doth countervail a faithful friend, and his excellency is invaluable. A faithful friend is the medicine of life; and they that fear the Lord shall find him."

Undeservedly, I found such a friend. Now he is gone, whither I know not.

Modern Art

SEPTEMBER 21, 1956

A Nashville newspaper reporter, according to a recent Associated Press dispatch, has dealt a foul blow to modern art in its more extravagant and incomprehensible manifestations.

The reporter makes a hobby of painting during his hours of release from his journalistic duties. In the course of applying himself seriously to art, he scraped off his palette with a knife and wiped the residue on an old piece of canvas.

The waste paint on the cloth made such a splash of inharmonious color that he was tempted to add a few more smears with a big brush. His overcoat accidentally touched the wet daubs when he picked up the canvas, making still more smears.

He submitted this painting to a Tennessee State Fair art exhibit. It won a prize, presumably as an outstanding work in the category of modern painting.

I do not know whether or not he intended a hoax on the judges, but knowing his journalistic tribe I suspect that he did. It doesn't matter. The essential fact is that a painting made by accidental smears, with the aid of a flapping overcoat, was awarded first honor in a State-sponsored art exhibit.

The painter says of his work, "It has no design or color scheme, and whatever paints used were slapped on the canvas at random."

The art expert who acted as judge disagrees. He says that he "gave it the prize because of the artist's excellent sensitivity in color," and he adds that "his sensitivity was so successful he created a complementing of colors that brought off a rather sophisticated painting."

The critic is enunciating a strange and revolutionary theory of art. He is implying that a distinguished painting can be created by accident, and that sophistication can be achieved by fortuitous circumstances which may descend alike on the trained and the untrained, the learned and the ignorant, the man and the child.

This thought will not be cheering to the thousands of artists who have studied and toiled for long years to learn their craft and given their days and nights to creating design, harmony, and meaning.

What is the use of all this labor and thought if the same result can be achieved by throwing daubs of paint haphazardly on a wall or a piece of cloth? You don't even need a brush. The effect can be obtained by squirting the paint, or applying it with the hands, or using an old overcoat.

Every artist in whatever field knows that this is nonsense. But how do you explain the reporter who won a first prize for painting by using some such methods?

It cannot be explained except by admitting that there is some element of nonsense in the current evolution and criteria of so-called modern art, which is not modern but primitive, not advanced by atavistic, not sophisticated but childish.

Of course, it would be absurd to apply this derogation to all art classified as "modern," but I suspect there is a good deal of the ridiculous in some of its weirder manifestations and that it will be so recognized in the course of time when its faddist elements have faded from fashion and common sense returns to the seat of judgment.

I think I am confirmed by history in believing that great and lasting art is popular art. It can be enjoyed and at least partly understood by anybody of ordinary intelligence and sensibility. It is not a cult for which you have to be specially trained and initiated by some mystic ceremony. The plays of Shakespeare, the paintings of Rembrandt, the sculptures of Michelangelo can be admired and understood by everybody without the use of a guidebook.

That is not true of much modern art, even that part of it which is now recognized as distinguished or great by those who are initiated into its mysteries. It has no general popularity and it is not readily intelligible, but it is being introduced by its partisans into wide public consciousness.

One of its eminent practitioners, Paul Klee, is ranked with Picasso as a great artist who has enlarged the field of human vision. *Time* magazine reproduced a few of his paintings in a recent issue, together with some laudatory comment. I confess that I could not make much of either.

One of the paintings is entitled, "She Howls, We Play." It consists of scrawls of two figures, constructed geometrically with what seem to be wires. I could find neither beauty nor any kind of meaning in it.

The explanatory comment was not of much help. It said: "The picture uses lines that are a cross between wire sculpture and children's sidewalk scrawls; the figures might as well be cow with heifers as dog with pups. The message is the same; adult overconcern vs. childhood unconcern."

I have nothing but admiration for the visual scope and the imagination of a critic who can see in a picture which might represent either dogs or cows a symbolization of adult worry and childhood unconcern. I envy him and I am sorry I cannot share either his pleasure or his understanding.

Old Books

JULY 30, 1958

In recent months I have spent all my waking hours in a room lined with books from floor to ceiling. Other books lie on tables, under tables, in chairs, and a few homeless volumes are stacked in corners on the floor.

Hundreds of books have overflowed into an adjoining room where they crowd the shelves and spill over into small mountains on the floor. I have enough book reading at hand to last a young man his lifetime and am in no urgent need of more.

The duchess thinks otherwise. A few days ago she visited a Salvation Army store and bought three secondhand books which she presented me with an air of having accomplished a good and worthy task. The books were Alexander Woollcott's *Long, Long Ago*, Arthur Morrison's *Tales of Mean Streets*, and Mark Twain's *Tom Sawyer and Other Stories*. I read two of the books and a considerable part of the third.

The price of the books disturbed me. They cost ten cents each. A man may put his life into a book. He may toil at it for years, pouring into it what is deepest and truest in his nature, his highest thought, his most poignant feeling, his hopes, his dreams, and all else that sets him apart as an individual human being.

Yet his life's blood is worth no more than ten cents when it is deposited on the shelves of a secondhand store.

Copies of an old newspaper bring more than that, and newspapers are supposed to be the most fleeting and ephemeral of printed matter. They last longer and have more readers than many a book solemnly embalmed in stout covers and classified as literature.

Sometimes a book that winds up on a secondhand shelf many years after its publication has never been read by anybody. That was true of the Mark Twain book which was thrust upon me. Its pages were uncut.

The original owner did not read it, nor did any of the probably numerous people into whose hands it had passed before it found a grave in a rummage store. In this case they did not miss much because the book is a miscellany of Twain's casual and lesser writings.

The Arthur Morrison book, *Tales of Mean Streets*, probably fared better. It consists of short, lively stories of the East London slums and it is set in large type, friendly to the eyes. H. L. Mencken wrote an introduction to this edition in which he commented on the endurance and the influence of the book which was written in the 1890's.

I doubt that many people read it today, or have even heard of it, though it stands up well as an amusing, sometimes tragic depiction of life in the curiously class-conscious, poverty-plagued environment of East London.

Of the three books, I was most interested in Woollcott's *Long, Long Ago*. It was published shortly after Woollcott's death in 1943. I had not read it before, though I was familiar with some of the pieces. They had been previously printed in magazines, or spoken by Woollcott when he was the town crier on a radio program.

The book is a reproduction of some of Woollcott's feebler essays, and I found it disquieting. It seemed faded and over-sentimentalized, like an old lace-bordered valentine.

While he lived, Woollcott's sentimentality was taken for granted, and it was an integral part of his pattern of writing which helped to charm a considerable public. Reading *Long, Long Ago* in the present era, the sentimentality seems exaggerated, obtrusive, and out of tune, and the book is only fifteen years old.

People are just as sentimental today as they were then. But the fashion of expressing sentimentality has changed and Woollcott's frank and joyous flaunting of it now seems forced and sugary.

Woollcott was a great raconteur. He was not a teller of tales, but a reteller. His rather florid style of writing had warmth, individuality, and persuasiveness. He had a most enviable attribute as a writer or speaker—he could communicate his enthusiasms to readers or audiences and make them feel as he felt, at least for the moment.

That is why he was so influential in his days as a drama critic. When he danced in the street, or threw his hat in the air to honor some play or book, people were infected by the obvious honesty and fervor of his enthusiasm and were inclined to go along with him.

There has been very little dancing in the streets among the critics since Woollcott gave up his portfolio on the old New York *World,* and perhaps today's readers would not accept the kind of vehement logrolling he used to practice when a personality or a play was caught in the glow of his approval.

Certainly, there is now nobody like Woollcott on radio or television. By mere skill in the use of words, coupled with the force of a singular temperament, he held an audience glued to the radio while he told some twice-told tale, or aired his views on a book, or a play, or on anything else that caught his fancy.

There is no reason why the contemporary radio or television could not provide a literature program of the sort that Woollcott used to furnish. No reason, that is, except that a man of Woollcott's skill and stature would have to be found. He was unique and the Creator who framed his fearful symmetry has not such another in his mold.

Old Book Marts

SEPTEMBER 3, 1958

The secondhand stores are hospitable to the seeker of books. They are the only merchandising institutions which encourage the visitor to taste and often consume their wares before making a purchase, or even without making one.

In the town where I was born nearly all the secondhand stores, dealing in used merchandise of all sorts, made a practice of displaying books on tables set on the pavement outside the establishment. You could leaf through a book without entering the premises or encountering a salesman. It was a golden opportunity for a schoolboy with a taste for reading and no money to buy books.

Over a period of some weeks I remember that I read all of

Jerome K. Jerome's *Three Men in a Boat* by surreptitiously turning its pages day after day on the pretense of examining it for the purpose of buying. I also read in this fashion a book about human anatomy, which I have now forgotten.

Of course, I might have borrowed from the public library the books I furtively read in the secondhand dealer's display. But that would not have been the same thing.

At that time you could not browse through the collections in public libraries and select what pleased you. The books were barricaded behind the librarian's desk. You had to ask for what you wanted, and the guardian of the collection would then retire into the secret recesses where the books were kept, dislodge the volume of your choice, and hand it over.

That is, she would do so if the book was in stock and not restricted to adult reading.

In that day and place the public library stocked the novels of Balzac and other masters of realism but it was forbidden to issue them to readers under the age of twenty-one. I believe our Cleveland Public Library was the first, or one of the first, great libraries to open its shelves for public examination and free choice. The British Museum still keeps its books locked up.

There was another reason in my youth for preferring the book collections in the secondhand stores to the larger assortments in the public libraries. When you glanced through a book in secondhand marts there was always the possibility, sometimes no more than a dream, that you might someday buy it and own it.

When I began to earn money the dream became a reality. The first purchase I made, of course, was the complete works of Balzac. I think the set was in thirty-two volumes and cost ten cents a volume.

I bought a set of Kipling in fifteen volumes for the same price. Secondhand books are one treasurable commodity which have not gone up much in price the past fifty years.

These old books, so highly cherished at the time, were not always the bargains they seemed. I had to get rid of the Balzac volumes some years ago because they were badly printed on poor paper which began to disintegrate.

The Kipling set I still have, but when I had occasion to refer to it not long ago I found that it was incomplete and lacked a famous ballad for which I was looking.

I have about a dozen different sets of Shakespeare's plays, some of them valuable and some of little worth, but all serving a particular purpose from easy legibility to distinguished prefaces or wealth of annotation.

The only set that I should like to surrender by throwing it in the publisher's face is a "complete" set in many volumes which a wormy editor has made useless by expurgating all the passages which offended his Grundyish sense of good taste.

I have spent many a pleasant hour in the secondhand bookstores in London, particularly Foyle's, which is said to be the biggest secondhand bookstore in the world. Foyle handles everything from rare first editions and beautifully bound masterpieces to trash, and the collection is scattered over many floors of crumbling buildings so that you have the feeling of plowing through old, neglected attics as you wander through the labyrinth.

I have picked up many a precious volume in Foyle's, particularly certain theatrical books which are unprocurable in the United States, although some of the books were written by Americans long since dead.

You cannot mention the secondhand book marts of Europe without thinking of the bookstalls that border the Seine. I never visit Paris without spending an afternoon walking this pleasantly shaded path by the water's edge, pausing at the bookstalls to examine the frayed and worn books or the ancient colored prints clipped from dead and forgotten magazines.

Here you are never asked to buy, and the sleepy, taciturn keeper of the kiosks plainly hopes that you will not bother him with a sordid commercial transaction.

Anatole France often wandered in this restful and reflective environment and he summed it up with the highest approbation at his command. "Here," he said, "are books and trees and women who pass."

MEMORIAL BY
PHILIP W. PORTER

"A Whole Man If There Ever Was One"

"A Whole Man If There Ever Was One"

⚔

William F. McDermott died on November 16, 1958. The following memorial by Philip W. Porter is reprinted from the
Cleveland Plain Dealer of November 20, 1958.

Bill McDermott was a small man physically, but a large one
intellectually. And he had more courage, pound for pound, than
any man I've ever known.

Mac was always a good-humored philosopher, but in his last
months on earth he proved it was possible for a man to die by
inches without one whimper. Never once did he complain. It
made you ashamed of so many humans, with so little to complain about, who moan so much about that little.

I am not certain that during his long ordeal Mac knew he
had cancer. You don't talk about things like that unless the victim wants to. Even his beloved and devoted Eva, who single-
handedly kept him alive for six months and who should have
four Congressional Medals of Honor, wasn't quite sure.

But Mac surely must have known, in those last few weeks,
when he had dwindled to practically a wisp and there was only
a great mind and a valorous spirit left, that he was on the way
out. He had had enough serious illness in the last eight years to
have accounted for his weakened condition. So perhaps it didn't
matter whether he knew exactly why.

What matters is that by sheer force of will he kept his spirits up and his column going for the last several months. When you saw him, you forgot he was dying and were fascinated as of old by his good talk. When he got too weak to sit up and type, he wrote in pencil and Eva copied it. And the last few he sent in were dictated from his couch, in a still small voice that could hardly be heard. But they still read like the flowing prose of the lusty, brilliant, much-traveled McDermott of days gone by.

Mac was without doubt the finest writer of simple, exact, descriptive prose who ever wrote for the *Plain Dealer*. He was one of the most adept users of English who ever wrote for any paper, book, or magazine. From his great erudition, he knew exactly what words meant. Few readers, except those who had read as much as Mac, ever realized what a magnificent stylist he was, or what a broad sweep his mind encompassed. It read as if he wrote easily, but he didn't. It was hard work.

But more than that, Mac was a kindly man who never as a dramatic critic got really rough with the actors he was evaluating. If the show was excellent, he said so. If it was mediocre, he let it down gently. If it stank, he wrote very little about it, and you had to read between the lines to know it stank. He hadn't the heart to blast a performance into which actors and writers had put their hearts and souls.

It was this lovable quality as well as his encyclopedic knowledge of the theater that endeared him to Katharine Cornell and her husband; the late Gertrude Lawrence, Mary Martin, and scores of others, and made Brooks Atkinson, the eminent critic of *The New York Times*, hold him in such high esteem.

Katharine Cornell once sent a taxicab all the way from Toledo to pick up Mac in time to see her opening there and send him back, after he had given some sage advice on how to improve it. Other producers often threw out whole scenes or altered them, after he told them what was wrong.

Mac was almost a legend around the *Plain Dealer*, for he was seldom in his office and did most of his column writing at home. He'd spend the day thinking about it, then in the afternoon he'd tap it out in a most laborious fashion—slowly and using three or four spaces between each word—then send it down to the office via taxicab.

He never learned to drive, so he knew most of the cab drivers around town. He never encouraged Eva to drive much, either. The result was that several years ago, they traded in a second-hand car they had owned for eight years that had only 12,000 miles on it.

About three years ago, when Mac was stricken with yellow jaundice or something similar while on a trip to New York, he was forbidden by the medics to drink anything alcoholic. This was quite a blow to the little guy, who loved life in all its delightful phases, and particularly good food and drink, for he was a gourmet, too. But he showed he could discipline himself. He swore off at once, and never touched a drop until last spring, when one of his doctors, knowing nothing could really hurt him then, ordered him to drink a small portion of bourbon each evening. He did it with a characteristic McDermott phrase:

"Those guys owe me a hogshead of this stuff by now," he grimaced.

Next to Eva, Mac most loved his library, overflowing with good books and overlooking Lake Erie. It was there that he spent all his days as he grew more and more ill. And in the few days before the end came, he firmly refused to stay upstairs. The old Westerners wanted to die with their boots on; Mac wanted to die among his books. He did.

It will be a long time before we know another man so sweet, so urbane, so unselfish, so brave. A whole man, if there ever was one.

About the Author

WILLIAM F. McDERMOTT was the drama critic and columnist of the *Cleveland Plain Dealer* for thirty-seven years. Born in Indianapolis in 1891, he studied at Butler University, and then served his apprenticeship as a journalist on the *Indianapolis News*, where for five years he was a critic and editorial writer. It was in 1921 that the editor of the *Plain Dealer*, in need of a new dramatic critic, took a poll of the leading theatrical figures in New York—men such as Klaw and Erlanger and the Shuberts. The answer was virtually unanimous in favor of McDermott, and McDermott moved to Cleveland in that year. But he did not confine himself there. He made thirty trips abroad. He traveled around the world three times. And the impact of his personality and of his writings was felt from coast to coast. Such personages as Alexander Woollcott, Brooks Atkinson, Katharine Cornell, Gertrude Lawrence, Mary Martin, and scores of others, all deeply respected and loved him for the wisdom of his comments and for his encyclopedic knowledge of the theater.

In the field of journalism, McDermott played many roles besides that of dramatic critic. In addition to his concern with political and social affairs at home, McDermott was a man who covered the horror of war overseas—both in Spain in the 1930s and in Europe in the 1940s. With the coming of an uneasy peace in 1945, he foresaw the impending conflict between the great power blocs of the world. It was the writing of McDermott, and of other newspapermen like him, that helped awaken America to her danger.

Dramatic critic or columnist, McDermott was first of all a newspaperman. His fondness for his profession increased with the years and he continued writing for the *Plain Dealer* until death claimed him in 1958. In the words of the man who wrote his obituary, McDermott was "one of the most adept users of English who ever wrote for any paper, book, or magazine."

*This book was set in
Caledonia and Caslon types
by Slugs Composition Company.
It was printed and bound by
The Haddon Craftsmen.
Typography and design are by
Lawrence S. Kamp*